TRAFALGAR

HAPPY VALLEY: The Story of the English in Kenya

'Nicholas Best tells an immensely entertaining tale'
– Max Hastings, *Evening Standard*

'Erudite, amusing and, even, gossipy' – Nigel Dempster, *Punch*

'First class . . . quite hilariously funny!' – *Melbourne Herald*

WHERE WERE YOU AT WATERLOO?

'As a satire on military bigotry and shambling officialdom,
Where Were You At Waterloo? is in places as sharp as Waugh and
sometimes better' – *Times Literary Supplement*

'Combines military satire with exotic thrills in a book reminiscent
at its best of that sublime beast *Black Mischief*' – *Financial Times*

'All good, clean fun and never heavy-handed' – *Daily Telegraph*

'Passages of pure comic pleasure' – *Spectator*

TENNIS AND THE MASAI

'Very good entertainment' – Sir Alec Guinness

'The funniest book of the year' – *Daily Telegraph*

'The funniest book I have read since David Lodge's *Small World*'
– *Sunday Times*

'Wickedly funny' – *Daily Mail*

'Less savage than Evelyn Waugh, Best is every bit as sharp . . .
an immensely enjoyable book' – *Evening Standard*

TRAFALGAR

The Untold Story of the
Greatest Sea Battle in History by

NICHOLAS BEST

TED SMART

First published in Great Britain in 2005
by Weidenfeld & Nicolson
The Orion Publishing Group Ltd
Orion House
5 Upper Saint Martin's Lane
London, WC2H 9EA

This edition produced for
The Book People Ltd
Hall Wood Avenue,
Haydock,
St Helens WA11 9UL

1 3 5 7 9 10 8 6 4 2

A CIP catalogue record for this book
is available from the British Library

ISBN 0 297 84622 1

Text design: www.carrstudio.co.uk
Printed in Great Britain by Clays Ltd, St Ives plc

www.orionbooks.co.uk

With thanks to Tom Sharpe, who lent me the book that got me started.

Thanks also to Nancy Sharpe, Tom Pocock, Mike Dover,
Tim Atkinson, Pam and Cavan Browne, Nick and Melanie Marden,
Professors Mike Bickle and Gareth Roberts, Hazel Bickle, Colin White
of the National Maritime Museum, and Kay Hoar, librarian of
the King's School, Canterbury.

Of Anglo-Irish origin, Nicholas Best grew up in Kenya, and was educated there, in England, and at Trinity College, Dublin. He served in the Grenadier Guards and worked in London as a financial journalist before becoming a full-time author. He writes mostly history books and fiction and lives now in Cambridge.

Boulogne, 1805. Napoleon studies Dover Castle through a giant telescope. Behind him stands an army of 167,000 men, superbly trained and itching to invade. Behind them Joseph Fouché, France's Minister of Police, who attends public executions with human ears dangling from his hat.

Across the Channel, William Pitt awaits the French with the Cinque Port Volunteers, a ragbag force of 3,000 yokels armed initially with pikes and pitchforks.

In between sails the Royal Navy, desperately short of ships and men, yet blessed in Lord Nelson with a leader of outstanding ability. All are adamant that English ears must never dangle from Fouché's hat.

This is the story of the men and women of many nations who fought at Trafalgar, told in their own dramatic words. It is also the wider story of characters as diverse as Madame Forty Thousand Men – doyenne of the Grand Army's prostitutes, Captain de l'Ort – Austrian eyewitness at Ulm, and the anonymous but beautiful English blonde who did her best to get Napoleon's invasion plan out of him at Boulogne. Unaccountably neglected by Trafalgar historians, their tales are all the more fascinating for being very rarely seen in print.

CONTENTS

'I do not say the French cannot come.
I only say they cannot come by sea.'
Admiral St Vincent

———◆◦◆◦◆———

'I made a mistake trying to conquer the English.
They are a brave people.'
Napoleon Bonaparte

CHAPTER 1

NAPOLEON REVIEWS THE ARMY OF ENGLAND

The Emperor was coming and all of Boulogne was *en fête*. Along the cliffs north of the town, the men of Napoleon's army awaited his arrival. Almost 100,000 soldiers – the greatest army France had ever assembled – were gathered for his inspection. There were regiments of Guards drawn up on the slopes of Terlincthun. There were regiments of dragoons and light infantry, companies of Voltigeurs and artillery, rows of prancing horses and squadrons of cavalry in outrageous uniforms. It was not just the French army that was assembled at Boulogne. It was the grandest military spectacle the world had ever seen.

For many of the troops, fidgeting nervously as they waited for Napoleon to arrive, 16 August 1804 was going to be a day they would remember for the rest of their lives. A day their descendants have remembered too, ever since. The day the Emperor embraced them personally and bestowed on them the newly founded Légion d'honneur, France's highest decoration.

The ceremony had been planned for months. Boulogne had been specially decorated for the occasion. There were flags at every window and swathes of coloured bunting across the streets. There were triumphal arches, allegorical statues and signs pointing out 'The Road to England' towards the harbour. The road was lined with excited crowds, the girls wearing traditional fête costumes and patriotic ribbons, the children clutching tricolours in their hands. In the vale of Terlincthun, the massed bands of sixty regiments were waiting to greet Napoleon. Along the cliff tops, batteries of guns stood ready to fire a salute in his honour. Everything was in place, just waiting for the Emperor to appear.

In the middle of the vale, where he was to address the troops, a magnificent podium had been erected at the summit of a small rise. The podium was twice the height of a man, approached on either side and from the front by three sets of wooden steps. On top of it stood a splendid throne, said to have been used 1,000 years earlier by Dagobert, the legendary king of the Franks.

Behind the throne stood a theatrical backdrop of statues in shining armour and imperial eagles crowned with laurel wreaths. There was also a display of military banners, more than 200 of them, arranged in a fan shape around the podium. The banners were bloodstained and riddled with shot. They had been captured at the battles of Lodi, Arcola, Marengo and a score of other French triumphs. Now they stood fluttering in the breeze of the English Channel, eloquent testimony to the courage of the army that had captured them.

The army itself stood facing the podium in a giant semicircle. It was a fine sight, the pick of French manhood. Almost all the officers and NCOs had seen active service in recent campaigns, as had more than half the men. Their commanders were Michel Ney, Nicolas Soult and Louis Davout, figures legendary in the annals of war. The army had been camped at Boulogne for more than a year, training furiously for the assault on England. The troops were fully prepared and ready to go. Only a few more days now, they had been promised, just a few more days and then the invasion would begin. Their day of glory would arrive.

From their vantage points around the valley, some 20,000 citizens of Boulogne watched adoringly as the troops went through their paces. Many of the spectators were women, for Boulogne was a great prostitutes' town. The army had tried to get rid of them at first, refusing residents' permits to any who didn't actually live in Boulogne. But some had been allowed to remain, making fortunes in the process. Chief among them was Madame Forty Thousand Men, an energetic twenty-two-year-old whose chamber pot never stopped ringing to the sound of the écus the troops flung in there. Recent analysis of some skeletons suggests that eighty per cent of the army had syphilis. Madame Forty Thousand was probably in the pay of the English.

But now here was Napoleon. They could hear the cheers in the distance. Cries of 'Vive l'Empereur!' and girls strewing flowers in his path. The army stiffened as the cheers drew nearer. The musicians picked up their instruments and the infantry shouldered their muskets. The officers unsheathed their swords, ready for the salute. Thousands of bayonets flashed as the men gripped their weapons, waiting for the order to present arms.

The Emperor was riding his favourite white horse. He wore the uniform of a Foot Guards general – coat, white waistcoat and breeches, shiny top boots and that famous black hat, the very image of Napoleon. He was accompanied by an escort of 300 glittering horsemen, grouped protectively around their new Emperor. Napoleon had only been an Emperor since May. He hadn't even been crowned yet.

A fanfare of trumpets greeted his arrival. Two thousand drummer boys raised their sticks and beat out the urgent rhythm of 'Aux Champs' as his entourage galloped at full speed towards the podium. The gun batteries fired their salute and church bells rang out across the town. As one man, the Grand Army crashed to attention and presented arms as Napoleon reined in at the saluting base. They watched with awe bordering on reverence as he dashed up the steps and turned to address them from the great throne of Dagobert on the top.

He spoke first to the recipients of the Légion d'honneur. There were more than 2,000 of them, almost the first to be awarded France's most prestigious decoration. One was an admiral, two – Ney and Soult – were marshals of France, and three were bishops. The rest were soldiers of all ranks, officers and men who had distinguished themselves in the service of their country and who now stood waiting to reap their reward.

Napoleon surveyed them proudly. Then he raised his hand and swore them to be true to the ideals of the Légion:

Commanders, officers, legionnaires, citizens, soldiers. Swear upon your honour to devote yourselves to the service of the Empire, to the preservation of the integrity of French territory, to the defence of the

Emperor, the laws of the Republic, and the property which they have made sacred. Swear to combat, by all the means which justice, reason and the law authorise, any attempt to re-establish the feudal system. In short, swear to concur with all your might in maintaining liberty and equality, the very bedrock of our institutions. Swear!

The recipients swore. Then Napoleon turned to the rest of the army:

And you, soldiers, swear to defend with your life the honour of the French name, your country, and your Emperor.

The soldiers swore, too. Few of them could actually hear what Napoleon was saying, but they took their cue from their officers, who shouted, 'We swear it!' with one voice. Then the bands struck up the 'Song of Departure' and the distribution of the Légion's crosses began.

The ceremony lasted for hours. The men climbed the steps at one side of the podium, bowed to Napoleon, received their cross, then descended the steps the other side, like a school prize-giving. The crosses were distributed from the helmet of Pierre Bayard, the 'chevalier sans peur' who had been the saviour of France in the 1520s. The helmet was carried on the shield of Bertrand Du Guesclin, the celebrated Constable of France. The new Emperor saw himself as the heir to these great Frenchmen. Whenever he recognised a soldier he knew, he exchanged a few words with him as he gave him his cross, reminiscing about times past, campaigns they had shared. Napoleon was said to have a gift for remembering the faces of ordinary soldiers. It was why the army loved him.

They never knew that actually Napoleon remembered very few of them. His aides simply primed him with the relevant information beforehand.

The afternoon was well advanced by the time all the crosses had been distributed. The weather was still fine, but rain clouds were gathering in the distance and a breeze was whipping up waves in the Channel. During a break in the proceedings, Napoleon took a telescope and turned towards the sea. He trained it on England, the object of his current preoccupations. The white cliffs of Dover were clearly visible in the sunlight, less than thirty miles from Boulogne. Napoleon had long been familiar with the sight:

I have seen the English coast as clearly as one can see the Calvary [at Fontainebleau] from the Tuileries. One could pick out the houses, and see plenty of movement. The Channel is a mere ditch. It will be crossed as soon as someone is brave enough to try it.

And who was brave enough? Napoleon, of course. The arrangements were already well in hand. A few more days and everything would be ready for the invasion.

It had been planned down to the last detail. Julius Caesar had invaded England from Boulogne. His troops had landed somewhere between Walmer and Deal, where the gently shelving beach had made it easy for the legions to swarm ashore. As Caesar had invaded, so would Napoleon. From Deal he would advance to Canterbury, and from there to Chatham, Rochester and London. The English did not possess an army capable of stopping him, any more than their ancestors had been able to stop Caesar.

The campaign had been planned so meticulously that test dies for a commemorative medal had already been made. The medal was a classical affair, with a picture of Napoleon crowned with laurels on one side and one of Hercules on the other, subduing England in the shape of a half-man, half-fish. 'Descente en Angleterre', said the medal. 'Frappée à Londres en 1804'. Not true, of course, but who would ever know?

Thus would France be avenged. Thus would ten centuries of insult be expunged (Napoleon varied this speech – sometimes he thought it was only six centuries). Several centuries anyway of English tyranny, armies of boorish Anglo-Saxons rampaging unrestrained through the civilisation of France. Hordes of shirtless English peasants, roaring drunk, fighting anyone they met. The embarrassment of Crécy, the cruelty of Henry V, the disrespect of the archers at Agincourt, giving the chivalry of France a two-fingered salute to show that they could still pull their bowstrings. The burghers of Calais, the capture of Boulogne by Henry VIII (the town still had the cannon balls). The loss of Canada and India. The French kings and nobles dragged across the Channel and held captive for years in the Tower of London, some to be heavily ransomed, others to die miserably in that terrible place. All of this and much, much more would be avenged by Napoleon. A calm sea, a few days of good weather, and he would be in

London, flying the tricolour from the flagpoles of that same Tower. Then would come the reckoning for all those years of insult.

Napoleon had already decided what he would do when he had conquered London: 'With God's help I will put an end to the future and very existence of England.' A republic would be proclaimed, with liberty, equality and fraternity for all. King George III would be removed from his throne, although allowed to live on as Citizen Hanover. The nobility would be abolished, along with the House of Lords. Their lands and fine houses would be redistributed among Napoleon's supporters. The House of Commons would be allowed to remain, but only after major reform. A proclamation would be issued announcing that the French had come as friends, to restore popular government and liberate the common people from a corrupt and wicked aristocracy. There would be democracy and a redistribution of property in favour of the ordinary working man. The treasures and fine arts of the aristocracy would be redistributed, too – taken to France, where they would be far better appreciated by their new owners than a lot of useless English lords.

Then what? With England out of the way, the world would belong to Napoleon. He would be master of the seas, Emperor of all he surveyed. The West Indies would be his, rich in slaves and sugar. The route to India would again be open, and Canada and South Africa. Trade, commerce, profit, and no one to oppose him. He would make France the richest, greatest, most powerful country on the face of the earth. He would make it the world's first and only superpower, far surpassing anything Caesar had known, with himself unrivalled at its head. The prospect was dazzling, to say the least.

There was, however, one small cloud on this agreeably sunny horizon.

Napoleon adjusted his telescope. Turning away from Dover, he refocused on a sight much closer to home – a line of warships cruising the open sea outside Boulogne harbour. The ships were Royal Navy vessels, blockading the port just out of range of the shore batteries. They had been there for more than a year, watching the French army's every move. They were so close that they had heard the cheers for Napoleon and seen the banners waving around his throne.

Napoleon closed his telescope. The Royal Navy was an irrelevance. He had already devised a plan to get rid of the blockade. The ships would be lured away on false pretences, and while they were gone he would invade England behind their backs. His admirals had the details.

He consulted his watch. The party wasn't over yet. By some accounts there was a grand finale still to come – the arrival of the invasion barges that would ferry his army across the Channel. Their arrival was a well-kept secret, a surprise to rally the troops. The barges would appear out of nowhere, to highly theatrical effect. The sailors manning them would leap ashore amid wild cheering to join forces with their brothers in the army, throwing their arms around each other and shedding brave tears. Then they would all march past Napoleon, the sailors leading the way with boarding axes at their shoulders. More than 100,000 soldiers and sailors would swing past the podium, while Napoleon took the salute from his throne. It would be a splendid climax to the day's festivities.

But the flotilla was late. It should have arrived as Napoleon finished distributing the crosses. Something had held it up – perhaps the breeze that was getting stronger every minute, stirring up the waters of the Channel.

Laure Junot, wife of one of Napoleon's generals, could see that something was wrong.

It was five o'clock, and for about an hour I had observed the Emperor turning repeatedly to M. Decrès, the Minister of Marine, and speaking to him in a low voice. Then he took a telescope and looked out to sea, as if he was hoping to see a distant sail. At length his impatience appeared to get the better of him. Berthier, too, who was biting his nails in spite of being a Marshal, was also looking out to sea. Junot was there as well, all of them talking privately among themselves. They were obviously waiting for something to happen.

At length the Minister of Marine got a message and immediately told the Emperor. Napoleon grabbed M. Decrès' telescope so violently that it fell and rolled down the steps of the throne. We all looked in the same direction and saw a flotilla of between 1,000 and 1,200 boats, advancing towards Boulogne from the other nearby ports and Holland.

It was an armada, of sorts. The barges were flat-bottomed, specially designed for the invasion. They were part of a larger fleet that would amount to more than 2,000 vessels when it was fully assembled. The coast of northern France had seen nothing like it since the days of William the Conqueror.

Other accounts, perhaps downplaying the incident, put the number of vessels at only forty-seven, bringing more troops from Le Havre. Whatever the true figure, they made a stirring sight as they approached the shore. They would put the fear of God into the watching English, who would be in no doubt as to what the barges were for. So many landing craft so close to England could mean only one thing.

But then something happened, one of those unfortunate accidents that could befall anyone, if they don't know what they're doing. The officer leading the first division of the flotilla was unfamiliar with the waters. Instead of waiting for a pilot to guide him in, he pressed on regardless, not realising that there were some new coastal works in the shallows that didn't appear on his chart. The leading barges bumped into them and promptly capsized. A number of soldiers vanished overboard, to loud cries of alarm from the watchers on land. The water was shallow, so most were able to make it ashore by themselves. Even so, one still managed to drown.

The onlookers rushed to help. Half of Boulogne hurried down to the seashore. They pulled the soldiers out of the water with a great deal of shouting and gesticulating, then turned their attention to the barges, now floating upside down on the swell. Admiral Decrès had warned Napoleon that the flat-bottomed design was not well suited to the open sea. But Napoleon hadn't listened. He wasn't interested in naval design.

Napoleon remained on his throne, appalled. To be humiliated thus, in front of the English! Caesar had had a slave at his elbow during his triumphs, whispering in his ear to remind him that he was still only mortal. Napoleon had the French navy.

Climbing down from his throne, he strode angrily towards the cliff top with Decrès and Marshal Berthier. The air was blue with obscenities as Napoleon watched the rescue operation. Onlookers agreed that he had not been in such a bad mood for a long time. There was to be a grand dinner for the soldiers that evening and a display of fireworks afterwards if the rain held off. Napoleon's mood did not improve as the heavens opened and the rain came pouring down. It grew worse, if anything, because he was not going to forget this day for a long time to come. The sniggers of the English, as they enjoyed the antics of the flotilla, had been more than he could bear.

CHAPTER 2

---•◦•---

BRITAIN AWAITS
THE INVASION

On the other side of the Channel, at the precise point between Walmer and Deal that Napoleon had chosen for the invasion, an ill-assorted collection of ploughboys and fishermen stood waiting to repel him. There were 3,000 of them when they all turned up, many armed only with pikes or pitchforks. They were the Cinque Port Volunteers and their leader was the Prime Minister himself, Mr William Pitt. He had a farm nearby.

Anyone less suited to the task of hurling the French back into the sea would have been difficult to imagine. William Pitt was forty-five in the summer of 1804, a spindly bachelor with gout and a racking cough. He had first become Prime Minister at twenty-four and with one short break had continued so ever since. He was worn out with long years of politics and strife. All he really wanted to do now was to retire to his farm and spend the rest of his life improving the estate and putting his affairs in order.

Indeed, Pitt had already retired once, resigning the premiership in 1801 to Henry Addington, a close political colleague. At Amiens the following year, England and France had agreed a peace for the first time in almost a decade. But the peace had not lasted and the two countries were at war again. Addington was not up to the job of wartime leader, so Pitt had returned to office in May 1804 – the same week that Napoleon had been elected Emperor of France.

As well as Prime Minister, Pitt was also Warden of the Cinque Ports, the seven Kent and Sussex ports, originally five, that had enjoyed financial privileges in the Middle Ages in return for providing seamen and ships against the French. The job was supposed to be a sinecure, a way of pensioning off political figures approaching the end of their public lives. It came with a handsome salary and an official residence at Walmer Castle, overlooking the English Channel.

In time of war, however, it was no sinecure. As Warden, William Pitt now found himself in charge of the Cinque Port Volunteers, civilians in uniform with no military experience to speak of. Without enough muskets to go round, some of them did not even have proper weapons and were armed only with whatever they could lay their hands on. But if the French arrived off the Kent coast, they were all that stood between Napoleon and an unopposed landing on the beach between Walmer and Deal.

The precedents were not encouraging. In 55 BC, Julius Caesar had invaded Britain, almost certainly intending to land at Dover harbour. But the cliffs had been so sheer, and the ancient Britons so menacing, that his fleet had continued northwards for another seven miles until they reached the shingle beach between Walmer and Deal. The ancient Britons had kept pace with them on land, driving their chariots along the cliff tops. They waded into the sea when the Romans attempted to land, fighting hand-to-hand in the shallows. For a while it had been touch and go, the Romans experiencing much tougher resistance than they were used to. But then the standard-bearer of the 10th Legion had leapt into the water, encouraging others to leave their boats and follow him. The Britons had been forced back on to dry land. Once ashore, the Romans had rapidly asserted themselves. The Britons were defeated and very quickly sued for peace. Many feared the same would happen again if Napoleon ever managed to get his army ashore and safely established on English soil.

The French army was terrifying, as the English were the first to admit. Soon to be retitled the Grand Army, it was the finest military machine in the world. The English were amateurs by comparison. They did possess a modest professional force, backed by local militias and a system of volunteers that could be called upon in times of emergency, but nothing on the English side of the Channel could compare with the massed ranks of Frenchmen drilling ominously on the cliffs between Boulogne and Calais.

Partly, it was a question of money. The British had long been reluctant to pay for an army if they could possibly avoid it. But mostly it was a dislike of militarism that harked back to Cromwellian times – a visceral contempt for the rule of the major-generals who had subverted Parliament and chopped the king's head off without any legitimate authority. If you had a powerful army, ran the argument, then sooner or later one of its generals would seize the throne and declare himself an emperor. That was all very well across the Channel, but in England it explained why commissions in the army were obtained by purchase rather than merit. Officers who could afford to buy their commissions came from the propertied classes and were unlikely to favour revolution. That many of them were not very good at their job was simply an unfortunate by-product of the system.

The polite name for such officers was 'gentleman amateurs'. None fitted the bill more than Mr Pitt himself. He was no fool, but no soldier, either. Long years in Downing Street had left him ill-prepared for the cut and thrust of military life. His talents lay elsewhere.

Needs must, however, and Pitt wore his colonel's uniform with pride. He took his duties very seriously, drilling the men every week and putting them through their paces along the Kent and Sussex coasts. His niece Hester Stanhope frequently accompanied him on his expeditions:

> Mr Pitt absolutely goes through the fatigue of a *drill-sergeant*. It is parade after parade, at fifteen or twenty miles distant from each other. I often attend him, and it is quite as much as I am equal to . . . If Mr Pitt does not overdo it and injure his health every other consideration becomes trifling . . . He is thin but certainly strong, and his spirits are excellent . . . Mr Pitt is determined to remain acting Colonel when his regiment is called into the field.

Others were less impressed. 'Can any thing equal the ridicule of Pitt riding about from Downing Street to Wimbledon, and from Wimbledon to Cox Heath, to inspect military carriages, impregnable batteries, and Lord Chatham's reviews?' asked his cousin Lord Grenville on 25 August. And Major-General John Moore, commanding the military base at Shorncliffe, was even more sceptical.

'On the very first alarm I shall march to aid you, with my Cinque Port regiments,' Pitt assured him there one day. 'You have never told me where you will place us.'

'Do you see that hill?' Moore replied. 'You and yours shall be drawn up on it. You will make a most formidable appearance to the enemy, while I, with the soldiers, shall be fighting on the beach.'

In truth, though, they would all be needed because there weren't nearly enough troops to go round. The Roman beach between Walmer and Deal was not the only place where Napoleon might land. He was also considering the much longer beach north of Deal, stretching up to Margate. Or he could land in Sussex, as William the Conqueror had done, or Essex, or the West Country, or Ireland. With the advantage of surprise, he could land 100,000 men anywhere he liked within a few short hours, while the English were wrong-footed elsewhere. It was a nightmare for those on the British side trying to guess where he might come.

But the most obvious landing point was somewhere in Kent or Sussex, the thirty miles of coastline directly opposite Boulogne and the other invasion ports. It was here that the British had amassed as many troops as they dared, without leaving other parts of the country undefended. From Kent or Sussex, the French could be in London in five days. Logic dictated that this was where they were most likely to land.

The coast was spectacularly unprepared for an invasion. Apart from Dover Castle, a crumbling fort at Sandgate, and the ancient Tudor forts at Walmer and Deal, it had no permanent defences at all. The dockyard at Chatham was unprotected, as were Woolwich arsenal and the naval base at Deptford. If once the French got ashore, there would be very little to stop them marching straight for London. All that would stand between Napoleon and victory were a few battalions of regular troops and a much larger number of volunteers, some of whom really didn't know one end of a musket from the other.

Part of the problem was the huge mass of volunteers. So many had offered their services – if only to avoid a compulsory ballot for the more onerous militia – that the government had been swamped. At first there weren't enough uniforms to go round, let alone muskets. England had been at peace until quite recently. It would take time to get the country on a war footing again, fully prepared for an invasion. And time was something they didn't have.

But the British were rallying, as they always did in times of crisis. If they didn't have enough muskets, then anything else would suffice, as a notice cheerfully proclaimed:

> You must train yourselves to wield a pitch-fork, or a hedgestake, if you cannot procure a musquet; practise the old English cudgel-play quarter staff: *Assemble together, and learn to march, to wheel, to form companies, and, in short, to become half Soldiers* – then, British Spirit and British Valour will supply the *other half*, and manifest themselves in a most formidable manner to the imperious, the ambitious, but *powerful* Foe!

Quite how long the Grand Army would be detained by a crowd of English yokels hacking at them with sticks was open to debate. 'You might as well suppose that the enemy was to be kept off by bodkins or knitting needles,' one Member of Parliament commented acidly. But sticks were all some of them had until more muskets arrived.

Their best hope of defeating the French was to be forewarned of their arrival. With enough notice of the invasion, the British could rush in reinforcements from elsewhere, hurrying troops to the spot to await the French landing. To this end, an elaborate early-warning system had been set up off the coast, composed of a chain of Royal Navy vessels primed for ship-to-shore communication. Once the invasion fleet had been sighted, the news could be relayed immediately to the shutter-telegraph station (a precursor of the semaphore) at Deal. From there, a short message – '100,000 French heading for Sandwich' – could reach London in just a few minutes. The final telegraph station stood on the Admiralty roof in Whitehall. Once received, the message could be rushed across the parade ground to the Prime Minister's office in Downing Street in another two or three minutes at most. With luck, London would know about the invasion before the French had even landed.

The shutter telegraph was supported by a network of beacons on every prominent hilltop – signal fires to announce the French arrival. There were fifteen beacons in Kent alone, among them Pluckley, Minster, Westwell and Lenham. Each was supplied with eight wagonloads of fuel and three or four barrels of tar. When the French came, they were to burn wood by night to produce a bright light, damp hay by day to produce thick smoke. The beacons were identified by a large pole in the middle, flying a white flag from the top.

From Kent, the beacons branched outwards to all parts of the country, everywhere from Cornwall to Scotland. Each stood within two or three miles of the next, in direct line of sight. From the Kentish coast they ran west to Sussex and north-west to the River Thames, and from there across the water to Essex, Hertfordshire and beyond. Where there were no hills, as in East Anglia, other means of signalling had been devised. The village of Great Snoring in Norfolk employed a large red flag on the church tower for the purpose, as did Mum's Hedge and Sewers End in Essex. But most parts of the country could be reached by beacon. The system had worked well during the Spanish Armada scare of 1588. It would work again when the French fleet appeared over the horizon.

For the inhabitants of the Kentish coast, however, none of this provided much comfort. They were first in line for attack, and they knew it. The Grand Army was camped out on the cliffs between Calais and Boulogne, its rows of whitewashed huts plainly visible to the people of Dover and Folkestone. Many of Folkestone's citizens had fled inland after one of Napoleon's visits to Boulogne. The French town had been illuminated for the occasion, its lights shining so brightly across the Channel that the English had assumed the worst. There had been similar scares at Dover and Eastbourne, people packing up their valuables and fleeing the coast, putting as much distance as possible between themselves and the French. They did not want to be there when the Grand Army landed.

Fear of Napoleon lay at the bottom of it, the great bogeyman of Europe. The French army was nothing without its leader. As one of his subordinates shrewdly observed, 'Napoleon's great-coat and hat placed on the end of a pole on the coast at Brest would make Europe run to arms from one end to another.' No one disagreed, least of all the British. He was the man they all hated – a Corsican, and according to *The Times*, a tyrant, usurper, and Mediterranean bandit without morals or scruple. A menace to civilisation and decent people everywhere.

Napoleon Bonaparte. The man from nowhere who now sat on a throne and called himself an emperor. The English were terrified of him as they had been terrified of nobody else for a very long time. All along the Channel coast, from Eastbourne and Hastings to Dungeness, New Romney, Folkestone, Dover and Margate, they cast anxious eyes towards France and asked themselves the same question over and over again. When was Bonaparte going to come?

CHAPTER 3

―――――・◆・―――――

NAPOLEON LAYS HIS PLANS

The fireworks at Boulogne had to be postponed because of the rain, but only for a day. At 9 the following evening, thousands of people returned to the cliff tops to watch the fun. It began with a loud bang, followed by a wonderful display of bombs and rockets exploding over the sea. At the end, a row of 15,000 soldiers fired a magnificent *feu de joie* into the air, their weapons loaded with Roman candles instead of musket balls. The people of Boulogne remembered the spectacle for years to come.

Napoleon watched the display from his pavilion on the cliff above the town. He had built it near the ruins of the Tour d'Ordre, a Roman lighthouse very similar to the one that still stands at Dover. It was close also to the telegraph signalling station that kept him in touch with Paris. The pavilion had a small bedroom at one end, but consisted mostly of a council chamber with a painted ceiling depicting an eagle hurling a thunderbolt at England, under Napoleon's direction. The chamber had a map of the Channel on the wall, and a green baize table for conferences. The room boasted only one chair, for the Emperor's exclusive use. Everyone else had to stand.

The pavilion also housed a powerful telescope, four feet long and a foot wide, that stood by the window on a mahogany tripod. On a clear day, it gave Napoleon an excellent view of Dover Castle across the Channel. He spent a lot of time looking that way, scanning the shores of England, so near across the water, and yet so far as well.

It was in the pavilion that he worked on his invasion plans. Napoleon's main headquarters was an eighteenth-century chateau at Pont-de-Briques,

29

a few miles outside Boulogne on the Paris road. There, his staff ran to five generals, eleven aides-de-camp and thirty other officers, all of them at work on the invasion of England. To these were added a constant procession of ships' pilots, harbour masters and other seafaring men who came to see him in the less formal pavilion above the town, each with something to say about the feasibility of the invasion. Napoleon heard them all, sometimes in silence, sometimes with sharp questioning. But the more he heard, the less he liked what they told him.

It was not as easy as it looked, invading Britain. The sailors could see all sorts of practical difficulties that had not occurred to the military men on Napoleon's staff. The wind for one thing, the tide for another. The impossibility of getting out of harbour in a hurry, with so many ships packed closely together. The need for a calm crossing and an unopposed landing, to prevent the troops getting their powder wet when they stormed ashore. The need for resupply from the sea, if the English burned their crops and drove away their livestock, as they almost certainly would. It was a mammoth undertaking, throwing an army across the Channel, not to be attempted lightly. The potential for disaster was endless.

Wind was a major factor. Even a light breeze could upset the invasion barges, as Napoleon had already seen. What they needed was a calm day – several calm days – to allow the barges to be rowed across the Channel while the English watched impotently, powerless to intervene. Either that or a good dose of winter fog, so that the barges could slip across unnoticed in the gloom.

Tides were a serious problem, too. A whole invasion fleet could not be embarked on one tide. It would require five or six, which meant the first soldiers would have been at sea for three days before the rearguard caught up. They would still have the Channel to cross, and surprise would have been lost because the Royal Navy would have sent word back to England as soon as it saw what was happening.

Even getting out of harbour was an issue. Down at Cadiz, it sometimes took three days to reach the open sea, and that was with room to manoeuvre. Boulogne and the other invasion ports were so tightly packed with landing craft that they would not enjoy that luxury. Once the barges did emerge, there were sandbanks to negotiate, and unpredictable coastal currents. Caesar had had trouble with the currents off the English coast. Napoleon would too.

He was no sailor, as his detractors never tired of pointing out. Admiral Decrès had counselled vehemently against the flat-bottomed barges, observing that what looked good on the Seine would be less impressive in the middle of the Channel, with a lot of seasick soldiers clinging on for dear life. But Napoleon saw everything in military terms. If you wanted to move a force from A to B, you gave the order and it was done. If you wanted them back again, back they came. He had little sympathy with admirals bleating about wind, or the lack of it, shaking their heads and saying that ships couldn't be moved just anywhere if the weather wasn't right. He found it hard to understand that the sea was a law unto itself, beyond anyone's control.

Yet he was not deterred. The invasion had to go ahead. Britain was France's only enemy. Once the British were defeated, there would be peace again – on Napoleon's terms. The invasion would be managed somehow, and then the world would belong to France. Any setbacks in crossing the Channel would be more than compensated for by the splendid prospects that beckoned thereafter.

His admirals had grave doubts, but didn't voice them as loudly as they should have done. Like most dictators, Napoleon was short-tempered and did not warm to nay-sayers. He sometimes threatened to hang his admirals if they didn't do what he wanted. It helped to concentrate their minds. And anyway, the invasion was perfectly feasible. There were problems, certainly, but they could be overcome. There was no situation that could not be remedied with a little ingenuity. That was what admirals were for.

The work had been going on for years. The fishing port of Boulogne had originally been quite unsuitable for the launching of an invasion fleet. But the harbour had been widened and deepened, with a great basin dug out and lined with stone to accommodate the landing craft. A breakwater had been installed, and a sluice. All being well, Boulogne would now be able to launch 300 vessels on a single tide. Similar work had been done at Étaples, Ambleteuse and Wimereux, further along the coast. The task had been laborious, the expense vast. The cost had been met by the sale of Louisiana, recently wrested from Spain, to the United States.

The invasion fleet was being assembled too, though not as swiftly as Napoleon wished. It was the despair of the sailors on his staff. Not only were the barges flat-bottomed, but they also had low gunwales for easy disembarkation. The soldiers could get out easily, but so could water get in. Even on a flat sea, the keel-less barges were virtually unmanoeuvrable in anything but a following wind. They were just the thing for running the troops ashore once the French reached England – but how many of them would survive the journey across the Channel?

The escort vessels were little better. The first troops ashore were to be provided with covering fire by *prames* – shallow-draught corvettes armed with twelve heavy cannon. But the *prames* too were unstable in heavy seas, as were the *chaloupes canonnières*, little more than floating gun platforms without a keel. The *bateaux canonniers* were more seaworthy, but could not traverse their guns. The whole boat had to be pointed towards the target. And all of these different craft were so heavily weighed down with cannon that the strain on their hulls was unacceptable.

With hindsight, Napoleon might have done better to build steam ships instead – the technology existed. A steam-powered ironclad could have towed any number of landing craft across the Channel without any need for a breeze. But the French still thought in terms of wooden ships and sail, as did the English across the Channel. Steam power had yet to catch on.

Or he could have dug a tunnel. All the labour that had gone into digging out Boulogne and the other harbours could have gone into burrowing under the sea, pushing forwards from Calais to the English coast. Plenty of people in England thought Napoleon was doing precisely that. Cartoons had been published in London, not all of them fanciful, showing the French army creeping along a Channel tunnel, ready to burst out at Dover and take the English by surprise.

He could have built a bridge, or a series of floating forts. He could even have come by air, as individual balloonists already had. The French inventor Jean-Charles Thilorier had proposed the construction of a huge balloon, capable of carrying 3,000 troops at a time. Napoleon had commissioned him to produce a quarter-scale model, but Thilorier had been defeated by the practicalities, although he clung stoutly to the theory.

So an invasion fleet it was, and the work continued apace – not only in Boulogne, but in all the ports from Étaples to Ostend. The total number of ships amounted to 2,293, a massive logistical headache for the harbour masters involved. The flotilla was divided into six divisions, of which only two came from Boulogne. The others were based at Wimereux, Étaples, Ambleteuse and Calais. No two divisions were the same. Some were to carry assault troops, some cavalry and reinforcements, others baggage and artillery. Some of the troops were Dutch, some Italian. In all, there were upwards of 150,000 men to be fed, trained and kept busy to prevent them from becoming bored and disruptive. The work went on around the clock.

Nobody worked harder than Napoleon himself. Fifteen hours a day was quite normal for him. His step-daughter Hortense observed him during her visits to the Pont-de-Briques chateau:

> Work occupied Napoleon entirely. He neither rested by day nor by night, everything was subordinated to his work. His hours of sleep were no more fixed than those of his meals. He always lunched alone, we only saw him at dinner. On the days when he was preoccupied with some problem, nobody dared interrupt him for fear of encroaching on a serious thought or of receiving a rebuke.

Fifteen minutes was usually enough for Napoleon to grab a bite to eat. Sleep never lasted more than a few hours a night. He was always up again at six.

But this was his moment and he was determined to seize it. The British were wide open to attack, as he kept pointing out to his staff:

> A nation is very foolish, when it has no fortifications and no army, to lay itself open to seeing an army of 100,000 veterans land on its shores. This is the masterpiece of the flotilla! It costs a great deal of money, but *it is necessary for us to be masters of the sea for six hours only, and England will have ceased to exist.*

Years later, looking back on his career, he revisited the subject again:

London is but a few miles from Calais; the English army, scattered along the coast, could not unite in time to cover the capital. Of course this expedition could not be attempted by a mere *corps d'armée*, but its success was almost certain with 150,000 men presenting themselves before London within five days of their landing. Flotillas were the only means by which these 150,000 men could be landed in a few hours, and possession gained of all the shallows . . . Only ten hours would be needed for landing 150,000 disciplined and victorious soldiers upon a coast destitute of fortifications and undefended by a regular army.

True enough. A day of calm weather and Napoleon would be master of England. But the autumn equinox was approaching – with its winds and storms – and the fleet wasn't fully operational yet. If they didn't sail soon, the invasion would have to be postponed, perhaps until the following year. And if they waited that long, who could say what might happen in the meantime?

While Napoleon's staff worked round the clock, the men of the Grand Army watched and waited, wondering when their day would come.

They were a tremendous army, as everyone agreed. Upwards of 80,000 of them were grouped along the cliff tops between Calais and Boulogne, with the rest accommodated at various locations inland. The Boulogne troops were commanded by Marshal Soult, still only in his thirties and known throughout the army as a hard taskmaster. He had built up a highly professional staff, selected on merit, and exercised his troops three times a week for twelve hours at a stretch. The men admired him for his courage, which was exemplary. Soult had been badly wounded during the Italian campaign while leading from the front. They appreciated that in a commander.

Ney too was a legend to his men. He commanded the camp at Montreuil. They called him the 'Red Lion' because of his hair, or the 'bravest of the brave' because of his unfailing courage. Ney was none too bright, but could always be seen in the thickest of the action. Every regiment under his command had a schoolroom for the officers, where they were required to discuss tactics and swap ideas. Ney might not be clever himself, but he understood the need for professionalism in others. It was mandatory for the officers under his command to have a firm grasp of their work and approach it in a proper manner.

Davout commanded the Ambleteuse camp under strict discipline. Marshal Jean Lannes, his head bent towards his left shoulder as the result of a wound, commanded at Wimereux. All of them were highly professional officers, risen on merit. They knew their business, and they had the trust of their men. Napoleon could not have asked for better commanders to lead his troops across the Channel. A junior officer admired them unreservedly:

I do not believe that there existed at any period, nor in any country, such an excellent military school as there was at the Boulogne camp. The general who had command of it, the generals under his orders, and the troops which it comprised were all drafted from the pick of the French army, and the greatest general that had ever appeared, Napoleon Bonaparte, used to come himself frequently to inspect those old troops and the young fighting men who were being formed under those excellent models.

The men were in splendid form. Those who had fought in Egypt or Italy never tired of telling the tale. Those who had seen no action longed to emulate them. They trained hard, practising embarkation and disembarkation, leaping in and out of their landing craft, learning to jump into the sea and wade ashore without losing formation or getting their powder wet. They learned how to lead their horses aboard the barges and how to bring the heavy artillery ashore. They practised the drill again and again, going through the motions repeatedly until they could almost have done it in their sleep. They practised sometimes under cannon fire, their own batteries shooting above their heads to give them a feel of what it would be like. They practised until they felt there was nothing they didn't know about seaborne assaults and how to conduct them.

The exercises were realistic in every detail, terrifyingly so to some of the younger men:

During a practice attack, I sniffed the scent of powder for the first time and received my baptism of fire. I hate to admit it, but I was really frightened! The terrible reality of danger, the brutality of cannon balls, bullets flying, corpses lying around would make any recruit's heart beat faster. But we soon got used to it. A searching look from the veterans, a scornful smile, above all the fear of ridicule, banished all nervousness and we ended up encouraging danger.

The men were feeling good. They lived well too. The camp at Boulogne was a model of its kind. The men had lived in tents at first, but these had swiftly been replaced by permanent wooden huts, walled with mud in the local style and roofed with thatch. It was alleged that artefacts from Caesar's army and William the Conqueror's had been dug up on the spot where Napoleon's tent had been pitched – an encouraging omen for the troops. Each hut was whitewashed and accommodated fifteen men much more comfortably than in barracks. There were metalled roads around the camp, named after the Grand Army's victories. There were gardens, villas for the officers, tree-lined walks and carefully maintained flower beds. Meals were regular and filling, announced by bugle three times a day. The men complained constantly about the food, but what happy army doesn't?

They were kept busy from morning until night, as soldiers have to be if they aren't fighting. When not training, or digging out the harbour, or building huts, or repairing boats, they were on barrack duty, gardening or tending poultry, tidying up the camp and keeping it in good order. There was always something to do. Their leisure time was organised as well – fencing, horse racing, foot races along the sands, with Napoleon himself distributing the prizes. Some of them made tiny yachts on wheels and ran them along the beach. They were allowed dances occasionally, the younger and prettier soldiers taking the girls' parts in fisherwomen's caps, dancing the quadrille to wild music. There were, of course, no real girls allowed in the camp. The army's commanders knew better than that.

The real girls lived not far away, in a place just outside Boulogne nicknamed 'Happy Valley'. Despite the army's best efforts, there were thousands of them, doing ten times more damage than the enemy ever would. During his Italian campaign, Napoleon had decreed that any woman caught near the army would be painted black, paraded through the camp and then expelled. The decree had been enforced for all of two weeks before he had given up in despair. Wherever the army went, a flock of women always followed, ready to tend to the men's needs. After all, the lads needed their washing done, didn't they, and their sewing?

So the girls lived in Happy Valley and the soldiers visited them there, not all of them carrying laundry. The officers kept well away, pursuing their own adventures in Boulogne or else at Pont-de-Briques, near the Emperor's headquarters, which was out of bounds to the other ranks. There were days for officers at certain brothels and days for the men. The girls worked with a will. Madame Forty Thousand was the star, beloved of the army, but there were plenty of others. The police expelled them regularly, with orders never to set foot in Boulogne again. Somehow, though, they always managed to return.

The provost marshal was busy, too, keeping military discipline in the town. It was difficult, with so many young men full of drink and looking for trouble. Rivalry between the regiments was intense. The Grenadiers considered themselves the finest troops that ever lived and offered to fight anybody who disagreed. The cavalry accepted the challenge, as did the infantry of the line. They all looked down on the artillery and the engineers, dull technicians in dull uniforms. The artillery and the engineers stood their ground, hitting back for the honour of their corps. Gangs from every regiment and corps thronged the streets at night, cheerfully insulting each other and seeking any excuse for a brawl. Many still wore their hair in old-fashioned *cadenette* plaits and responded violently to any mockery. The military police did their best, but it was impossible to keep the gangs apart. Blood was often spilt when they met, and bones broken. Sometimes there was rape and murder too. Armies are difficult to manage when they're not in action. All those young men, in such a small town – there was bound to be trouble.

When it was over, the last bottle drained and the last head broken, they picked themselves up and rolled back to camp, lurching unsteadily up the hill to report in at the guardroom at the top. Often it was still light when they returned, the long summer evening not yet over, the sun still glinting across the sea towards England, where they expected to be in a few days' time. Sometimes they could make out the Dungeness lighthouse in the gloaming, twinkling at them from the opposite shore.

Their thoughts turned often to England, and the challenge that lay ahead. They would be in London soon, most of whom had never been in Paris. London was the biggest city on earth, and the richest. The Emperor had promised it to them, when they captured it – theirs for the looting. They could take everything they could carry away, and then come back for more. They could steal everything worth stealing and bring it in triumph back to France. There would be enough to buy each of them a farm, or an inn, or anything they wanted. Enough for everyone to retire on the proceeds, once they had conquered the English capital. It was a mouth-watering prospect for illiterate peasant boys without a sou to their name, an opportunity that would never come their way again. And the women, too. There would be plenty of women. The Grand Army was counting the days.

CHAPTER 4

———— ·•◆•· ————

BRITAIN'S MILITARY
DEFENCES

In his office overlooking Horse Guards Parade, the Duke of York, commander-in-chief of the British army, viewed the arrival of the French with rather less enthusiasm. He was only too aware of what would happen if they captured London. It was his job to stop them.

The view from the duke's office has changed very little in the past 200 years. His desk was probably the one still being used in the room today. It looks out across the parade ground towards Buckingham Palace, where his parents lived, at the far end of St James's Park. To the left of the window, No. 10 Downing Street – where William Pitt had his office – still stands 100 yards away. To the right, also 100 yards away, the Admiralty is still there as well, the shutter telegraph on the roof replaced now by a forest of radio antennas. For more than 250 years, the Prime Minister and the heads of the army and navy have worked within a few minutes' walk of each other, able to confer at a moment's notice if need be. In August 1804, they needed to confer more often than not.

The Duke of York was George III's second son. He had been appointed commander-in-chief of the army at thirty-five. Not for him the hard slog and promotion on merit that had accompanied Ney and Soult's rise to the top. He was commander-in-chief because his father was king.

The duke's active service record was not distinguished. He was the grand old Duke of York of the nursery rhyme who marched his men to the top of the hill and marched them down again. He had campaigned without distinction in Flanders and Holland, lurching from one disaster to the next until eventually he had had to be recalled. Promotion had swiftly covered his embarrassment. The duke was now the man in charge of defending England against the Grand Army – perhaps the most professional army the world had ever seen.

In fairness to the duke, not everything in Flanders had been his fault. The British army had been incompetent to an astonishing degree. He had done his best with very poor material against an enemy fired with revolutionary zeal. And if he was not very good in the field, he was much better as an administrator. On promotion to commander-in-chief, he had set in motion a wholesale programme of reform, drawing on his experiences in Flanders. He had worked hard to reduce corruption, weeding out the bad officers and rewarding the good, and improving the care of the men. The programme had been under way for several years, but was still very far from complete.

The officers were the biggest headache. Taken collectively, they were idle, ignorant, incompetent and undisciplined, the products of a system that depended entirely on money for promotion, rather than aptitude. The duke himself had been a colonel at seventeen. Others had been bought colonelcies while still at school or even, in one or two cases, while still in the nursery. If their parents had money, it took less than a month to advance from a civilian with no military experience to lieutenant-colonel in a smart regiment. If they didn't have money, they could serve competently for forty years and never reach that rank.

The system was too entrenched for the duke to abolish it overnight. Instead, he was gradually increasing the possibility of promotion on merit and establishing the principle that commissions could no longer be held by children or others unsuitable for the task. His reforms were beginning to have effect, as the *British Military Journal* gratefully acknowledged:

We no longer hear of captains at the boarding school, of majors spinning their tops, and of beardless lieutenant-colonels lording it over veterans. An officer cannot now obtain rank but by actual residence with his regiment and he is prevented from skipping from one step to another by being obliged to serve a certain time in each previous to his promotion.

There were exceptions, of course, even in the duke's own household. His mistress Mary Anne Clarke took advantage of her position to obtain promotions and appointments for officers willing to bribe her for the privilege. It was said that she had even arranged a commission for her own footman, for no other reason than that he thought he might look good in military uniform. Plenty of other officers joined the army for similar reasons. They were always the first to sell out at the prospect of any fighting, hastily disposing of their commissions to the highest bidder and returning to civilian life. Even with the duke's reforms, there were still a great many officers in the army who really should not have been there.

The duke himself probably knew nothing of his mistress's activities. He was a nice man, well liked by almost everyone who knew him. 'Big, burly, loud, jolly, cursing, courageous; he had a most affectionate and lovable disposition, was noble and generous to a fault, and was never known to break a promise.' The duke had many friends and very few enemies, which made him the antithesis of Napoleon. But his personal pleasantness was not an advantage in his profession. He lacked the killer instinct of the best generals. No one was in any doubt as to what the outcome would be if he and Napoleon ever faced each other in the green fields of southern England or even – God forbid – at the gates of Buckingham Palace.

Fortunately for the army, there was a scattering of highly competent officers in influential positions who knew their business and were just as professional as the French. One was John Moore, who had introduced the Light Infantry to the British army, a new breed of soldier inspired by the French Voltigeurs and the Indians and backwoodsmen of the American wars. The Light Infantry wore green uniforms and travelled light and fast, trotting where others walked, covering long distances with astonishing speed. Another good officer was Sir Arthur Wellesley, unfortunately not in England at the moment, but making a reputation for himself in India. A third was Major Henry Shrapnel, a resourceful artilleryman working on interesting new ways of blowing the French to pieces. These officers and others like them were the glue that held the rest of the army together.

But the fact remained that it was not much of an army compared to the French. No matter how fast they could march, the Light Infantry were not equipped to delay Napoleon for long. The country lay wide open to attack and everyone knew it. For the Duke of York and his staff, the problem was how to react if once the French got ashore and came heading straight for London.

The obvious place to stop them was on the coast, before they could get more than a toehold on dry land. Armies are at their most vulnerable when coming ashore. But the English coastline was long and virtually undefended. What it needed was a series of interlocking strongpoints, mini-castles that the French could neither bypass nor capture quickly. Something that would break up the momentum of their advance and delay them long enough for British reinforcements to arrive.

The idea for such strongpoints – known as Martello towers – was not new. It had been suggested by a tower at Mortella Point in Corsica, Napoleon's home ground. The British had attacked the tower in 1794 and found it difficult to capture – the tower's tiny garrison had held out for two days before surrendering. John Moore had been one of the officers involved in the attack, and the idea had been brought back to England. A wooden model of the tower had been passed around various government departments, with the recommendation that similar towers should be built all along the invasion coast. But the expense was considered prohibitive, so nothing had been done.

With Napoleon at the gates, however, the idea had been revived. In August 1803, the Duke of York had urged the immediate construction of a chain of Martello towers along the south coast. Again, nothing had been done, largely as a result of bureaucracy and interdepartmental rivalry. The duke had persevered, however, and at long last the Board of Ordnance had been goaded into action. A committee was even now considering what to do. It was planning to report in September 1804 – provided Napoleon hadn't invaded by then, of course.

What the duke wanted – as a matter of the utmost priority – was a series of military strongpoints along the Kent and Sussex coasts, each no more than 500 or 600 yards from the next, so as to provide each other with covering fire. Garrisoned by one officer and twenty-four men, well supplied with grapeshot and canister, such strongpoints could hold out for days behind thick walls, while the enemy found little shelter on the beach. The towers would pose a serious problem for the French, one they could not easily surmount. The expense was still prodigious, particularly if the towers were going to be square, as originally proposed. A square tower with four big guns would be very costly, but an elliptical tower with one gun and two carronades could be built for a fifth of the price, while guaranteeing three-quarters of the fire power. It was problems of this kind that the committee was considering while the Duke of York fretted and the rest of the country waited daily for Napoleon to arrive.

Whatever the committee decided, it would take time for the towers to be built. The French would encounter little immediate opposition when they stormed ashore. But there were other ways to defeat them, or at least impede their progress. One was a scorched-earth strategy, destroying the harvest and driving the livestock away to prevent the enemy living off the land. Another was to break up the roads, delaying the French advance while British reinforcements arrived from elsewhere to intercept them.

A third possibility open to the duke was the flooding of Romney Marsh. It occupied much of the Dungeness peninsula, an area so wide and flat that it was an obvious landing ground for the French. The marsh was good farming land as well, 28,000 acres of excellent pasture reclaimed from the sea and protected by a sea wall. It was drained through five sluices that let the water out at low tide. But if the sluices were left open, the marsh would fill again with sea water, making it impossible for the French to land.

The trouble was, it would take a while to flood – perhaps three or four tides in all. The process would have to be set in motion before the French put to sea. And once the land was flooded with salt water, it would take a long time to reclaim when the war was over. The farmers would have to be compensated, but the government was not prepared to find the money. The Cabinet had been adamant about that.

So a compromise was being discussed. If flooding the land was too costly, it could still be rendered useless by digging a canal across the Grand Army's line of advance. The entire Dungeness peninsula could be cut off by a canal from Hythe to Rye. The proposed waterway would be nineteen miles long, but it would neutralise a good thirty miles of invasion beach.

The canal would present a considerable impediment to the French, while allowing British reinforcements to arrive quickly by barge. With a military road running parallel to it on the landward side and a rampart made of spoil from the canal, it would be an excellent defensive position from which to harass the French. Napoleon would surely think twice about landing at Romney Marsh if he knew there was a fortified canal further inland.

At the moment, however, the idea was still on the drawing board. The indications were that the canal would gain official approval, but nothing had actually been done yet. Not a spadeful of earth dug, or even the route drawn up and surveyed. The canal existed only in the minds of the officers who had proposed it.

Fortunately, the French weren't ready either. According to intelligence reports from Boulogne, they were still putting their fleet together, assembling the landing craft for the invasion. The British didn't have any defences, the French didn't have enough ships. It was going to be a race to see who could complete their preparations first.

If the French won? If they succeeded in getting ashore before the British could stop them? Where else could the Duke of York block their progress along the approaches to London?

To some extent, it depended on where they came ashore. If the French landed west of Hythe, the North Downs stood in their way – a range of hills that would have to be wrested from the British army before they could go any further. The South Downs presented a similar obstacle if the French landed west of Beachy Head, and the Weald of Kent if they landed west of Hastings. If they arrived in east Kent, however, as seemed most likely, the only natural barrier to their progress was the River Medway. The betting was that none of these physical obstacles would hold Napoleon up for long.

What might delay him was the garrison at Dover. It amounted to 4,000 men, safe behind the walls of the castle. Napoleon needed to capture a port before advancing on London, and Dover was the obvious choice. Even if he captured another port nearby, he still wouldn't feel secure with so many British troops in his rear. He would have to eliminate them before advancing further inland. The garrison could probably hold out for three weeks in the event of attack – more than enough time for reinforcements to arrive from elsewhere.

If they lost the opening battle against Napoleon, the duke's strategy was for the Kent troops under General Sir David Dundas to withdraw towards Dover rather than London, creating a military threat in the French rear that they could not ignore on their way to the capital. Dover was dominated by its castle on one side and by a cliff known as the Western Heights on the other. Various generals had been campaigning for years to have the Heights fortified against invasion, and the work was finally under way. The Western Heights were being strengthened with a citadel, a drop redoubt and a barracks for 1,300 men. The work would take several years to complete, but Dover would be virtually impregnable when it was done.

But if Dover failed to delay Napoleon, nothing else would on the way to London. Both sides calculated that if the French invaded immediately, they would almost certainly reach London within five days. Once they arrived, the capital would be almost defenceless. In medieval times it had been protected by stout walls, but these were no defence against artillery and had long since been dismantled. In any case, the city had outgrown them. It sprawled in every direction, the greatest metropolis on earth, yet without any permanent fortifications against an invading army. It hadn't needed any, for centuries.

Too late to start now. Instead, the duke placed his faith in 'field' fortifications – a series of wooden palisades, earthworks and gun platforms that could be erected very quickly. They were much cheaper than permanent fortifications, which was an important consideration. Provided the materials had already been assembled at the chosen site, no further expense need be incurred until the French had actually landed. The duke had reported to William Pitt in July that the defences on the north side of London could probably be completed in four days by 5,000 men and 800 horses. Those on the south could be completed in three days with just 500 men and 300 horses. No rent had to be paid to landowners until the fortifications were actually erected – and if the work was left until the last minute, it would provide 'useful and animating labour to an overgrown population that might otherwise become dangerous and desponding'. In other words, it would involve Londoners in their own defence, giving them something to do instead of worrying about Napoleon.

The duke's plan was to defend the approaches to the city first, falling back if necessary on to London itself. Shooter's Hill would dominate the approaches to the south, but the north was more of a problem. The Lea Valley could be flooded and a camp dug in at Brentwood, but there were no obvious defensive points along the East Anglian coast. The duke toyed with Colchester, Sudbury and Braintree before settling on 'an Entrenched Camp in Front of Dunmow'. The choice was not entirely satisfactory, but nobody could think of anywhere better.

As for London, the duke defined its perimeter thus:

> On the Right bank of the Thames the Line rests upon the River above Deptford and passes along the ridge of the Norwood hills, then turning by Streatham and Tooting to the River behind Wandsworth Crick. The continuation of the Line upon the Left bank of the Thames in front of London passes behind the River Lea by Stratford and Lea Bridge to Stamford Hill; from thence it takes the ridge of Ground by Hornsey Wood, Highgate and Wilsden Green; and again turns by Holland House and Little Chelsea to the Thames.

The duke calculated that he would need 180,000 men to defend this area, most of whom would be drawn from the volunteers. There were no artillerymen among the volunteers, and not enough in the regular army, so he had called on all Londoners who knew how to work a cannon to come forward and offer their services. The response had been swift, but not large. His hope was that the French would only attack on one front at a time, giving him a chance to concentrate his gunners where they were most needed. If they attacked on more than one front, he would just have to rely on musket fire instead . . . assuming the muskets had arrived by then.

It was a grave situation. Not enough had been done, and nothing was ready yet. No matter how confident Britain's leaders appeared in public, they all suspected privately that the French might well be marching up the Mall within a week of coming ashore. The British were under no illusion as to what would happen if Napoleon did capture London. Caricaturist James Gillray had caught the public mood with his cartoon of a guillotine outside St James's Palace. So had a newspaper article, with its gloomy forecast of the likely outcome once the Grand Army had taken the city:

London, 10th Thermidor
General Bonaparte made his public entrance into the Capital over London Bridge, upon a charger from His Britannic Majesty's stables at Hanover, preceded by a detachment of Mamelukes. He stopped upon the bridge a few seconds to survey the number of ships in the river; and beckoning to one of his Aides-de-Camp, ordered the French flag to be hoisted above the English – the English sailors on board who attempted to resist the execution of this order were bayoneted and thrown overboard.

When he came to the Bank, he smiled with complaisance upon a detachment of French grenadiers who had been sent to load all the bullion in wagons . . . From the Bank the First Consul proceeded in grand procession along Cheapside, St Paul's, Ludgate-hill, Fleet-street, and the Strand, to St James's Palace. He there held a grand Circle, which was attended by all his Officers, whose congratulations he received upon his entrance into the Capital of these once proud islanders . . .

11th Thermidor
Bonaparte, at five o'clock in the morning, reviewed the French troops on the Esplanade at the Horse Guards . . .

12th, 13th, 14th Thermidor
LONDON PILLAGED. The doors of private houses forced. Bands of drunken soldiers dragging wives and daughters from the arms of husbands and fathers. Many husbands who had the *temerity* to resist, butchered in the presence of their children. Flames seen in a hundred different places . . . churches broken open and the church-plate plundered . . .

16th Thermidor

A plot discovered by Fouché against the First Consul, and three hundred, supposed to be implicated, sent to the Tower . . . Lords Nelson, St Vincent, and Melville, Messrs Addington, Pitt, Sheridan, Grey, twenty Peers and Commoners tried by the Military Tribunals for having been concerned in the *insurrection* against France, and sentenced to be shot. Sentence was immediately carried into execution in Hyde Park.

Would it ever happen? Of course it would. Napoleon was a ruthless man. Joseph Fouché was his Minister of Police, a charmless revolutionary who had attended the massacres at Lyons with a pair of human ears dangling from each side of his hat. Between them they would eliminate all opposition within a few days of their arrival. Nobody would be safe with the French loose in the town. The Terror would have come to London.

But it hadn't come yet. Perhaps English ears would never dangle from Fouché's hat. The feeling among military men was that London might actually be the best place to stop Napoleon. He would have to take the capital house by house and street by street, and that would not be easy – Londoners would fight him every yard of the way. Greenwich, Southwark and Lambeth formed the likely battleground. The battle would continue day after day, night after night, for as long as it took. Hundreds of houses would be burned to the ground, if need be, and thousands of people would die, but nothing would be surrendered willingly. The British were too fond of their freedom to give it up without a struggle.

The hope was that Napoleon would find the price of victory too high, if he had to lose half his army in the process. With luck, he just might turn tail and flee instead, hurrying his troops back to the coast while he still could. Or he might even do what he had done in Egypt – flee himself and leave them to find their own way home. Napoleon was a formidable commander, but he was not invincible. There was still a chance for the British, in the generals' sober assessment. They were not beaten yet.

CHAPTER 5

---•◦•---

LORD MELVILLE AT
THE ADMIRALTY

In his office next door to the Horse Guards, the First Lord of the Admiralty was contemplating the same problems as the Duke of York, but from a naval perspective. He too was short of public money, trying to do too much with too little. He was worried that if the French invaded, the Royal Navy might be spread too thinly to stop them.

Like its neighbouring buildings, the Admiralty has changed little in 250 years. It was here that Captain Cook returned from the South Seas in the 1770s, bringing improbable stories of kangaroos and other discoveries. Here, too, that a messenger arrived from Falmouth in 1781, bearing the less welcome news that Lord Cornwallis had surrendered to the American rebels at a place called Yorktown. The news should have been taken straight to Downing Street, but instead had travelled halfway round London first, being passed from one cabinet minister's house to the next because none of them wanted to be the one to tell the Prime Minister. He reacted as if he had been shot when they did finally break it to him.

But that was all in the past now and the British were fighting a new war against a much more formidable opponent. It was the First Lord's job to ensure that not a single French soldier set foot on British soil during the coming crisis. For a man who knew next to nothing about the sea, this was a daunting task.

Lord Melville had never served in the navy. He was a Scottish lawyer who had entered Parliament in 1774 and had been in government on and off ever since. He had twice been Treasurer of the Navy and had served also as Secretary of State for War, but his record at both was dismal. Melville was a politician to his fingertips and a masterly fixer, but he was not a fighting man. He had no practical experience of warfare and no aptitude, either. His list of failures was long, particularly as Secretary for War. Disasters attributable to his ineptitude had been suffered in the West Indies, the East Indies, the Netherlands, India, Ireland and the Mediterranean. He was not greatly admired by those who had to serve under him. They reckoned his interference did more harm than good.

Melville had become a peer during the Addington administration, but his closest ally in politics was William Pitt. The Prime Minister had appointed him to the Admiralty in May 1804, with a brief to restore the fleet to its former glory and put it on a war footing as quickly as possible. Melville's predecessor in the job, Lord St Vincent, had been rather too complacent about the Royal Navy's state of readiness for Pitt's liking. 'I do not say the French cannot come,' St Vincent had airily announced one day. 'I only say they cannot come by sea.' He had said that before Napoleon built his invasion fleet. Melville's job was to make certain that St Vincent's words came true.

The fleet was in an appalling state when he inherited it, partly as a result of well-intentioned reforms by his predecessor. St Vincent had set out to tackle corruption among the navy's suppliers, but had succeeded only in alienating them. Shipbuilders and dockyard workers alike had withdrawn their cooperation. Even more seriously, so had the timber suppliers who provided the navy with its raw material. The ships were built of oak because nothing resisted a cannon ball better than a stout piece of oak. Timber merchants all over the country understood this and had banded together to force the price up, knowing the navy couldn't go elsewhere. Appeals to their patriotism had fallen on deaf ears. If there was going to be a war, they might as well make a profit out of it.

It was not only oak that was in short supply. Pine for the masts had to be imported either from the United States or, more often, the Baltic. There was a severe shortage too of compass timber – naturally curved pieces of wood essential for the construction of the hull. And even if there had been enough wood, it needed to be seasoned for at least three years before it could be used. The Royal Navy's policy of keeping three years' supply in hand had been allowed to lapse after the Peace of Amiens. Stocks had dwindled to a mere nine months' worth – little short of disastrous after the resumption of hostilities, when Britain needed more ships than ever. At Sheerness dockyard, they had run out of wood altogether.

The effect on the navy had been catastrophic. Some of its ships were floating death traps. Older vessels were waterlogged and riddled with dry rot. Newer ones had been built of green timber that was still warping as it aged. Many had been patched with wood cannibalised from other ships. Their frames were braced internally and their hulls sheathed with additional planking. Carpenters were kept busy throughout the fleet, filling in the holes and praying their work would keep the ships afloat. An inspection of one vessel at this time was typical of many:

> We began by discovering slight defects in the ship, and the farther we went in the examination the more important they appeared until at last she was discovered to be so completely rotten as to be unfit for sea. We have been sailing for the last six months with only a copper sheet between us and eternity.

But timber was not the navy's only problem. The manpower shortage was just as serious. The navy was always chronically in need of seamen. Conditions afloat were so unpleasant that volunteers never came forward in sufficient numbers, although there had been a surge during the invasion scare. The shortfall was made up of 'quota' men, mostly miscreants sentenced to join the navy as an alternative to prison, and pressed men, who had been conscripted against their will. They deserted in droves whenever they had the chance. Sometimes whole crews vanished in foreign ports, leaving their officers stranded. The navy responded by refusing to allow them ashore and discouraging them from learning to swim. Now and again, it even pressed foreign nationals into service, hauling them off the streets or from other ships. There were many hundreds of Americans in the Royal Navy. There were even a few French.

The Americans were probably the largest group of foreigners. Most were volunteers, but some had been kidnapped by the navy and were outraged at their treatment. Others were not American at all, but British sailors claiming US citizenship in order to avoid their obligations. The Royal Navy asserted its right to impress any sailor of British origin found aboard an American vessel. The Americans disagreed, insisting that the neutrality of their ships should be respected. The matter was taken seriously on both sides. It was shaping up to be a major bone of contention between the two governments.

The British view was summed up by James Monroe, the US ambassador in London. Reporting back to Washington, he noted that:

> If the British should consent to make our commercial navy a floating asylum for all the British seamen who, tempted by higher wages, should quit their service for ours, the effect on their maritime strength, on which Great Britain depends, might be fatal . . . they might be deprived, to an extent impossible to calculate, of their only means of security.

In short, British sailors might be safer and better paid working for Yankee merchantmen, but the Royal Navy needed them in time of war and it wouldn't think twice about seizing them whenever it could.

The issue rankled with Americans, particularly French-leaning Republicans, but they were not yet disposed to come to blows about it. The two governments were on friendly terms. The British had privately congratulated the Americans on the Louisiana Purchase, although they were less happy about the invasion fleet that Napoleon was building with the proceeds. President Jefferson in turn was hoping for an alliance with the British, implying formal approval of the Purchase and support for the United States' territorial ambitions in Florida. In the view of some, it would be like the old days again if the two peoples fought the French side by side, as they had in the past.

For the moment, however, the Royal Navy needed manpower and would continue to seize men from American ships. It had Lord Melville's full backing, because there was really no alternative if the navy was to keep its ships at sea. The navy had to take men wherever it could find them.

And the ships *were* at sea – almost all of them. The majority were long overdue for a return to base and a refit, but could not be spared from duty. The British were at war all over the world. The immediate threat came from France's Channel ports, but the French were active too in the West Indies and capable of threatening British trade routes via South Africa to India. The Mediterranean had to be policed as well, to keep the French fleet there firmly tied down. The Royal Navy was stretched to full capacity, in ships full of worm holes, manned by underpaid crews who in most cases were only there because they had to be. It was not a recipe for success, with an invasion imminent.

These were the problems faced by Lord Melville when he arrived at the Admiralty. His primary task as the new First Lord was to build more ships and restore the fleet without delay. To this end, he had quietly postponed Lord St Vincent's attempts at reform and had come to terms with the dockyards and the navy's timber suppliers. Reform would have to wait for another time. Nothing mattered now except getting new ships built and repairing old ones so that they could return to service. Melville had no talent for warfare, but he knew how to make things happen on the home front. A new building programme was under way and the fleet was being rapidly expanded. It would take time, perhaps a year or so, but Melville was confident of meeting the challenge that Pitt had set him. He would do everything that had been asked of him – always assuming, of course, that the French did not invade before he had got the job done.

Melville was heavily dependent on his admirals for an assessment of the invasion threat. They were taking it very seriously, particularly after the reports of Napoleon at Boulogne. The Royal Navy had between fifteen and twenty ships off Boulogne that August, most of them anchored ten miles to the north-west. A detachment of five or six ships operated up front, cruising the harbour mouth just beyond reach of the French guns. It was this detachment, under Captain Edward Owen, that had witnessed Napoleon's visit to review his troops. They had seen the unusual activity on shore and guessed that something must be up. It did not take a genius to work out what.

But when would Napoleon come? And where? The navy had no better idea than the army. The English coastline was just as long and undefended on the seaward side as the land. Wherever Napoleon did come, the navy would be there to try to prevent it, but so much depended on the wind and the tide, elements beyond anyone's control. The prospect of a huge invasion fleet crossing the Channel was just as much a nightmare for the Royal Navy as it was for the army.

In Lord Nelson's view, the shortest route across the Channel was the most likely. He had told the Admiralty so in 1801:

> Supposing London the object of surprise, I am of opinion that the enemy's object ought to be the getting on shore as speedily as possible, for the dangers of navigation of forty-eight hours appear to me an insurmountable objection to the rowing from Boulogne to the coast of Essex. It is therefore most probable that from Boulogne, Calais and even Havre, the enemy will try to land in Sussex, or the lower part of Kent; and from Dunkirk, Ostend and other ports of Flanders to land on the coast of Essex or Suffolk.

Nelson estimated that the French could row the Channel in twelve hours, if the sea remained calm. He was in no doubt as to how the Royal Navy should react: 'If a breeze springs up, our ships are to deal *destruction*; no delicacy can be observed on this great occasion.'

The one advantage the British did have was their knowledge of the invasion's starting point. They had seen the barges at Boulogne and the other ports and had made a guess at their numbers. In theory, therefore, it should have been easy to prevent the invasion from happening. All the navy had to do was gather its ships outside the invasion ports and wait for the barges to emerge.

But that was easier said than done, because with all its other commitments the navy did not have enough ships for the task. And even if it had, a total blockade of the Channel ports was impossible for geographical reasons – wind and tide again, and shifting sands. Not even the Royal Navy could have managed it.

The worst scenario of all, from the British point of view, would see the French battle fleet putting to sea as well – all of it, in one combined showing. At present, the French squadrons were widely dispersed, some in the Channel ports, others at Brest and Toulon, where the Royal Navy was making every effort to keep them blockaded. But if the Brest and Toulon fleets fought their way out, making common cause for the Channel, the Royal Navy might find itself outnumbered on its own doorstep. The consequences did not bear thinking about.

British strategy, therefore, was to keep the French blockaded wherever they were. Ships were usually allowed into French ports, but not out again. They were left bottled up in harbour, reluctant to face the Royal Navy on the open sea. It was vital for the British to keep the French fleet divided, unable to join forces in the Channel.

So far the strategy was working well, but it was extremely demanding of ships and manpower. Until Lord Melville's building programme bore fruit, the navy was desperately short of the vessels it needed for the job. The shortage made itself felt in all sorts of ways, not least the leaky British warships prowling the Channel opposite the invasion ports. Until the problem was solved, as Lord Melville was uncomfortably aware, there could be no guarantee that the bulk of Napoleon's armada would not successfully make it to England, if and when the invasion was launched.

CHAPTER 6

———◆·◆·◆———

THE NAVY'S THREE LINES
OF DEFENCE

While Lord Melville sat at his desk, the Royal Navy was patrolling the English Channel, well aware of the difficulties it faced, but determined that the French would never set foot ashore while it still had ships to stop them.

The navy had prepared three lines of defence against a French invasion. The first was the blockade, a permanent patrol of frigates and gunships operating the length of the French and Dutch coasts, so close to the enemy that at Boulogne its sailors could read the signals from the telegraph station on the cliff next to Napoleon's pavilion. The patrols were there to prevent any enemy ships from putting to sea – even ordinary fishing boats. The task was difficult, but the patrols were largely successful, forcing most shipping to keep close inshore, under the protection of the shore batteries. Any stray fishermen the British captured were closely interrogated about the situation on land. The patrols also took soundings, measuring the constantly shifting sandbanks and observing the layout of the invasion fleet, keeping a sharp eye on everything that was happening on shore.

The navy's second line of defence was much closer to home. It comprised a squadron of frigates and ships of the line under Admiral Lord Keith anchored in the Downs, off Deal. The squadron could scud across the North Sea or down into the Channel at a moment's notice. It was a rapid-reaction force, poised to go into action as soon as the invasion sails were sighted on the horizon.

The third line of defence was even closer still. It consisted of the Sea Fencibles, several hundred river craft and fishing boats armed with cannon and manned by volunteers. The Sea Fencibles were responsible for patrolling the estuaries and inlets of southern Britain, all the way from Great Yarmouth to Swansea in South Wales. There were even a few of them as far north as the Firth of Forth. They were unlikely to see any action against the French, in the Admiralty's view. They had been formed to give the local fishermen something to do more than anything, a way of soaking up manpower that was keen to be involved but would otherwise be sitting around idle.

The blockade was the navy's chief weapon against the French. Apart from a break during the Peace of Amiens, it had been in place for many years. The blockade kept the French fleet permanently in port, rendering it useless for all practical purposes. It also stifled the coastal economy and inhibited communications with France's overseas possessions. More than that, it presented an all too visible curb on Napoleon's global ambitions, a reminder that his writ did not run on the high seas and never would while the Royal Navy had anything to do with it. The blockade was a formidable instrument of war.

In practice, however, it was hardly ever a total blockade. A tight grip was maintained around the invasion ports wherever possible, but in the Mediterranean the British were usually careful to leave at least one channel open, in the hope of tempting French warships out to sea. Once out of harbour, the French could have a discussion with the British as to precisely which of the two navies ruled the waves. It was an invitation the French wisely declined. They preferred to remain safely in port, consoling themselves with the thought that it was the Royal Navy whose ships were permanently at sea, slowly disintegrating in the bad weather while the French kept their powder dry for another day.

There was a good deal of truth in this. The wear and tear on the Royal Navy was considerable, and likely to remain so for the foreseeable future. Many of its ships were inferior to the French navy's – older, creakier and less well designed. Some of the Royal Navy's best ships were actually French, captured in action and recommissioned under the White Ensign. But whatever their provenance, they were all suffering the effects of being forever at sea. Every major storm produced its share of mishaps – sails cut to ribbons, ships dismasted, hulls collapsing under the strain. The Royal Navy was taking a constant battering on blockade duties, its vessels gradually being torn to pieces while the French remained snugly in harbour. Often it was only the skill of the navy's carpenters and sailmakers that kept them in business at all.

Vice-Admiral Cuthbert Collingwood regularly went a week at a time without taking his clothes off on blockade duty and was often on deck all night. He was forthright in his condemnation of the politicians who had allowed the situation to develop. In his view, the navy's masters at home did not understand how much of a beating their ships were taking. Nor did they realise

> how little practicable it is to block up a port in winter. To sail from one blockaded port, and enter another, where the whole fleet is, without being seen, does not come within the comprehension of the city politicians. Their idea is that we are like sentinels standing at a door, who must see, and may intercept, all who attempt to go into it. But so long as the ships are at sea they are content, little considering that every one of the blasts which we endure lessens the security of the country.

Yet the navy was equal to the challenge. The deficiencies of its ships were more than compensated for by the quality of its men. The officers of the Royal Navy went to sea at the age of twelve, and many of the men not much older. Long years afloat had given them skills and seamanship second to none. As the Grand Army predominated on land, so did the Royal Navy at sea – there wasn't another navy in the world that could compare. The men of the blockade were well-drilled professionals, supremely confident of their own ability. They could clear a ship for action in six minutes flat, which was no mean achievement. Their gunnery was excellent, too, even in rough seas when the pitch and roll made it difficult to aim properly. They had had plenty of time to practise, perfecting their technique in every kind of weather. All they wanted now was a chance to show what they could do. And for that, they needed the French navy to show itself out of port.

*

In Brest, Boulogne and elsewhere, the French navy stubbornly refused to do anything of the sort. The French had persuaded themselves that they were playing a much more cunning game by sitting tight in harbour. They might have better ships, but their navy was no match for the British, as even the most patriotic Frenchmen privately acknowledged. It was a formidable force on paper, with plenty of fighting vessels under command. In practice, however, its ships had serious problems competing with the Royal Navy. For one thing, the British were an island people, with a maritime heritage stretching back to their Viking ancestors. There was no such tradition in France.

For another, the French navy had suffered grievously during the Revolution. Its officers had been drawn from the upper class and duly paid the price. Large numbers had been guillotined or forced to resign, leaving vacancies that had been filled by a new breed of officer, noted more for revolutionary zeal than seamanship. Promotion had been swift, with so many vacancies to fill. Officers were now in command who had not put in long years at sea and lacked the expertise of their British counterparts. Quarterdecks were crowded with Jacobins instead of disciplinarians. The names of French ships, proudly handed down over the centuries, had been unceremoniously dumped in favour of revolutionary slogans. The red cap of liberty was worn on deck, and everybody regarded themselves as the equal of everybody else. But equality was no compensation for the professionalism that had been lost with the execution of so many good officers. An awful lot of French seamanship had dropped into the guillotine basket during the years of terror.

Worst of all, the matelots of the lower decks could not compare with their British counterparts. They came from similar backgrounds, but where the British spent months and sometimes years at sea, training hard and honing their skills, the French often didn't go to sea at all. How could they, with the Royal Navy blockading the ports? And if they didn't go to sea, how could they learn about wind and tide, or the best way to ride out a storm? How could they practise gun drills if they never got out of harbour?

The British knew how to sail their ships and fire their guns in all kinds of weather. The French did not. They had been hopelessly outclassed at the Battle of the Nile, when Lord Nelson attacked them from the landward side, in the dark, and still managed to blow them out of the water. They feared they would be outclassed again, if they ever came out of port. Much better to sit tight and let the Royal Navy take the strain, falling to pieces on the high seas while the French stayed safely in harbour and watched them suffer.

Even so, morale was not high in the French navy. Nobody enjoyed being stuck in port all the time. Enthusiasm for the Revolution had also waned, although support for Napoleon's new empire was not much greater. One admiral had openly objected to the election of Napoleon as Emperor, arguing that this was hardly what the Revolution had been about. He had promptly been dismissed, as a warning to the others. They had duly taken heed and kept their mouths shut, even among themselves. Very few admirals were prepared to stand up to Napoleon and speak the truth to him. Very few had his respect.

One who did was René Latouche-Tréville, probably the best admiral in the French navy. He had once got the better of Lord Nelson at Boulogne and never let anyone forget it. Latouche-Tréville commanded now at Toulon in the Mediterranean, where Nelson was doing his best to lure him out of harbour for a fight. The Toulon fleet was crucial to Napoleon's invasion plan. Under Latouche-Tréville's command, it was to sail up to Boulogne when the time came and keep the Royal Navy occupied while the invasion barges crossed the Channel. If anyone could handle the operation successfully, it was Latouche-Tréville.

Unfortunately for the French, he died on 18 August. He suffered a heart attack after climbing the hill to the signal station to get a view of the English out to sea. It was a major blow for Napoleon – a man of Latouche-Tréville's calibre was not easy to replace. At the very least, it would take several weeks to find another admiral and send him down to Toulon. Several weeks would bring them to the autumn equinox, with all its bad weather at sea. Latouche-Tréville's heart attack could hardly have come at a more inconvenient time for the invasion plan.

———•◆•———

CHAPTER 7

NAPOLEON VISITS CHARLEMAGNE'S TOMB

Not yet aware of Latouche-Tréville's death, Napoleon remained a few more days with the army at Boulogne, continuing his inspection of the invasion force. Then he left earlier than planned and set off for a tour of the German principalities in the Rhineland.

He was going to collect his wife Josephine on the way. The new Empress was taking the waters at Aix-la-Chapelle. At Napoleon's insistence, her retinue for her sojourn at Aix numbered almost 100, including chefs, maids, footmen, ladies-in-waiting, a chamberlain, her personal physician, the master of the horse and many others. At his insistence also, towns along the route had been decorated with bunting for her arrival, bands had played to welcome her and guns had fired a salute at every stop. Josephine had come a long way from her modest origins in Martinique. She was now the wife of the Emperor of France, and had to be seen as such.

Napoleon wrote to her from Boulogne on 20 August:

In ten days I will be at Aix-la-Chapelle. From there, I will go with you to Cologne, Coblenz, Mainz, Trier and Luxembourg . . . I am anxious to see you, to tell you everything you inspire in me, and to cover you with kisses. A bachelor's life is a miserable one, and nothing is worth so much as a good wife, beautiful and loving.

Four days later, he wrote again:

> I may arrive at night, so let lovers beware . . . ! My health is good and
> I am working hard, but I am too well behaved. That has a bad effect
> on me, so I am anxious to see you.

He left Boulogne on 27 August, travelling in a yellow berline drawn by
four horses. Other carriages followed with his staff. Napoleon's coach was
fitted out as an office, with a filing cabinet, oil lamp and portable lavatory.
He worked non-stop as he travelled, issuing a stream of directives through
the window to the aides-de-camp and dispatch riders keeping pace
alongside. He liked to maintain a cracking pace along the road,
complaining constantly that the carriages weren't moving fast enough.

Via St-Omer and Arras, he reached Aix on 2 September. Josephine had
cried for joy at the news that he was coming to see her. She was a mature
lady in 1804, forty-one years old and nervous of her position, well aware
that she had still not provided Napoleon with a son. She was hoping a
miracle might yet happen. If it didn't, she was worried he would not want
her by his side when he was crowned Emperor later in the year.

Josephine had good reason to be nervous, because it wasn't for her that
Napoleon had come to Aix. Despite his effusions to Josephine, it was one
of her ladies-in-waiting that he wanted to see. Elisabeth de Vaudey was a
beautiful young aristocrat with extravagant tastes, and Napoleon had had
his eye on her for some time. At Aix, he pursued her relentlessly, regardless
of his wife's feelings. Josephine reacted as she usually did, complaining of
severe headaches and claiming she couldn't rise from her sick bed.

But Madame de Vaudey did not occupy Napoleon for long. Really he
was in Aix because it was the city of Charlemagne, the great king of the
Franks who had united all of Western Europe under his rule. The
medieval town hall still stood on the ruins of his palace. Thirty-five kings
had banqueted there after their coronations in the cathedral. If kings could
be crowned in Charlemagne's footsteps, why not the new Emperor of
France as well? Why not Aix for his coronation, instead of Paris?

Soon after his arrival, he and Josephine attended a *Te Deum* in the
cathedral, where Charlemagne was buried. Various relics were produced for

their inspection, including Charlemagne's skull and a bone from his arm. Josephine had earlier refused to touch the bone, insisting that she was supported by an arm quite as strong as Charlemagne's. Napoleon was more interested in other relics – the regalia used at Charlemagne's coronation. A crown, orb, sceptre, sword and spurs still existed, although they had been scattered during the Revolution. Most of the relics were kept now at Nuremberg, beyond Napoleon's reach. It would be good to get them back again and be crowned in Charlemagne's capital wearing Charlemagne's spurs and holding Charlemagne's sword. If nothing else, it would annoy the people of Paris, with whom Napoleon had a very uneasy relationship. He was not popular in the French capital. They saw him there as a Corsican upstart and laughed at his pretensions. It would be a tremendous snub to them if he chose to be crowned in Aix cathedral instead of Notre Dame – 'if only to make the Parisians see that one can govern without them'.

Best of all, though, would be to conquer England before his coronation. If he could capture London in the next few months, then he could come to his coronation as master of the English and everyone in France would love him for it, even the people of Paris. Wherever he was crowned, it would be a master stroke to arrive at the ceremony as the man who had defeated France's bitterest enemy and brought victory to the French-speaking world. Perhaps the logistics were against an invasion of England just yet, with the military preparations incomplete and the year so far advanced, but Napoleon could always dream. His dreams tended towards the grandiose. It was in a bullish mood that he left Aix after a few days and set off to Cologne for a quick tour of the lower Rhine and a series of official visits to some very apprehensive German princelings.

News of his departure took several days to reach England. It was greeted with relief, mingled with more than a little misgiving. Was he really heading off down the Rhine on a cruise? Or was his absence from Boulogne merely an elaborate ruse, designed to lull the British into a false sense of security? Would he return suddenly and launch his troops across the Channel without warning? Anything seemed possible, where Napoleon was concerned.

For William Pitt, now spending most of his time in London, the dilemma was acute. As Prime Minister at this time of crisis, it was his duty to remain in the capital, at the heart of government. If the French invaded, he was to take to the field with the king and remain with him at his headquarters. But the action was far more likely to take place in Kent, on the shingle beach just across from Walmer Castle. As the man who had raised the Cinque Port Volunteers, Pitt was longing to be at the head of his troops when the French landed. And even if he was not directly involved in the fighting, it would be useful to be on the spot, to see at first hand how things were going. He could keep in touch with London through the telegraph station at Deal – just so long as the French didn't capture it in the first wave of fighting.

Pitt worried constantly about where he ought to be. It was his practice at Walmer never to travel too far from the castle, so that he could be called back in a hurry if necessary. He varied this habit only when the weather was bad, or the tides weren't right for an invasion. Then he felt free to leave Walmer for longer, or even to go back to London for a few days. It was impossible to be everywhere at once.

Walmer had been dubbed 'the most dangerous place in the whole kingdom' during the invasion scare. The castle itself was a modest creation, little more than a fort, a relic of the Tudor era. It had become domesticated since then, and by 1804 was really only a gentleman's residence with a few gunports attached. It boasted several cannon and a row of firing loops to cover the moat, but was hardly a great fortress. The permanent garrison numbered fewer than twenty.

William Pitt had lived there intermittently since 1792, largely because it was cheaper than anywhere else. Constantly in debt, he depended on the income from his Wardenship of the Cinque Ports to make ends meet. The castle came with the job, which helped considerably. He inhabited bachelor quarters over the gatehouse and used the drawing and dining rooms off the north bastion for official entertaining (his dining table and chairs are still used today).

The threat of invasion had hung over Pitt's head for most of his time at Walmer. As early as 1799, the Astronomer Royal had sent him a reflecting telescope to watch for an invading fleet. The telescope had arrived with a list of assembly instructions in six easy stages. George Canning, himself a future Prime Minister, had been staying at the castle at the time, but neither he nor Pitt had been able to put the thing together. They had both abandoned it after a while, leaving the telescope in bits in the corner.

But the invasion threat remained. The beach was just a stone's throw from Walmer Castle. There would be hand-to-hand combat if the French came ashore, grenades lobbed on to the terrace and muskets fired from the dining-room windows. If Pitt was present at the time, there was every possibility that he might be killed in the crossfire. It was probably this that made General Moore emphatic that the Prime Minister should play no real part in the fighting when it came.

Moore was a frequent guest at the castle. He commanded the Light Infantry brigade at Shorncliffe, near Hythe, and was highly intelligent for an army officer. He and Pitt got on well. Moore was full of ideas for improving the army, everything from camouflage and a revision of tactics to the use of rifles by the infantry instead of smooth-bore muskets. He didn't think much of Pitt's Volunteers, but had plenty of confidence in his own troops, so much so that he advocated offensive action against the French, a policy of carrying the war to the enemy instead of being permanently on the defensive. He considered a military attack on Boulogne perfectly feasible. He also pressed the case for Martello towers, drawing on his own experience in Corsica. Pitt listened to everything he had to say, and valued his opinion.

Pitt listened to others as well, a constant procession of militia colonels, sea captains and undercover agents who dined at his table. Walmer was the de facto headquarters for operations against the French. All sorts of people arrived to give him their views, some of them amateur, some professional. A great many of the militia colonels were simply landowners, with no real idea of what they were talking about. But they were accustomed to being heard because of their standing in society. Pitt listened to them patiently, as he listened to everyone else.

He listened to relatively junior officers, too, often with unorthodox ideas. To the dismay of Admiral Lord Keith, in command of the home waters, Pitt had long taken an interest in clandestine operations against the French, a war of secret agents and gold bullion aimed at fomenting an anti-Napoleonic movement in France. The Pas de Calais was a staunchly Royalist area, whose people had never approved of the Revolution or the execution of Louis XVI. They approved of Napoleon even less and looked to Britain for help in getting rid of him. So did people elsewhere in France, even in the army. Quite a few generals despaired of Napoleon, resenting the way this obscure Corsican had seized command of the armed forces and now declared himself Emperor as well. With help from the British, they might be persuaded to overthrow Napoleon before he was crowned and restore the monarchy instead. Anything to distract them from invading England.

In fact, something of the sort had recently been tried, with disastrous results. In August 1803, the Royal Navy had landed the Royalist General Georges Cadoudal on the French coast near Abbeville. He had been joined in January 1804 by General Charles Pichegru, once a colleague of Napoleon's but now a bitter opponent. The two of them had set off for Paris to organise the tyrant's assassination, but had been caught and imprisoned. Pichegru was too popular with the army to be executed publicly, so Napoleon had had him strangled instead – probably by four Mamelukes, who were immediately shot in turn to prevent them talking. He then announced that Pichegru had committed suicide.

Cadoudal had been guillotined in June. Some 354 other conspirators had also been arrested, among them the Duc d'Enghien, heir to the Bourbon dynasty. D'Enghien almost certainly had nothing to do with the plot against Napoleon and was living peaceably in the neutral territory of Baden. But he was the descendant of French kings, and that was enough to condemn him in Napoleon's eyes. He had been kidnapped from Baden in March 1804 and shot out of hand in the moat at Vincennes – a cold-blooded murder that had outraged all of Europe. It had been a bad mistake on Napoleon's part, because it had lost him widespread support among influential people who had hitherto seen him as a force for good. His own wife Josephine had been appalled by the murder, as had Fouché, his Minister of Police. So had Ludwig van Beethoven, who had just composed his Third Symphony in Napoleon's honour. Unimpressed by the murder, or by Napoleon's imperial pretensions, Beethoven had retitled it the 'Eroica' Symphony instead.

Despite the executions, however, the threat to Napoleon had not been extinguished. The rumblings had continued, so much so that for a time

Napoleon had been afraid to appear in public. The British had been delighted, doing everything they could to make things worse for him. Charles Talleyrand, the French foreign minister, had lodged a formal protest, accusing the British of interfering in France's internal affairs by plotting to assassinate Napoleon and overthrow his government. The British had huffed and puffed, but had been unable to deny this diplomatic faux pas. 'It is an acknowledged Right of Belligerent Powers to avail themselves of any discontents existing in the countries with which they happen to be at war,' they had claimed. In any case, the French were doing the same with the rebels in Ireland.

Pitt himself had kept aloof from plans to assassinate Napoleon, but was privately sympathetic to the idea of destabilising his regime. It had not escaped his notice that the cheapest way to thwart Napoleon's invasion plans would be to get rid of the man himself by financing his enemies at home. To this end, large quantities of gold coin had been stored at Walmer Castle, to be smuggled into France by night. There were numerous secret landing places along the coast between Calais and Boulogne, and the Royal Navy knew them all. The navy was well used to running bullion ashore, and spies, both English and French. Its cloak-and-dagger operations greatly annoyed Admiral Lord Keith, who preferred a more open kind of warfare, fully above board. He was annoyed also that the operations were run by officers much junior to himself, who appeared to have Pitt's approval for their activities. Lord Keith found the whole business highly irregular.

But Pitt was always open to new ideas, however unorthodox. Among those who came to see him at Walmer was the American inventor Robert Fulton. They had breakfast together while Fulton tried to interest Pitt in 'a submarine expedition to destroy the fleets of Boulogne and Brest'. Fulton had already designed several submarines and a range of torpedoes. He was convinced they would do great damage, if the Royal Navy would only give him the go-ahead.

Fulton was a remarkable man. Initially enthused by the French Revolution, he had gone to Paris in 1797 to try to sell his submarine to the French as a way of breaking the British blockade of French ports. In 1800 he had built a submarine called the *Nautilus*, with a crew of three and a hand-cranked propeller four feet wide. Tests on the Seine and at Brest had been encouraging, but with peace coming the French had not been interested in his plan to blockade the Thames with a fleet of submersible warships.

Fulton had turned his mind to steam power instead. After the resumption of hostilities, he had attempted to interest Napoleon in a flotilla of paddle steamers to tow the invasion barges across the Channel, but again without success. In May 1804, therefore, Fulton had allowed himself to be wooed to London, where the maritime British were far more receptive to his ideas. They at once granted him a licence to work on steamship design, and took a keen interest in his other projects as well.

The Royal Navy's view of his submarines was that they might well work, but would probably be more trouble than they were worth. Rather more promising were his torpedoes, boat-shaped 'carcasses' loaded with gunpowder and a clockwork fuse. Over breakfast at Walmer, Fulton persuaded the Prime Minister that these were just the job to set among the French in Boulogne harbour. A few torpedoes could cause untold damage to the tightly packed invasion vessels. Pitt agreed, not least because Admiral Keith disapproved of Fulton. A few days after the meeting, the American had received a contract for the development and production of torpedoes in several different designs. He was hard at work now, using the *nom de guerre* of 'Mr Francis' in case his erstwhile French employers got wind of what he was up to.

But Fulton's were not the only ideas for attacking the French at Boulogne. Another American named Mumford had proposed sinking blockships loaded with stone in the harbour mouth, to keep the invasion fleet bottled up. Someone else had suggested rocket-carrying balloons, to be released over Boulogne at night and detonated by clockwork. Others put their faith in fireships, launched against the French exactly as they had been against the Spanish Armada. There was no shortage of ideas for carrying the war to the French. Pitt's task as Prime Minister was to choose between them, deciding which of the many schemes were worth pursuing.

Pitt was a lifelong bachelor, but he did not live alone at Walmer. With him as he grappled with invasion problems was his niece, Lady Hester Stanhope. She acted as his hostess at dinner, presiding at the other end of the table as Pitt entertained his generals and admirals, retiring afterwards to the drawing room with the ladies while the men sat over the port and discussed strategy. Hester Stanhope was twenty-eight in 1804, a forthright character who had quarrelled with her father and had little money of her own. She had taken advantage of the Peace of Amiens to travel abroad, but had returned to England in 1803 with nowhere to go. Pitt had taken pity on her and invited her to live with him, even though it meant changing the habits of a lifetime.

To his surprise, the relationship had prospered. Hester was his sister's child, a difficult woman who irritated many people while captivating others, but she and Pitt had taken to each other at once. She adored him, and he looked upon her as a daughter. They shared a roof quite happily together.

For Hester, the idea of being invaded by the French was too thrilling for words. It was wonderful to be a part of it, so close to Walmer and everything that was going on:

> Bonaparte was said to be at Boulogne a few days ago; the officers patrolled all night with the men, which was pleasant. I have my orders how to act in case of real alarm in Mr Pitt's absence, and also a promise from him never to be further from the army than a two hours' ride. This is all I wish. I should break my heart to be driven up the country like a sheep when everything I most love was in danger.

She often accompanied Pitt on his inspections of the Volunteers, sometimes riding twenty miles at a stretch without complaint – 'the hard riding I do not mind, but to remain almost *still* so many hours on horseback is an incomprehensible bore'. And she had been with him when one of Napoleon's flat-bottomed barges was captured in the Channel and brought back to England.

> As soon as she came in Mr Pitt, Charles, Lord Camden and myself took a Deal boat and rowed alongside of her. She had two large guns on board, thirty soldiers, and four sailors. She is about thirty feet long, and only draws about four feet of water; an ill-contrived thing,

and so little above the water that, had she as many men on board as she could really carry, a moderate storm would wash them overboard.

Having seen enough of their rascally regiments, I certainly pronounce these picked men. They were well clothed and provided with everything – an immense cask of brandy, and a certain quantity of provisions. They appeared neither low nor mortified at being stared at or talked to, nor did they sham spirits. They simply said they should be retaken, for it would all be over in less than two months . . .

The Frenchmen thought one of the Volunteers guarding them so puny that they advised him to go home and eat more pudding.

But it was British troops, rather than the rascally French, who had given Lady Hester her most exciting moment of the invasion so far. On a visit to Ramsgate with her maid, she was accosted one day by some troopers of the Royal Horse Guards, plainly the worse for wear:

Five of the Blues, half-drunk, not knowing who I was, walked after me, and pursued me to my door. They had the impertinence to follow me upstairs, and one of them took hold of my gown.

Lady Hester's maid shrank back, terrified, but her mistress was equal to the occasion. The Prime Minister's niece did what any well-bred Englishwoman would have done in the circumstances. She turned around and punched the man hard, right in the face.

I sent him rolling over the others down stairs, with their swords rattling against the balusters. Next day, he appeared with a black patch as big as a saucer over his face; and, when I went out, there were the glasses looking at me, and footmen pointing me out – quite a sensation!

Lady Hester Stanhope would be taking no prisoners if the French army landed anywhere near her.

CHAPTER 8

———◆———

SPYING OUT THE LAND

Off Boulogne, the Royal Navy remained on full alert after Napoleon's departure for Aix, convinced that he might double back at any moment and launch the invasion. It was obvious that something was in the wind, with all the military activity on shore.

The navy's chief concern was the assembly of invasion barges moored in the inner harbour. They were protected from the open sea by a double line of warships anchored nose to tail across the harbour mouth. The warships in turn were protected by a formidable array of gun batteries along the cliff tops. A frontal assault against such a target would have been suicidal, which was why the navy was taking such an interest in Robert Fulton's torpedoes and other clandestine means of warfare.

Early in August, the *Immortalité* – a captured French frigate now commanded by Captain Edward Owen – had arrived off Boulogne with a mysterious passenger on board. He never gave his name and no one dared ask – the midshipmen called him Mr Nobody for want of anything better. Their mission was to sail as close to Boulogne as possible, so that their passenger could study the port's layout and make sketches of the defences. It was a hazardous undertaking, as sixteen-year-old midshipman Abraham Crawford recalled:

During the fortnight that this gentleman passed on board the *Immortalité*, she was kept constantly close inshore, whenever the state of the tide and weather would permit, in order to give him an opportunity of pursuing certain researches upon which he seemed

71

intent, and which, to give him his due praise, he did with the greatest earnestness and coolness, unruffled and undisturbed by the showers of shot and shells that fell around the ship, splashing the water about her at every instant. The object of this scrutiny seemed to be to ascertain, as correctly as he could, the fortifications around Boulogne, and the position and bearings of the different batteries which faced the sea, and also the exact distance at which the flotilla in the roads was anchored from the shore.

Mr Nobody may have been unruffled by the bombardment, but the ship's crew was less amused. The men resented his presence if it drew so much attention to themselves. They wondered who he was, and why he wanted to know so much about Boulogne's defences. They were glad to see the back of Mr Nobody when at last he decided he had seen enough and asked to be taken back to England.

The *Immortalité* was back off Boulogne by the middle of August, exchanging fire with the French flotilla. As Crawford remembered it, they were harried for three days in a row by the French, responding with unaccustomed vigour to the presence of British ships so close inshore:

> The enemy, although he did not venture from under the shelter of his batteries, was unusually bold, and boats, having officers of rank on board them, were seen frequently to pass along their line. From these circumstances it was thought that Bonaparte was present at the time, and that, under the eye of their newly elected Emperor, they fought with a resolution and boldness unknown to them before.

This was Napoleon's trip to Boulogne to review his forces and distribute the Légions d'honneur. It was a relief to everyone when he took himself off to Aix, leaving both sides free to relax again. Even so, the British remained on high alert. They were convinced something important was going to happen soon. Why else were Mr Nobody and others like him taking such a keen interest in the defences of Boulogne?

*

The Grand Army had arrived at the same conclusion. With so much British activity along the coast, so many spies and saboteurs being put ashore, something was certainly being planned. Whatever it was, the Grand Army was determined not to be taken by surprise when it happened.

The area between Boulogne and Calais teemed with British spies. The Royal Navy was putting them ashore almost every day. A surprising number were French – Royalists with little love for Napoleon or the Revolution. They did not love the English either, but saw them as useful allies in the struggle to restore the French monarchy. The English were a libertarian people who had restored their own monarch after the unfortunate incident with Charles I. They did not desecrate churches or guillotine the innocent, as French revolutionaries had done. They also had plenty of gold, which they distributed generously to anyone prepared to help overthrow Napoleon.

But most of the spies were English, sent ashore by the Royal Navy to inspect the defences of Boulogne and the other invasion ports. They desperately needed information about the ports and the invasion fleet – how many barges each port had, how many men they held, what kind of guns they carried, what kind of keel. They needed to know how the warships were painted (useful for recognition at sea), how they were rigged, how deep they lay in the water. They needed the enemy's signal codes and newspapers, access to local gossip. The only way to gather such information was to send people in to see what they could learn.

So the area teemed with spies, both English and French. They came in a variety of disguises, with telescopes hidden in their boots and maps sewn into the lining of their waistcoats. By night they signalled to the Royal Navy from the cliff tops, opening and closing windows or waving lights in a prearranged pattern. They came and went in the dark, sneaking ashore in a Royal Navy cutter or else rowing out to sea with the latest newspapers from Paris. The deserted beaches north of Boulogne were ideal for clandestine operations of that kind.

It was the Grand Army's job to stop them. The troops kept constant watch along the cliff tops, looking out for landing parties or signals from the coast – bonfires or flashing lights answered by English ships out at sea.

The army identified the most likely landing places along the shore and ambushed them at night. Once, they found two small boats on the beach, hidden under canvas. Another time, a spent signal rocket lying in a field. They had had their most spectacular success in June, when they captured no fewer than eight spies – eight well-dressed Englishmen carrying sulphur matches hidden in their clothes that could have been used for setting fire to the invasion barges. The English were shot within the hour. They found a Boulogne schoolmaster as well, signalling with his arms on the cliff top facing out to sea. The man protested his innocence, but with letters in his pocket connecting him to the enemy was executed next day.

The English would stop at nothing, in the view of the Grand Army. It was even rumoured that they had resorted to germ warfare, landing bales of cotton impregnated with disease on the coast. A notice to that effect had been posted in Boulogne and the other ports in March:

> Remain at your posts, Citizens, and increase your vigilance.
>
> The English, unable to conquer us by force, are employing their last resource: *the Plague.*
>
> Five bales of cotton have just been thrown upon our coast.
>
> All are hereby forbidden to approach any boats or objects that may be cast on shore. Let patrols be instantly afoot; let them be accompanied by customs-house officers.

But nothing had been found except an old hammock, the source of the alarm. It had not been impregnated with plague and nobody had died. The English were not that heinous.

Yet they remained active along the coast – increasingly so as August turned to September and the nights began to draw in. If the invasion was going to come this year, it would have to come sooner rather than later, with autumn fast approaching. The Grand Army knew it, and was expecting to put to sea at any moment. The British knew it, too, and were determined to prevent it by any means within their power.

They had decided to attack Boulogne. The decision had been taken at Walmer to launch a pre-emptive strike against the invasion flotilla. It was a tall order, with the flotilla so heavily defended, but the English were not deterred. It was imperative to attack the French and knock them off balance before they could put to sea. Doubly imperative after the reports of Napoleon at Boulogne and the imminent threat of invasion.

The attack was set for early October. It would not be a conventional operation – Boulogne was too well prepared for that. Lord Nelson himself had been one of several commanders who had failed to breach the harbour's defences by conventional means, losing so many men in the attempt that posters had been put up in British ports accusing him of butchery. But where a frontal assault could never succeed, a less orthodox approach just might. Unmanned fireships, for instance, or the new explosive torpedoes that Robert Fulton had been secretly constructing all summer. It was a dirty way to fight, in the view of many naval officers, but it was better than doing nothing with the French about to invade.

In the last days of September, a strike force of British ships slipped quietly across the Channel and converged on Boulogne from several different directions. The force was equipped with fireships, explosive devices and torpedo-catamarans. Its orders were to sail into Boulogne after dark and attack the line of warships protecting the invasion barges. The attack was scheduled for the night of 2 October.

CHAPTER 9

THE BOULOGNE RAID

The plan was to send in the fireships under cover of darkness and release them close to the row of French guardships, leaving the tide to do the rest. Torpedo-catamarans would be released as well, and a number of forty-gallon casks filled with explosives. The aim was to test Fulton's new weapons against the flotilla, to see how they performed under operational conditions.

The plan had been carefully thought out, but it got off to an awkward start. For reasons best known to himself, Admiral Lord Keith saw no need to conceal his intentions from the French. For several days before the assault, he allowed British ships to assemble in plain view of Boulogne, anchoring five miles out while they gathered for the attack. Perhaps he thought a show of force was a good idea with an invasion in the offing. Whatever the reason, it was obvious to the French, studying the sudden appearance of so many English ships through their telescopes, that something untoward was about to happen.

Abraham Crawford, the teenage midshipman aboard the *Immortalité*, could hardly believe what he was seeing.

There was a great display of our force before Boulogne, amounting to between fifty and sixty vessels of all kinds, for no object that I can conceive, except to put the enemy on his guard, and give him timely notice of our intentions. Besides the *Monarch*, Lord Keith's flagship, this force consisted of two or three ships of fifty and sixty-four guns, four or five frigates, a few sloops of war, and the remainder of bombs, armed ships and gun-brigs. Besides these there were a few sloop-rigged vessels, prepared as fire, or rather explosion vessels . . . not exceeding, I think, four or five. These vessels were filled with combustibles and powder, and supplied with explosive machinery similar to that which was fitted to the carcasses or coffers.

This explosive machinery was at the heart of the attack. Robert Fulton had been busy in Portsmouth all summer, building catamaran-torpedoes (known also as carcasses or coffers) designed to explode on contact with the enemy. The idea of sneaking up on the French and blowing them to pieces while they slept seemed distinctly unsporting to many officers, but their objections had been overruled. The new weapons were a fact of life and Fulton had been agitating to show what he could do. Government policy was to play along with him in case he took his inventions elsewhere and sold them to Britain's enemies. It was better to have him onside than selling his dreadful machines to anyone else.

Fulton had driven a hard bargain with the British government. As well as a monthly salary of £200, he had negotiated a bounty of £40,000 for the first decked vessel destroyed by one of his machines, and half the value of all enemy shipping destroyed under his supervision. He only needed to sink one French ship to live like a king for the rest of his life. It was no surprise that Fulton himself was present off Boulogne, working with the task force as it waited for a suitable wind to launch his catamarans against the enemy.

Also present, much more surprisingly, was Lord Melville, the First Lord of the Admiralty. It was not the First Lord's job to go to sea, and most unusual for a politician to join an assault force, but nevertheless Melville was aboard Admiral Keith's flagship the *Monarch*. He wanted to witness the action for himself, to form an idea of just how useful Fulton's new weapons would be in practice.

The attack began soon after 9 p.m., with light wind and a favourable tide. The British force advanced in three divisions. The fireships sailed towards Boulogne with an escort of gun brigs, accompanied by four or five torpedo-catamarans, each packed with forty barrels of gunpowder, activated by a clock-and-flintlock firing mechanism. The British ships also carried ten forty-gallon hogsheads crammed with a mixture of gunpowder, ballast and combustible balls. These were to be thrown overboard when they reached the enemy, rather like Second-World-War depth charges.

The men in control of these new weapons had been specially trained for the task. The bravest of them handled the torpedo-catamarans. These coffer-like devices were called catamarans because they were carried by two parallel wooden floats, steered by a man with a paddle. He wore black clothes and a black cap pulled over his face, so as not to stand out in the dark. The torpedoes too were lined with lead to give them a low profile in the water. The man's task was to paddle his torpedo towards the enemy and hook it on to a French ship's anchor cable so that it would swing alongside the hull. He was then to disengage the catamaran and steer back to his own ship, hoping to be out of range before the torpedo blew up.

But the French were ready and waiting. They had already taken the precaution of anchoring their own ships closer inshore, to make an attack more difficult. Their sentries were on full alert and they had launched a protective screen of pinnaces to patrol the approaches to Boulogne in the darkness. They soon spotted the Royal Navy. The shooting started at once, the whole shore lit up so brightly that it seemed almost like noon to the watching sailors. There was no chance now of taking the French by surprise. All they could do instead was head straight for the enemy and hope for the best.

They did so, the fireships advancing at full speed, straight for the French line. Their passage was disputed by French gunboats. The British activated the clockwork firing mechanisms aboard the fireships, primed to go off in six to eight minutes' time. Then they leapt into their longboats and left the ships to their fate.

The explosions were not long in coming. They looked magnificent to the watching British – great columns of flame shooting hundreds of feet into the air, like meteors or fireworks. The display was spectacular, but the damage done was minimal. One fireship blew up between two French gunboats. Another passed straight through the French line and appeared to explode harmlessly beyond. A third was boarded by French sailors and blew up while they were searching it. The result was a number of French casualties, but no real harm done to the flotilla. The line of gunboats remained as steady as ever, undisturbed by the assault.

The torpedo-catamarans had little success either, and the hogshead casks did no damage at all. They were activated by removing a pin to start the fuse – a task so dangerous that the sailors were required to keep the pin as evidence that they had actually armed the devices. John Allison, a junior officer aboard the *Leopard*, never received the order to keep the pins:

> I proceeded with two casks in the *Leopard's* long cutter, one in the bow, the other in the stern sheets, stood inshore and made the round battery to the southward. I dropped down until I could plainly see the flotilla, and driving directly for them by the tide, at the distance of about half a cable, I took the pin out of the machine on the aftermost cask.
>
> William Bailey, boatswain, laid hold of it after it was out. I put my ear to the machinery and heard it going, then ordered it to be thrown overboard and told Mr Gilbert, Midshipman, with William Rogers (whom I had stationed forward) to take the pin out of the cask in the bow. They answered it was out. I then ordered the cask to be thrown overboard. Mr Gilbert reported to me that he heard the machinery going.
>
> I think they must have heard the splashing of the casks from the shore, as they commenced firing musketry immediately, the balls coming over the boats. This was the first firing that took place . . . Having only had time to have the machinery explained (which I perfectly understood) I received no instructions to preserve the pins, nor did I think it necessary.

But none of this achieved anything. Despite all the effort that had gone into the raid, the damage to the French flotilla was negligible. Midshipman Crawford scanned the French line next morning and noticed no difference at all, although a count revealed one pinnace missing. This had been lying alongside a British fireship when it blew up. It was the only vessel sunk on the French side – not much of a return for months of British planning and preparation. In terms of tonnage destroyed, the attack had been a failure.

In Robert Fulton's view, this was partly because his weapons had not been used properly in action. He immediately began a programme of refinements to make them easier to handle. Even Admiral Keith, no fan of the new technology, thought they had been unlucky and might do better next time. And Lord Melville later argued that although little physical damage had been done, the Boulogne attacks had at least created panic in the Grand Army.

Melville was putting a politician's gloss on a failure by his department, but to an extent he may have been right. French reaction to the raid was to install an elaborate system of booms and chain cables across the harbour mouth, to frustrate any further intrusions. The new arrangements took time to set up and succeeded in putting the French on the defensive when they were supposed to be thinking about attack. With the year drawing on and winter approaching, it meant with luck that the invasion of England would now have to be postponed for several months, probably until the spring of 1805 at the earliest.

CHAPTER 10

———•◦•———

SPAIN ENTERS THE WAR

Three days after the Boulogne raid, the Royal Navy was in action again. The target this time was not the French, but four Spanish treasure ships on their way from South America to Cadiz.

Britain was not at war with Spain, but relations between the two countries had been fraught for some time. By a treaty of 1796, the Spanish were obliged to supply a number of ships and soldiers to the French on demand. Napoleon had asked for cash instead, thus enabling Spain to remain nominally neutral in his war against Britain. The Spanish had complied with reluctance, knowing full well that whatever they did to appease Napoleon would antagonise the British. They had chosen what they hoped would be the lesser of two evils.

The British had responded by reserving the right to treat any cash payment to Napoleon as a potential act of war. Alarmed by the growing amount of naval activity in Spanish ports, they had set out to intercept the treasure ships en route from Montevideo with a cargo of specie ultimately destined for Napoleon. A Royal Navy squadron had hurried to Cadiz to detain the ships 'by force or otherwise' before they could reach port.

About 6 a.m. on 5 October, they sighted the Spanish south-west of Cape Santa Maria. Two hours later, they caught up with them and ordered the Spanish to shorten sail. Admiral Bustamente refused until the British put a shot across his bows. Captain Graham Moore of the *Indefatigable* then sent a boat across to ask for his surrender. Bustamente refused again, and at 9.30 a.m. the fighting began.

A few minutes later, the *Mercedes* blew up, killing more than 200 people including women and children. It also killed some friends of the Spanish royal family. Two of the other Spanish ships surrendered by 10 a.m. The third made a run for it and was not captured until 1 p.m. In addition to all the lives lost, the cost to the Spanish treasury was well over £1 million – an immense sum by the standards of the day.

The Spanish were naturally outraged. The British were no better than pirates. One Spaniard aboard the *Mercedes* had lost his wife, his life savings and eight of his family of nine. The British paid him compensation, but the damage had been done. Spain formally declared war on 12 December.

This was dreadful news for the British. It meant that the long Spanish coastline was now enemy territory. The declaration of war was quickly followed by a naval agreement with France whereby the Spanish undertook to equip and maintain a substantial part of Napoleon's fleet, effectively placing their ships and ports at his disposal. The hostile shore facing the British stretched now from the Friesian Islands in the north all the way down to Corunna, and from Cadiz to the Italian border. For a Royal Navy already operating at full capacity, this was nothing less than a disaster.

For Napoleon, however, the news was much more encouraging. With Spain now on France's side, the number of capital ships available for the invasion of England had almost doubled overnight. The Spanish could bring more than thirty ships of the line to the task, and a navy with a long tradition of seafaring. They were a substantial fighting force, with plenty of secure anchorages along the Spanish coastline that the Royal Navy could never penetrate. It was just the fillip Napoleon needed.

But it meant his plans would need rethinking. With so many extra ships at his disposal, he could make life much more difficult for the Royal Navy, but it would take time to organise. The death of Admiral Latouche-Tréville, the only French sailor capable of taking on Nelson, had delayed Napoleon for a while. He had toyed briefly with the idea of postponing the invasion of Britain until November, then launching a two-pronged attack on both England and Ireland in the hope that one or the other would succeed. But November was very late in the year to launch an invasion, and his fleet was still hopelessly divided between several different ports. The Royal Navy was doing its utmost to keep it that way. Better perhaps to wait now until next spring, when the Spanish fleet would be ready to sail and the British would be that much more weary, their ships much closer to breaking point. It was exhausting for the British just waiting for Napoleon, never knowing when he would come. He was costing them money by doing nothing at all.

Napoleon decided to wait. Spring 1805 was the time. Meanwhile, he had other things on his mind. His coronation was fast approaching. He had been hoping to be crowned in November, but negotiations with the Pope had taken longer than expected, so now his big day was fixed for 2 December instead.

For William Pitt, at 10 Downing Street, the situation was looking graver by the minute. He had not expected Spain to react so badly to the attack on the treasure ships. The incident had been intended merely as a warning, a sharp reminder to the Spanish that Britain would not sit idly by while they kept Napoleon's war machine supplied. But the killing of women and children had been a dreadful mistake. If it meant that the Spanish navy was now to join forces with Napoleon, the implications for the invasion of England would be disastrous.

The war was escalating alarmingly, with Britain still standing alone. Napoleon had plenty of enemies in Europe, but no one else had declared war. The Austrian Emperor lived in fear of him. The Russians had interests in the Mediterranean that were threatened by the French. Both these countries wanted to see France restrained and its monarchy restored. It was in their interests to form an alliance with Britain to see Napoleon off – particularly if they could persuade William Pitt to subsidise their armies with British gold, something he was very loath to do.

All three countries had reservations about an alliance, which would be based more on dislike of Napoleon than enthusiasm for each other. The Russians were putting out feelers to London to see how things lay. Pitt was responding cautiously, not wanting to rush into anything that might cost the British money. He took the view that Napoleon would force the Russians' hand, sooner or later. They would certainly need an alliance with

Britain at some point, but on better terms than they were contemplating at the moment.

Meantime, Pitt turned his attention to the defences of Kent and Sussex. The defences were of paramount importance now, with the Spanish fleet likely to join the invasion. On 21 October 1804, a fortnight after the capture of the treasure ships, Pitt attended a conference at Rochester with the Duke of York, General Sir David Dundas (the officer commanding the area) and General William Twiss, a Royal Engineer. The meeting gave the green light for construction of eighty-one Martello towers along the invasion coast. This was an astonishingly large number, by far the biggest defensive programme the country had undertaken since Henry VIII's coastal forts of the 1540s. The towers were to be built along the seafront at 600-yard intervals, to a design already being tested at Woolwich, where cannon balls fired at various ranges simply bounced off the walls. Thirty million bricks were needed for the project, of which two and a half million had already been ordered. It was too late in the year to begin work now, but sites were already being leased and materials gathered together. Construction was due to begin in the spring of 1805.

Three days later, Pitt attended another conference, this time at Dymchurch in Romney Marsh. General Dundas was present again, and General Moore (it was his brother, aboard the *Indefatigable*, who had captured the Spanish treasure). The purpose of this second conference was to give the go-ahead for a military canal from Sandgate to Rye to cut off the Romney Marsh peninsula from the rest of the country, so rendering it useless to the French.

The canal qualified as a field work, which meant the cost would come straight out of the army budget without any bureaucratic delays. The work could begin at once. The first ground was broken on 30 October, and the task was considered so urgent that the labourers were to work on Sundays until the job was done. They were joined later by hundreds of soldiers, drafted in to do most of the spadework and build guardhouses and gun emplacements at every crossing.

The work progressed so quickly that the first stretch of the nineteen-mile canal was due for completion by 1 March 1805. The rest was to be finished by 1 June. That was a very tight schedule, but with Spain up in arms and Napoleon about to invade, there was no more time to waste. As he headed for Walmer after the Dymchurch meeting, Pitt could only hope that all these defences, so long in the gestation, would now be completed before the French arrived.

At the Admiralty, Lord Melville redoubled his efforts after the attack on the Spanish treasure ships. He had already instituted a substantial programme of shipbuilding to restore the deficiencies of the British fleet. He had given commissions to private yards to get the work force employed again, and had come to terms with the timber suppliers and others to ensure an adequate flow of building materials to the government yards. He was satisfied that warships would soon be rolling off the production line again in sufficient numbers to put the navy back on its feet, fully equipped and able to do its job properly. But soon, unfortunately, was not quickly enough.

It took three years to build a seventy-four-gunner. Melville needed ships in three months – three weeks if he could get them. He needed ships *now* to counter a threat that was suddenly all too clear and immediate. He could not afford to wait.

His most burning priority was to get all existing ships out of reserve and back to sea again. Many were long overdue for the scrap yard – the average life of a wooden ship was only seven years – but there was no question of scrapping them now, with England's fate in the balance. They had to be patched up instead, before they rotted any further, and sent back to work. In an emergency, their hulls could be resheathed with three-inch planking and their frames reinforced internally with diagonal bracing. It was a stop-gap measure, in every sense of the term, but it would do for the time being. Nothing else mattered for the moment, except getting the ships back to sea again. Lord Melville was working round the clock to make sure it happened.

CHAPTER 11

———◆◆◆———

NAPOLEON CROWNS HIMSELF

In Paris, Napoleon was crowned Emperor on 2 December. The Pope himself travelled from Rome to officiate at the ceremony.

The pontiff arrived with deep misgivings, knowing full well that other European monarchs would be reluctant to recognise Napoleon's coronation when the French already had a royal family in exile. He had misgivings about France as well, a country that had guillotined its priests and ransacked its churches in the all too recent past. Napoleon had since mended fences with the Catholic Church with a carefully negotiated Concordat, but the Pope still had his doubts, although he kept them to himself. He was grateful to Napoleon for the victory at Marengo, which had driven the Austrian army out of Italy. He needed to remain on good terms with the most powerful man in Europe.

The ceremony was held at Notre Dame, Napoleon having decided against Aix-la-Chapelle. But he retained his enthusiasm for Charlemagne. Unable to wear the great man's spurs because of the royal fleurs-de-lis on them, he had elected instead to wield Charlemagne's sword and sceptre, the only other relics available to him. The sword had arrived in state from Aix, only to be challenged by two other swords, both also alleged to have been Charlemagne's. After some debate, one had been selected and solemnly brought to Notre Dame the night before the coronation. Comte Louis de Ségur had had to admonish two young officers for having a fight with it when they thought no one was looking.

The cathedral itself, stripped of much of its finery during the Revolution, had been refurbished for the ceremony. Houses near the entrance had been demolished and a Gothic annexe added to the west front. The choir screen and two altars had been removed to make a bigger central space, filled with thrones, chairs, a dais and all the trappings of a great state occasion. Napoleon's sense of theatre would not let him settle for anything less.

He wore satin for the occasion, a silk shirt and stockings, a velvet coat and a black felt hat topped with enormous white plumes. He was decorated with so much jewellery that he looked like 'the King of Diamonds' or 'a walking mirror'. His elder brother Joseph looked much the same. They stood admiring each other as Joseph joined him for the procession to Notre Dame. 'If only our father could see us now!' Napoleon told him. For impoverished Corsican gentry, they had come a long way indeed.

The ceremony was arranged for noon. Before setting out for the cathedral, Napoleon summoned a man called Raguideau to him. Raguideau was Josephine's notary, a virtual dwarf who lived in the rue Saint-Honoré. Many years earlier, on the announcement of her engagement to Napoleon, Josephine had asked Raguideau to draw up the marriage contract. Napoleon had eavesdropped as Raguideau tried to talk her out of it, telling her she was mad to marry a man who had only his army cloak and sword to offer. He had advised her to marry an army contractor instead – far better prospects all round.

Raguideau arrived at the Tuileries full of trepidation. He was horribly aware that Napoleon had never forgotten the insult. He wondered what was going to happen, the Emperor calling for him on this of all days.

He found Napoleon pacing up and down in his pantaloons. The Emperor drew himself up to his full five feet and a bit and glowered down at the dwarf. 'Well, Monsieur Raguideau?' he demanded. 'Have I nothing now but my cape and sword?' Raguideau could only gibber in reply. He was glad to get out of the room in one piece.

The imperial state coach took Napoleon and Josephine to Notre Dame. It was decorated with bees (a symbol of assiduity used by Charlemagne), golden eagles and a replica of Charlemagne's crown. The crowds along the procession route cheered loudly enough, but more for Josephine than Napoleon. There was no real enthusiasm for either of them, as he noted afterwards. Perhaps it would have been different if he had been able to conquer England before the ceremony.

At the cathedral, cannon boomed and bells rang out as they arrived. They went first to the archbishop's palace to change into their coronation robes. Napoleon's was royal purple, lined with ermine and embroidered with the letter 'N' and a swarm of golden bees. It was so long that it needed four train-bearers to carry it into the cathedral. Eight thousand people stood up and clapped as he and Josephine entered Notre Dame, proceeding up the aisle towards their thrones in front of the altar.

The ceremony followed the usual course, except that Napoleon declined to lie flat on his face in front of the Pope, as custom demanded. He accepted a papal blessing, but placed the crown on his own head rather than receive it from the Church. In the absence of Charlemagne's, a new crown had been specially made for the occasion, a laurel wreath of solid gold designed to make him look like Caesar on a gold coin. Napoleon crowned Josephine as well, taking great trouble to make sure hers sat comfortably on her curls. She was delighted that he did so, scarcely concealing her relief that she was still his wife for the occasion, despite her inability to give him a son.

Afterwards they drove through the streets again, the crowds more enthusiastic this time, particularly in working-class areas. Their procession was lit by 500 torches as the winter afternoon gave way to night. There were fireworks in the city that evening, and fêtes and illuminations, but Napoleon and Josephine saw little of them. Back at the Tuileries, they decided to dine alone instead. At Napoleon's insistence, Josephine wore her crown throughout the meal, because it made her look so pretty.

Three days later, Napoleon was on parade again, distributing new eagle standards to colour parties from the regiments of the French army. A glittering assembly was held on the Champ de Mars, where the Eiffel Tower now stands. It poured with rain throughout, but the new Emperor was not perturbed. His address to the troops was stirring:

Soldiers, here are your colours! These eagles will always be your rallying point. They will fly wherever your Emperor deems it necessary for the defence of the throne and his people. Do you swear to lay down your lives in their defence, and by your courage to keep them ever on the road to victory?

The colour parties swore. The tricolours were raised aloft in the rain and everyone cheered. Then they went back to their regiments, proudly taking the eagles with them.

The celebrations continued for the rest of the month, an endless round of balls, dinners and receptions to mark the inauguration of the Bonaparte dynasty. It was a new beginning for France. The country was still a republic, but once again with a dynastic family at its head. After Napoleon would come his son, if he had one, or his brother's son if he did not. For a nation that had been without a real head of state since the execution of Louis XVI, the new order promised stability, where for years there had been only chaos. It came as a relief to some – although not all.

Napoleon was now one of the crowned heads of Europe. As far as he was concerned, that meant he was free to address the others on equal terms, whether they liked it or not. And none of them did. To the other monarchs, he was still General Bonaparte, the revolutionary soldier who had seized power by force of arms rather than constitutional right. They were reluctant to recognise the legitimacy of his coronation, for all that the Pope had officiated at the ceremony.

But Napoleon was undeterred. He dashed off letters to all and sundry, signing himself Napoleon at the end, as he had done since becoming Consul for Life. If other monarchs signed themselves thus, so would he.

One of the letters he wrote, exactly a month after his coronation, was to the king of England. It was a remarkable missive, astonishing in its disingenuousness. Napoleon proposed peace between the two countries, an end to all hostilities. Coming from a general with 150,000 troops poised to invade, it was not to be taken seriously. For political reasons, however, Napoleon needed to propose peace to the British. A large body of French opinion was in favour of peace. If he proposed peace and the British turned him down, it would not be his fault if the war continued. It would be theirs, and he could say as much to his critics. Napoleon's spies had told him also that the British were in secret negotiations with the Russians. By writing to George III, he could test the waters and find out how badly they wanted peace. Napoleon dictated the letter on 2 January 1805.

My Brother,

Called by Providence, and by the voice of the Senate, the people and the army, to occupy the throne of France, my chief desire is for peace. France and England are wasting their wealth. The struggle between them may last for years. But are their respective governments fulfilling their most sacred duty? And all the blood which has been so ruthlessly shed, for no particular purpose, does it not accuse them in their own conscience . . . ?

Circumstances were never so favourable, nor the time ever so propitious, for calming passions, and listening to the dictates of humanity and reason. Once let this opportunity pass, and who can say when the war, which all my efforts were powerless to prevent, is likely to cease? Within the last ten years your Majesty has acquired vast wealth, and an extent of territory larger than that of Europe. Your nation is at the height of prosperity. What can you hope to gain by war . . . ?

If your Majesty will but consider the question, you will agree that you have nothing to gain. And what a melancholy prospect, that nations should war with each other simply for the sake of fighting! The world is large enough for our two nations; and reason should have sufficient influence to enable us to conciliate our differences, if there be a sincere wish on both sides to do so . . . I trust your Majesty will believe in the sincerity of my sentiments, and my earnest desire to give a proof thereof.

The letter was signed 'Napoleon', in the Emperor's own hand. It was taken to Boulogne and delivered under flag of truce to a ship of the Royal Navy's blockade. From there it was ferried across the Channel to England. French soldiers and British sailors alike watched it go, wondering darkly what was in the letter and what it might mean for them.

CHAPTER 12

NAPOLEON'S OPENING
GAMBIT

The letter reached London late on the night of 7 January 1805, the same day as news of Spain's formal declaration of war. It did not go to King George III. His Majesty did not open post from dictators. It went instead to the Foreign Office, the department of the outgoing under-secretary, Lord Harrowby.

From there it was taken across to 10 Downing Street for the Prime Minister to see. William Pitt was shaken by Napoleon's presumption. Early next morning, he forwarded the letter to the king at Windsor Castle, with a recommendation that no answer be given until the British had consulted Russia and Austria, their potential allies in a coalition against Napoleon.

King George in turn was outraged 'that the French usurper had addressed himself to him'. Not only that, but Napoleon had called him 'brother'. They were far from being brothers, in King George's opinion. No kin at all.

The king was old and ill in 1805. He had been suffering for years from intermittent bouts of madness and he had cataract problems that would eventually turn him blind. But his heart was still in the right place. 'I should like to fight Boney single-handed. I'm sure I should. I should give him a good hiding.' Although almost sixty-seven, George was in no doubt as to what he must do if Napoleon invaded: 'Should his troops effect a landing, I shall certainly put myself at the head of mine, and my other armed subjects, to repel them.' The king intended to set up his headquarters in Chelmsford, if the French landed in Essex, or Dartford, if they landed in Kent. He was ready to move at thirty minutes' notice, if necessary.

But now here was Napoleon proposing peace, even if no one believed a word of it. Napoleon's idea of peace was not anyone else's. The British government responded accordingly with a letter that reached Paris on 14 January. It was not written by King George, and it was not addressed to Napoleon. It was sent instead to 'the Chief of the French Government', care of Foreign Minister Talleyrand:

> His Britannic Majesty has received the letter addressed to him by the Chief of the French Government. There is nothing which his Majesty has more at heart than to seize the first opportunity of restoring to his subjects the blessings of peace, provided it is founded upon a basis not incompatible with the permanent interests and security of his dominions. His Majesty is persuaded that that object cannot be attained but by arrangements which may at the same time provide for the future peace and security of Europe, and prevent a renewal of the dangers and misfortunes by which it is now overwhelmed.
>
> In conformity with these sentiments, his Majesty feels that he cannot give a more specific answer to the overture which he has received, until he has had time to communicate with the continental Powers, to whom he is united in the most confidential manner, and particularly the Emperor of Russia, who has given the strongest proofs of the wisdom and elevation of the sentiments by which he is animated, and of the lively interest which he takes in the security and independence of Europe.

In other words, the British were contemplating a new coalition against France. Even with the threat of an invasion hanging over them, there could be no peace on Napoleon's terms. The war would go on.

Napoleon had expected nothing else. He was already finalising his plans for the invasion of England. It was scheduled now to go ahead in the spring or early summer of 1805, when the weather would be more reliable.

Napoleon's initial idea had been to assemble a huge fleet in the Channel and push straight across to England, brushing aside any opposition from the Royal Navy. But his admirals had managed to talk him out of it, arguing that a frontal assault was far too risky – even if they could get all their ships out of harbour. The Royal Navy was too formidable for such blunt tactics. Subtler methods were needed if the operation was to be a success.

After brooding about it, Napoleon had decided on a diversionary strategy instead – luring the Royal Navy away from the Channel, then doubling back and launching the invasion barges across the Straits of Dover while the navy was looking the other way. It was a standard manoeuvre in military terms, one that Napoleon had practised often enough on land. It could work at sea as well.

His admirals had been labouring for months on different versions of the plan. The essence of it was to land French troops in places as far afield as South America, the West Indies, West Africa and a small Atlantic island named St Helena – all areas of commercial interest to the British. The troops would attack British settlements and threaten their security, leaving the Royal Navy no choice but to abandon its blockade and chase after them. While the navy was away, the French fleet would give it the slip and hurry back to launch an invasion of the thinly guarded British Isles. What could be simpler?

Almost anything, in the view of the admirals charged with making it happen. But Napoleon wanted it, and no one was prepared to gainsay him. On the same day that he proposed peace to King George, Napoleon instructed his admirals at Rochefort and Toulon to sail independently for the West Indies and create havoc among the British there. They were to attack the sugar islands because sugar was important to the British economy. If the merchants of the City of London saw their commercial interests being threatened, they would put pressure on William Pitt to make peace, if necessary on terms favourable to Napoleon. If they did that, then perhaps Napoleon would get everything he wanted without the bother of an invasion.

The expedition, in effect, was a dress rehearsal for the invasion. Napoleon was literally testing the waters, seeing what the British reaction would be. The Rochefort fleet was to head straight for the West Indies, while the Toulon ships were to raid the coast of South America first. They would then join forces for further operations in the Caribbean before making the long haul back to Rochefort, in the Bay of Biscay, to await the invasion of England. Further orders would follow as and when the situation developed.

The Rochefort fleet was the first to put to sea. With 3,500 troops on board, ten ships under Rear-Admiral Burgues Missiessy nosed out of harbour on 11 January 1805, in the middle of a snowstorm. They had been waiting for bad weather in the hope of slipping out unnoticed by the British blockade. They had almost made it when they were spotted by two Royal Navy vessels, one of which was storm-damaged. Escorted by the other, it limped back towards the British squadron to fetch help, but had to be abandoned on the way. The delay meant that five days had elapsed before the main British force learned what had happened. It was enough for the French to make good their escape and sail unpursued for the West Indies. They arrived off Martinique on 20 February.

The Toulon fleet had less success. Under their new admiral, Pierre Villeneuve (he had dropped the aristocratic 'de' after the Revolution), they slipped out of harbour on 18 January, emerging cautiously into a strong north-westerly wind. Lord Nelson's blockade was nowhere in sight. He had temporarily withdrawn his ships to Sardinia to take on fresh water. Two lookout frigates remained on guard, but they were no danger to Villeneuve's force. In any case, they disappeared next morning, peeling off to report to Nelson. Villeneuve was free to head for South America.

But he was unable to go anywhere by then. The weather had deteriorated sharply during his first night at sea. A howling gale had torn through a fleet crammed with seasick soldiers and manned by sailors who had scarcely been out of harbour before. The weather was routine for the Royal Navy, but an uncomfortable revelation to the French. They had no idea how to ride it out. By dawn next morning, only four of the eleven ships of the line were still together. The rest were scattered in disarray, picking up the pieces. One had lost her mainmast, another a topmast. Most had decks littered with torn rigging and bits of broken spar. They were in no position to sail for South America. Some would be hard pushed to sail anywhere at all.

Villeneuve took the only sensible decision and ordered them back to port. Reluctantly, they turned about and headed for Toulon, arriving back there only three days after setting out. It was not an impressive start to the invasion of Britain.

CHAPTER 13

———•◆•———

LORD NELSON ABOARD
THE *VICTORY*

Aboard his flagship *Victory*, Lord Nelson had no idea that Villeneuve's force had returned to base so quickly. The last his frigates had seen of the French, they appeared to be heading south of Sardinia. Nelson had sent his own ships that way as well, scouring the waters between there and Sicily for a sight of the enemy. He spent weeks chasing all over the Mediterranean, literally worrying himself sick as to where they might have gone – 'I am in a fever. God send I may find them.' It wasn't until 19 February that he reached Malta and learned that the French had been back in harbour all the time – news he greeted with incredulity. 'Those gentlemen are not accustomed to a Gulf of Lyons gale, which we have buffeted for twenty-one months, and not carried away a spar.'

Nelson himself had not set foot on dry land in all that time. He had been commander-in-chief of the Mediterranean fleet since the resumption of the war in 1803 and had been aboard the *Victory* ever since. He had spent two unhappy winters at sea – a combination of boredom, ill health and weather of the kind that had defeated Villeneuve – and was longing to go home to his mistress Lady Hamilton. But he could not go home while the Toulon fleet remained a threat. Duty required him to remain where he was.

Nelson had jumped at the command when it was first offered to him. After a year ashore on half-pay, and with seventy-three admirals senior to him on the flag list, he had badly needed to go to war again. His mistress had extravagant tastes, and he had a wife to support as well. The only way he could do so was by taking the admiral's share of any prize money awarded to the fleet. The war was a commercial proposition for Nelson, as well as a patriotic duty.

He had been offered the Mediterranean because that was Latouche-Tréville's beat, the only French admiral capable of meeting Nelson on equal terms. They had fought an elaborate duel for months, Latouche-Tréville in Toulon with his fleet, Nelson patrolling outside, usually so far offshore that there wasn't a British sail in sight. He had hoped thus to tempt the French out of harbour, drawing them out to sea where the Royal Navy was lying in wait for them. The French had emerged once or twice, but had always scuttled back in as soon as the British reappeared. Latouche-Tréville had written to Napoleon after one of these encounters, boasting that Nelson had run away the moment he saw the French. When Nelson heard about it, he had promised to make Latouche-Tréville eat the letter when he caught up with him.

But now Latouche-Tréville was dead, 'and all his lies with him'. Villeneuve was the new man in Toulon. He was an unknown quantity to Nelson, although he had been present at the Battle of the Nile in 1798. Villeneuve had been at the rear of the French line on that occasion, powerless to influence the fight one way or the other. He had escaped the general annihilation either because it was the sensible thing to do (Villeneuve's view) or because he had cut the cables of his ship and run away (the view of many others). Either way, Villeneuve had extracted his ship and lived to fight another day, which was more than could be said for many of his colleagues.

He was not Napoleon's first choice for the Toulon command. Other, better officers had either just taken command elsewhere or were out of favour with the Emperor. Villeneuve was an able officer, but not an outstanding commander. He himself had had considerable doubts about taking the job, between Napoleon and Nelson, but had allowed ambition to overcome his better judgement. Accepting the appointment, Villeneuve had hoisted his flag aboard the *Bucentaure* in Toulon.

It was embarrassing to slink back into harbour after only three days at sea. As soon as he was ashore again, Villeneuve lost no time getting his version of events in the post to Admiral Decrès, the Minister of Marine. After less than a month in command, he blamed the debacle on poor equipment and untrained men, rather than himself:

> I declare to you that ships of the line thus equipped, short-handed, encumbered with troops, with superannuated or bad materials, vessels which lose their masts or sails at every puff of wind, and which in fine weather are constantly engaged in repairing the damages caused by the wind, or the inexperience of their sailors, are not fit to undertake anything.

Decrès privately agreed. He was an old shipmate of Villeneuve's and understood only too well the problems he faced. Napoleon, however, did not. He made no attempt to conceal his anger when he heard what had happened:

> The great evil of our Navy is that the men who command it are unused to the risks of command. What is to be done with admirals who allow their spirits to sink and resolve to be beaten home at the first damage they suffer?

Napoleon thought hanging might be the answer, although he didn't mention it to Villeneuve. The English had shot Admiral Byng in similar circumstances.

Villeneuve offered his resignation, but Napoleon declined to accept it. There was no one better to replace him. The wretched admiral would just have to put to sea again, and sooner rather than later. There was no more time to waste if the invasion was to go ahead on schedule. The whole plan depended on the Toulon fleet breaking out and making its way to the West Indies to support Missiessy. Villeneuve must try again, and this time he must succeed. Napoleon was counting on it.

Nelson's fleet, meanwhile, was back in position off Toulon, waiting for the French to emerge again. Nelson was irritated that he had missed the chance of a fight. As well as the prize money, he would have had a chance to go home if the Toulon fleet had ceased to be a threat. On 9 March, he wrote to Lady Hamilton in despair:

I shall ever be uneasy at not having fallen in with them. I know, my dear Emma, that it is in vain to repine; but my feelings are alive to meeting those fellows, after near two years' hard service. What a time! I could not have thought it possible that I should have been so long absent; unwell, and uncomfortable, in many respects. However, when I calculate upon the French Fleet's not coming to sea for this summer, I shall certainly go for dear England.

Nelson was due for a rest. He was forty-six years old, blind in one eye, going blind in the other. He had lost an arm in battle and endured recurring pain in his side from an old stomach wound. His hernia produced a lump the size of his fist every time he coughed. He suffered headaches from a head wound and was prone to regular bouts of fever, toothache and depression. For a man who had been in action 120 times by the age of thirty-nine, Nelson was bearing up well, but he was long overdue for an honourable retirement. It was only the war that kept him at sea.

But there was no rest for Nelson, or anyone else, for that matter. They had all been at sea far too long. Officers and men alike were dreadfully bored, cold and wet for much of the time, overworked and undermanned for the rest. They were longing for the French to come out and fight, so that the issue could be decided once and for all and everyone could go home. It was not an exciting life, constantly patrolling the same monotonous stretch of coastline. For most of them, the world had narrowed to the mastheads, rigging and lower decks of their own ship. They had no life beyond it.

Yet morale was high in the fleet, largely as a result of Nelson's leadership. He was an inspired commander and everyone under him knew it. The atmosphere was particularly happy aboard the *Victory*. Most of the crew were from the British Isles, but there were also Norwegians, Germans, Canadians and many other nationalities, including at least one Brazilian and twenty-two Americans. Several were black and one was a woman in disguise. Wherever they came from, they were all delighted to be aboard the flagship, serving under Nelson. He inspired their confidence in a way no other commander did.

Leonard Gillespie, a Scottish physician, spent some time aboard the *Victory* early in 1805. He was struck at once by the happiness of the crew. A good test of morale was the number of men who had reported sick for one reason or another. Gillespie found only one man confined to his bed aboard the *Victory*, out of a crew of 840. It was much the same on the other ships as well. They were all in 'the best possible order as to health, discipline, spirits and disposition towards our gallant and revered commander, Lord Nelson'. In a world where fever and scurvy were still commonplace at sea, it was a remarkable achievement.

Gillespie wrote home to his sister, outlining his daily routine aboard the *Victory*:

At six o'clock my servant brings a light and informs me of the hour, wind, weather and course of the ship, when I immediately dress and generally repair to the deck . . . Breakfast is announced in the Admiral's cabin, where Lord Nelson, Rear-Admiral Murray, the Captain of the Fleet, Captain Hardy, Commander of the *Victory*, the chaplain, secretary, one or two officers of the ship, and your humble servant assemble and breakfast on tea, hot rolls, toast, cold tongue, &c . . . Between the hours of seven and two there is plenty of time for business, study, writing and exercise . . . At two o'clock a band of music plays till within a quarter to three, when the drum beats the tune called 'The Roast Beef of Old England', to announce the Admiral's dinner, which is served up exactly at three o'clock, and which generally consists of three courses and a dessert of the choicest fruit, together with three or four of the best wines, champagne and claret not excepted . . .

Coffee and liqueurs close the dinner about half-past four or five o'clock, after which the company generally walk the deck, where the band of music plays for near an hour. At six o'clock tea is announced, when the company again assemble in the Admiral's cabin, where tea is served up before seven o'clock, and as we are inclined, the party continue to converse with his lordship, who at this time generally unbends himself, although he is at all times as free from stiffness and pomp as a regard to proper dignity will permit, and is very communicative. At eight o'clock a rummer of punch with cake or biscuit is served up, soon after which we wish the Admiral a good night, who is generally in bed before nine o'clock.

Off Brest at the same time, eleven-year-old midshipmen were eating ship's biscuit so cold and full of weevils that it reminded them of their mothers' calves' foot jelly. Nelson had eaten weevils too, when he was a midshipman. As admiral, though, he had clearly decided that comfort food should be the order of the day.

CHAPTER 14

POLITICAL MANOEUVRES

In London, following his rejection of Napoleon's peace offer, William Pitt was turning his mind to a military alliance with Russia. It was increasingly important now that Spain was in the war as well. Negotiations were stalled at the moment, but Pitt was optimistic about the eventual outcome. If it came off, Russia would provide the manpower for a new land campaign against Napoleon while Britain would supply the money – £1,250,000 a year for every 100,000 soldiers the Russians put in the field. If the Austrians joined as well, it could amount to half a million men, a formidable alliance against Napoleon. The fighting would all be in mainland Europe, taking the pressure off the English coast. The expense was horrific to a money-minded Prime Minister, but it would be cash well spent if it kept the country from being invaded. Napoleon was not the only one who could employ diversionary tactics to achieve his ends.

The timetable was crucial to the British. Much depended on how quickly the Spanish could put to sea. As with Boulogne and the Channel ports, the British had sent spies ashore to find out. The newly knighted Sir John Moore had been one of them. On 18 December 1804, unaware that Spain had already declared war, he had landed near the port of Ferrol with his brother and Admiral Cochrane. With fowling pieces and gundogs, they were ostensibly a shooting party, but their real purpose was to see how the land lay for an attack on Ferrol. They had been spotted before they could learn anything useful and had had to run for the beach to escape back to sea.

The Spanish were certainly mobilising for war, but faced the same problems as everyone else in getting their ships out of harbour. Nothing could be done in a hurry. Like the French and British, they had a manpower shortage that could not be addressed overnight. The Spanish were so short of sailors that they had recruited British seamen who for one reason or another were refugees from the Royal Navy. Lord Nelson had warned his men against this before the Spanish entered the war:

> When British Seamen and Marines so far degrade themselves in time of War, as to desert from the Service of their own Country, and enter into that of Spain; when they leave one shilling per day, and plenty of the very best provisions, with every comfort that can be thought of for them – for two-pence a day, black bread, horse beans and stinking oil for their food . . . To put himself under the lash of a Frenchman or Spaniard must be more degrading to any man of spirit than any punishment I should inflict on their bodies.

With no other means of leaving the navy, however, British sailors had continued to desert, so many that Nelson had had to insist on death for any who were recaptured and court-martialled. If they were convicted, there could be no question of their sentences being commuted to any lesser punishment.

The best guess in London was that the Spanish fleet would be ready for war any time from March onwards. After that, there would be nothing to prevent it joining Napoleon's Channel fleet for an assault on England. If Villeneuve managed to join as well, their combined firepower – perhaps fifty capital ships – would dwarf anything the Royal Navy could produce. It would need a miracle to save the navy from annihilation.

The shore defences were not ready either. Work had begun on the Martello towers, but it would be two years at least before they were completed. The Royal Military Canal had run into trouble too. The task was proving more complex than at first thought and the target dates would not be met. The men digging it did not even know the canal's true purpose. They thought it was just a communications channel for moving military stores about. The work was under way, but for the moment the Romney

Marsh peninsula was still wide open to attack, with nothing to stop the French from landing and proceeding immediately inland. It was not a comfortable thought for William Pitt, conferring with the Duke of York and his other military advisers in Downing Street.

To cap it all, Pitt was about to lose one of his closest allies in the fight against Napoleon. Lord Melville was an efficient First Lord of the Admiralty, but his past was catching up with him. As Treasurer of the Navy, he had years ago allowed one of his officials to use public money for private speculation. Melville himself had not benefited directly, although he had borrowed money from the man. But he had been a party to unacceptable behaviour. A report into the affair had been published on 18 March. It had come down heavily against Melville and the issue was now before Parliament. The indications were that the House of Commons would vote for his impeachment. If it did, Pitt would lose his First Lord of the Admiralty at the worst possible juncture, with the Royal Navy still not up to strength and the French and Spanish poised to invade at any moment. It could hardly have happened at a more awkward time.

At the Tuileries, surrounded by a court that was looking more imperial by the day, Napoleon was putting the finishing touches to his final plan for the invasion. It was his seventh plan, by some estimates. One of the problems his admirals faced was that the plan kept changing from day to day. Napoleon sparked off ideas in all directions, but did not always remember what he had said. He contradicted himself sometimes, or changed the details, or issued orders that were impossible to carry out. It did not make life any easier for his staff.

The current plan was much the same as the previous one, except that Villeneuve was no longer to sail to South America. He was to head for Cadiz first, to collect a Spanish squadron under Admiral Don Federico Gravina. He would be followed by Vice-Admiral Honoré Ganteaume with six frigates and twenty-one ships of the line from Brest. They were all to cross the Atlantic and link up with Admiral Missiessy off Martinique. This monster force would then turn about and return to Europe under Ganteaume's command, aiming for the English Channel. Its ultimate destination was top secret, contained in sealed orders that were not to be opened until they were at sea. In fact the destination was Boulogne, where Napoleon would be waiting for them from 10 June onwards. From Boulogne, with a huge armada at his disposal, he would make short work of the final leg of the journey – the hop across the Channel to England.

But Napoleon was aware that it might not work out exactly as planned. His orders to Ganteaume and Villeneuve contained elaborate instructions as to what to do in Martinique if the other fleets didn't show up. Essentially they were to wait for a while and then proceed independently back to Europe, doing whatever was necessary to arrive in strength off Boulogne in the middle of June. Arriving off Boulogne in June or early July was the important part to Napoleon. It was the new date he had set for the invasion.

That was the plan, but neither Ganteaume nor Villeneuve was overwhelmed by it. Napoleon was thinking like a soldier rather than a sailor, in their opinion, running his dividers across a map of the Atlantic and calculating how many leagues his ships could cover each day. It didn't work like that at sea. Ships were not formations of troops that could be moved across the board at will. They were more complicated altogether.

Yet the admirals had to make it work somehow. In Brest, Ganteaume dutifully began to prepare for sea. 'Do not forget the great destinies which you hold in your hands,' Napoleon wrote to him. 'If you are not wanting in enterprise, success is certain.' In reply, Ganteaume telegraphed Paris on 24 March, pointing out that fifteen British warships were lying in wait for him outside Brest harbour. Was he supposed to fight them on his way out?

'*Sortez sans combat*,' came Napoleon's reply. There was nothing to be gained from fighting the British off Brest. Ganteaume agreed, but couldn't see how to get his fleet out of harbour without a fight. Easier said than done, with the Royal Navy sitting there, watching his every move.

Villeneuve was little happier. Acutely aware of the need to redeem himself in the Emperor's eyes, he was determined to make a success of his second escape from Toulon. But the omens were not good. As if anticipating a breakout, Nelson's fleet had been spotted off the Spanish coast, barring the way to the Atlantic. Villeneuve had been hoping to stick close to a friendly shore, creeping along the coast until making his final dash for the Straits of Gibraltar. Now he would have to go due south instead, around the outside of Majorca and Ibiza – pirate waters, in Villeneuve's view, no place to be with untrained crews and the Royal Navy prowling the horizon. He would much rather have stuck to the coast.

In Cadiz, the Spanish commander too was facing problems putting to sea. Admiral Gravina was a forty-nine-year-old aristocrat, so grand that he had the right to keep his hat on in the presence chamber of the king. He had been in the navy since he was twelve and was Spain's most highly respected sailor. He had fifteen ships in Cadiz, and more at Ferrol and Cartegena. All were nominally available to join the invasion fleet, but in practice Gravina would count himself lucky if half the ships at Cadiz were ready in time. Even with a few renegade Englishmen, the shortage of trained crews was acute.

'Fine and powerful ships,' Villeneuve said later, when he saw the Spanish fleet, but 'manned with herdsmen and beggars.' It was horribly true. They were so short of sailors that the guns were operated by untrained landsmen with little idea of what they were doing. A few artillerymen had been co-opted from the Spanish army, but they were soldiers and had no experience of conditions afloat. The crews were seriously deficient. The Spanish operated the same press-gang system as the Royal Navy, but where the British employed strict discipline and long months at sea to lick unpromising material into shape, the Spanish did not. Some of their sailors hadn't been to sea for eight years.

Gravina's orders were to join Villeneuve and sail for the West Indies with as many ships as possible. Yet the manpower shortage left him little option but to pay off half the ships under his command and use whatever crews he could muster to man the other half. By his calculation, only six or seven ships would be ready for sea by the time Villeneuve reached Cadiz on his way to the Indies. It was a disappointing figure, but the best Gravina could manage in the circumstances. Whatever else happened, he was determined not to disgrace Spain when the ships under his command finally put to sea.

CHAPTER 15

THE ENEMY PUT TO SEA

The breakout was set for the last week in March. Admiral Ganteaume's Brest fleet was the first to move. Ganteaume had twenty-one fighting ships under his command, but trained crews for only seven. He had been forced to make up the difference with landsmen and soldiers. On 23 March he began loading troops on board, prior to leaving harbour. Next day, he signalled to Napoleon his readiness to sail. All it needed now was a favourable wind and the fleet would put to sea.

The crews were longing to go. Everywhere there was a keen sense of anticipation, a feeling that at last they were going into action, after so long cooped up in port. The Royal Navy was waiting for them outside, but its ships were thinly spread and heavily outnumbered. There would surely be safety in numbers when the entire French fleet emerged from harbour.

But the situation changed dramatically on 27 March. Twenty-eight British ships suddenly appeared from nowhere off the Île de Beniguet. Ganteaume counted them with a sinking heart. There was no way he could slip past that many without a fight – and he had strict orders not to fight. It would be foolish even to try.

Swallowing his disappointment, Ganteaume ordered his ships to stand down. They would try again another day. Meantime, they would just have to remain in harbour, tying up British ships on the blockade that could not be released for anything else. It was not what Ganteaume had intended, but it was better than losing half his force on his first day at sea. No sensible officer would risk his fleet for a fight he could never hope to win.

*

In Toulon, Villeneuve was rather luckier in his second attempt at escape. There was a brisk north-easterly blowing on the evening of 29 March, just right for putting to sea. Nelson's fleet was nowhere to be seen, presumably still off Spain somewhere. Villeneuve gave the order to weigh anchor that evening and began moving his ships out under cover of darkness. By dawn next morning, they had cleared the harbour and were well out to sea, heading south-west for the gap between Minorca and Sardinia. There wasn't an English sail in sight.

'May fortune fulfil the hopes which the Emperor has founded upon the destination of this squadron,' wrote Villeneuve, wishing he could believe it. He had the same manpower problems as Gravina at Cadiz and Ganteaume at Brest – too few trained seamen and too many landlubbers who didn't know what they were doing. He was also carrying thousands of troops, who cluttered the decks and got in the way of the professionals. More than that, he had been saddled with a spy for the voyage as well, an agent of Napoleon's who had been seconded to the *Bucentaure* to keep an eye on Villeneuve and report back to his master. It was the ultimate insult for a career naval officer far more competent than Napoleon gave him credit for.

The spy was General Alexandre de Lauriston, commander of the troops aboard the fleet. He was an aide-de-camp to Napoleon and had direct access to the Emperor. Villeneuve, by contrast, reported only to Admiral Decrès. Lauriston carried the sealed orders containing the expedition's final destination, which were only to be opened after they had put to sea. But Lauriston already knew the destination because he had been told before they left port. He enjoyed the Emperor's confidence in a way that Villeneuve never would. He also shared the Emperor's contempt for the navy. His brief was to dine at Villeneuve's table and report back at every opportunity, confirming Napoleon's opinion as to the uselessness of his admirals and the navy in general. It did not make for a relaxed atmosphere as the *Bucentaure* headed southwards for the Minorca–Sardinia gap.

They were going that way because Villeneuve believed Nelson was somewhere off Barcelona, covering the coastal route to Gibraltar. In fact, Nelson's fleet had just finished revictualling in Sardinia and Villeneuve was sailing right towards it. Nelson was desperately short of ships, particularly speedy frigates. Unable to keep everything covered, he had sailed to Spain first, making sure his fleet was widely observed on shore and the news passed to Villeneuve. Then he had doubled back towards Sardinia, guessing correctly that Villeneuve would go this way if he broke out. The French were sailing straight into a trap.

They were already thirty miles out of Toulon before they were spotted by two Royal Navy frigates. HMS *Phoebe* turned round at once and headed back to Nelson to warn him the French were out. HMS *Active* stayed with the French, shadowing them all day and watching their every move.

It took the *Phoebe* five days to find Nelson. He immediately ordered his own ships westward, into the path of the French. He guessed that Villeneuve was aiming for Egypt, or maybe Sicily or Naples. Nothing in the French fleet's course suggested that Gibraltar was the real destination.

But Villeneuve had already changed tack and was heading straight for Gibraltar. A chance meeting with a merchantman had alerted him to Nelson's true position. Shaking off HMS *Active* in the darkness, his fleet switched course abruptly and crammed on sail for the Atlantic. When the sun came up next morning, HMS *Active* was faced with an empty horizon and no idea of where the French had gone.

Nelson was horrified. He immediately sent ships out in all directions, but there was no sign of Villeneuve anywhere. He decided to position his own fleet between Sardinia and Sicily until he heard something, but he was kicking himself with frustration. His job was to keep the French from breaking out and he had failed again, for the second time in two months. More than that, he didn't even know where they were now. The whole of the Mediterranean to look in, and Nelson had no idea where to begin.

In Gibraltar, the frigate HMS *Fisgard* was refitting after a spell at sea escorting Nelson's supply ships. Half her gear lay on the quayside, including her launch, barge, anchor and twenty-two tons of water casks. The frigate was commanded by the Marquess of Lothian's son, Lord Mark Kerr. On 9 April, he was busy with the refitting when he noticed a crowd of sails to the east, coming up past Gibraltar at full speed. A quick count revealed two brigs, seven frigates and eleven ships of the line. It certainly wasn't Nelson's fleet. It could only be Villeneuve's.

Kerr didn't waste a moment. His own ship lay in bits, but that didn't deter him. Quickly hiring a brig, he shoved a lieutenant into it with orders to go and tell Nelson. Then he set his crew to work to put the *Fisgard* back together, ready for sea. They sailed within four hours, abandoning much of their equipment on the dockside in their haste. Kerr turned at once towards the Atlantic, heading up past Cape Trafalgar in pursuit of Villeneuve. His duty was clear: he had to catch up with the French and see where they were going. Failing that, he would sail for the western approaches, locate the rest of the Royal Navy and warn them that the Toulon fleet was out.

Aboard the *Bucentaure*, Villeneuve maintained full speed past Gibraltar, well aware that he had been spotted and would quickly be pursued. His fleet continued headlong towards Cadiz, just up the coast, where it was to join forces with Admiral Gravina's squadron and proceed without delay to Martinique. Villeneuve had sent a frigate ahead to warn the Spanish he was coming.

It was getting dark by the time he arrived. The British were nowhere in sight, but they couldn't be far behind. As soon as the French came into harbour, Villeneuve was informed that the Spanish would have six ships of the line and a frigate ready to sail by midnight. He sent his flag-lieutenant hurrying ashore to remind Gravina that every minute was precious. It was essential to be back at sea before the British appeared from the Mediterranean.

By 2 a.m. on 10 April, Villeneuve's ships were under way again, heading for Martinique. The Spanish would follow as soon as they could. When the sun came up, however, only one Spanish ship was in sight – the *Argonaute*, Gravina's flagship. Villeneuve reduced sail to let the rest catch up, but only one more Spanish ship appeared in the next twenty-four hours. He gave up waiting after that and set course for the West Indies. His fleet was safely over the horizon before the British knew which way it had gone.

CHAPTER 16

NAPOLEON TAKES ANOTHER CROWN

Napoleon, meanwhile, was in Italy. He was on his way to Milan to be crowned. There had not been a king in north Italy for centuries. Napoleon was going to rectify that omission.

He had offered the Iron Crown of Italy to his brother Joseph first, in return for Joseph resigning his right to succeed him as Emperor of France. But Joseph had declined, so Napoleon was taking the crown for himself. It had belonged to Charlemagne in its time and was said to have been made from the nails that had pinned Jesus to the cross.

Napoleon left Paris at the end of March, accompanied by a large retinue and his wife Josephine. He intended to be away two or three months, long enough for Villeneuve and the other admirals to sail to the West Indies and back for their rendezvous off Boulogne. It was a carefully calculated move. The British would be lulled into a false sense of security if they knew Napoleon was in Italy. They would think he had forgotten about the invasion. But nothing could be further from the truth. Far from forgetting the invasion, Napoleon was planning to return unexpectedly and catch the British by surprise, popping up in Boulogne to mastermind the assault on England while they thought he was still sunning himself across the Alps. It was a clever idea, just the kind of outflanking manoeuvre Napoleon delighted in.

He travelled to Italy via Brienne and Troyes. As the newly crowned Emperor of France, it was his first tour of the provinces and he was wondering how he would be received by ordinary people. In the event, all went well. No one booed as he passed and his carriage was cheered at Lyon. People seemed to approve of their new Emperor. Ever sensitive to popular opinion, Napoleon took the cheers as a good omen.

In Italy, he stayed in Turin for several days before taking Josephine to see the battlefield of Marengo, where he had defeated the Austrians in 1800. He put on his old uniform for the occasion and wore the same cavalry sword and decaying lace hat that he had at the battle. Thirty thousand soldiers were on parade when he arrived, ready for a re-enactment of their triumph. Josephine did her best to look fascinated as Napoleon took her through it blow by blow, explaining in lavish detail how the French had been outnumbered two to one and by his account had retreated four times before he rallied them to victory. Then he inspected the troops and distributed Légions d'honneur before laying the foundation stone for a memorial to the fallen.

From Marengo he continued to Milan, where he stayed for a month. He was crowned in the cathedral there on 26 May 1805, with Josephine watching from the side. Napoleon marched up the aisle with the Iron Crown under his arm and put it on his own head after the archbishop had blessed it. Fluent in Italian, Napoleon repeated the inscription on the crown to the congregation: 'God gave it to me. Woe to him who touches it.' Napoleon hoped it would be prophetic.

That night he chased Josephine around their apartments, repeating the words on the crown and tickling her until she begged him to stop. The ceremony had gone well and Napoleon was pleased. As a gesture of goodwill, he had decided to finance the completion of the cathedral's western façade, with a tasteful statue of himself on the roof.

But others were less happy. A few days after Napoleon had crowned himself, the little republic of Genoa was coerced into joining his ever-expanding empire. It was this that finally persuaded the Czar of Russia that Napoleon's ambition knew no bounds. The man was insatiable. He would keep going until he was stopped. It would take a war to stop him, in the Czar's sober assessment. And that, for the Russians, meant an urgent alliance with England.

*

In London, Lord Melville was fighting for his political life. The report into his conduct as Treasurer of the Navy was being debated in Parliament. A motion of censure had been tabled in the House of Commons. Preliminary soundings by the party managers suggested the vote could go either way.

The motion was discussed on 8 April. The House was packed for the occasion, as was the strangers' gallery. The Prince of Wales sat watching, along with half of fashionable London. Melville had many enemies in the Commons, but he had friends as well, notably William Pitt. The Prime Minister was not going to desert him in his hour of need. Pitt's advisers had urged him to abandon Melville, but he would do no such thing. Melville may have been negligent in handling the navy's money but he had not been corrupt. He had served the country faithfully for many years without profiting himself and he had been a staunch ally of Pitt's in times of stress. Pitt wouldn't disown him now.

But the opposition was determined to bring Melville down. The motion was proposed by Samuel Whitbread, a nonconformist brewer's son and a lifelong opponent of corruption. He was supported by Charles James Fox and other leading MPs. The debate began at 9 a.m. and raged for twenty hours while Pitt sat on the government benches, grey with fatigue. From time to time his people whispered in his ear, still counting heads. The vote could still go either way.

At 4 a.m. on 9 April, the great anti-slavery campaigner William Wilberforce rose to speak. Wilberforce was a principled man. He spoke and voted according to his conscience and was highly respected in the House of Commons. Members on both sides craned forward to hear what he had to say.

Wilberforce came down against Melville. Pitt slumped back in despair. Wilberforce was his friend, but he was voting against Pitt's wishes. So would many others, following Wilberforce's lead.

The vote was taken shortly afterwards. Two hundred and sixteen Members of Parliament voted in favour of censuring Lord Melville. Two hundred and sixteen voted against. The result was a tie.

All eyes turned to Speaker Charles Abbot, who paled at the responsibility. After a pause of several minutes, during which Abbot looked as if he had been struck by a thunderbolt, he took a deep breath and gave his casting vote in favour of the motion. Melville was to be formally censured by the House.

The opposition exploded. Baying in triumph, they crowded round and yelled at Pitt to resign. Unable to stop a flow of tears, he hid his face behind his hat. Some of his supporters ran to help, shielding him from the opposition as they escorted him from the chamber. They got him out of the House and calmed him down, but the damage had been done. Melville resigned next day and Britain was without a First Lord of the Admiralty at a time when the country needed a First Lord more than ever before. The feeling in the Commons was that it wouldn't be much longer before the rest of the government fell as well.

The news took several weeks to reach the ships at sea – Nelson did not learn about it until early May. 'I have just heard that Lord Melville has left the Admiralty . . . His Lordship was doing much for the Service, and now we have to look forward to someone else.' From the sailors' point of view, it was not a good time for a change of leadership.

Nelson had been in a state of deep anxiety all month, ever since Villeneuve's escape from Toulon. His ships had been all over the Mediterranean looking for him, but without success. He had finally learned of Villeneuve's whereabouts on 18 April, when word reached him that the French had slipped past Gibraltar nine days earlier. Even then, though, he had not been able to set off in pursuit immediately. The wind had turned against him, blowing strongly from the west, just where he needed to go. It continued for several days, adding to his frustration. Nelson was in despair by the time it veered at last and he was able to get his fleet through the Straits on 6 May and out into the Atlantic. But he still had no idea which way to go to follow Villeneuve. North, towards England and Ireland? Or west, across the Atlantic?

It was an acute dilemma for Nelson. If he went north while Villeneuve went to the West Indies, he would be pilloried at home for allowing the French to ravage Britain's colonies. But if he headed for the West Indies, leaving Villeneuve free to join the Boulogne invasion, he would be castigated even more. 'If I fail, if they are not gone to the West Indies, I shall be blamed; to be burnt in effigy or Westminster Abbey is my alternative.'

Nelson couldn't decide between the two. He personally thought the French had sailed north:

> The circumstances of their having taken the Spanish Ships which were for sea, from Cadiz, satisfies my mind that they are not bound to the West Indies (nor probably the Brazils), but intend forming a junction at Ferrol, and pushing direct for Ireland or Brest.

That was Nelson's opinion, but it was only an opinion. He didn't know for sure.

Desperate for more information, he had sent ships ahead to see what they could learn. On 9 May, he received a note from the *Orpheus* saying that an American sea captain had been in Cadiz on the day Villeneuve sailed. According to the captain, Villeneuve had departed on 9 April amid scenes of chaos. Several Spanish ships had followed unwillingly, their crews 'forced with great reluctance aboard the men-of-war'. Both the French and Spanish ships had been carrying troops, some of them cavalry. The word in Cadiz was that they were bound either for Ireland or the West Indies, but the captain couldn't say which.

Nor could anyone else. No one knew where they had gone. A Portuguese man-of-war had seen them sailing west, but they might easily have changed course over the horizon to confuse the pursuit. On the other hand, Nelson had received no word from the north that they had gone that way. Surely a frigate would have been sent to tell him if the French had been seen heading for the Channel? Or was one on its way to him even now?

Exactly a month after Villeneuve's disappearance, Nelson anchored his fleet in Lagos Bay, off Portugal's southern tip. Sick with worry – 'disappointment has worn me to a skeleton' – he sat pondering his options while the fleet took on provisions to last five months. Where was Villeneuve now? Standing off Walmer or some Irish beach while the Grand Army swarmed ashore in an orgy of rape and destruction? Rampaging through the West Indies, annexing island after island for France with no one to stop him? The possibilities were too awful to contemplate.

Alone in his cabin, Nelson came to his decision. The decision was his to make and no one else's. He had nobody to help him, no real information to go on. All he had was thousands of men who would go wherever he told them, without demur. But the call was his to make. Nelson had got it horribly wrong when he thought Villeneuve was bound for Egypt or Sicily. The country would have his head if he got it wrong again.

He made up his mind on the morning of 11 May: they would go to the West Indies. God help them all if he hadn't got it right this time.

CHAPTER 17

———•◦•◦•———

VILLENEUVE IN THE
WEST INDIES

Three days later, Villeneuve arrived in Martinique after a panic-stricken voyage across the Atlantic. He had spent much of it looking over his shoulder, terrified that Nelson was about to appear at any moment. Villeneuve had seen what Nelson had done at the Nile, sailing inshore of the French in the darkness and catching them disastrously off-guard. The battle had left a huge impression on him. He didn't want anything like it to happen again.

But there had been no sign of the Royal Navy coming after him, or anyone else either. Villeneuve was on his own. Once safely at sea, he had taken the opportunity to shake his crews down, working on their seagoing skills during the five-week voyage. Most had never been out of sight of land before, but were soon cured of that. Villeneuve pushed them hard, preparing them for the battle that undoubtedly lay ahead.

It was also a chance to fire his guns, now that they were on the open sea. It was important for his men to know what a real broadside felt like, and he hadn't been able to show them in harbour. Even at sea he couldn't fire more than once or twice because of the need to conserve ammunition, but at least his men could feel the shudder as the guns recoiled and see the fall of shot on the wave tops. It wouldn't come as a total surprise when they had to do it for real.

They reached Martinique on 14 May to discover that Admiral Missiessy's fleet had long since returned to Europe. After attacking a few

British islands, Missiessy had given up waiting for Villeneuve and set off for home at the end of March. He was probably back in Rochefort by now. Villeneuve was still on his own.

Two days later, however, he was joined by the remainder of the Spanish squadron, which had been trailing after him all the way from Cadiz. The Spanish contingent was now six ships of the line and one frigate. The Spaniards spoke a different language from the French and employed different tactics. The two navies did not even have a signal book in common. But Admiral Gravina was a good officer with a long career behind him. In 1793, he had cooperated with the Royal Navy in supporting royalist Toulon against the excesses of the French Revolution. Times had changed since then. He was with the French now.

Their orders were to wait at Martinique until joined by Admiral Ganteaume's fleet from Brest. They did not yet know that Ganteaume had never left harbour. With time on his hands, Villeneuve turned his attention to HMS *Diamond Rock*, an outcrop off the tip of Martinique, 600 feet high, which had been occupied by the Royal Navy for the past sixteen months. The British had fired on the Spanish ships as they came into harbour. It was time the rock was recaptured for France.

Villeneuve assigned a sizeable task force to the operation – two ships of the line, three other ships and eleven gunboats, together with several hundred assault troops. They approached the rock on 31 May and began a bombardment at 8 a.m. The British promptly abandoned the lower reaches and retreated towards the summit, taking their ladders with them. The French troops landed quickly enough, but took another two days to scale the rock face. The Royal Navy's ammunition was almost exhausted by then, and an earth tremor had cracked the garrison's cistern. Further resistance was impossible without drinking water, so the *Diamond Rock*'s commander hoisted the white flag and negotiated an honourable surrender. The British had lost two men killed and one wounded in the action. The French acknowledged at least fifty casualties, although the British reckoned it was more.

While this small triumph was taking place, Villeneuve had received fresh orders from Napoleon. Ganteaume was still stuck in Brest, but Rear-Admiral Charles de Magon was coming instead, bringing extra troops to help Villeneuve continue his attacks on British colonies. There would be enough troops, Napoleon calculated, for Villeneuve to expel the British from all the Leeward Islands and probably Trinidad as well.

Villeneuve was shaken. This was the first he had heard of clearing the British out of the islands. His previous orders had simply told him to wait at Martinique until Ganteaume arrived. There had been nothing about attacking the British. Yet here was Napoleon thinking he had been clearing British colonies all this time. Had he missed a set of orders somewhere? Or had Napoleon simply forgotten what his original plan had been?

Admiral Magon arrived on 4 June but could shed no light on the matter. Anxious to make up for lost time, Villeneuve decided to attack the British at once. Combining forces with Magon, he sailed north on 5 June and arrived off Antigua next day. Jane Kerby, daughter of a judge on the island, reported their arrival to a friend:

> You will have heard how the combined fleet escaped by magic; how in reality (for I counted them myself – twenty-four of the line) they rode triumphant on *our element* for some weeks . . . how they peeped into the beautiful harbour of St John's, missed the rich sugar-loaded ships . . . tried to look warlike and form a line of battle, but they could not; but how, alas! they scampered after our sugar, took fourteen ships full of that and various good things going to our friends; and how to our great joy they burnt this treasure on its way to some of these islands by the manoeuvres of a sloop of war, who, afraid of being taken, threw out signals as for approaching friends, and they, *toujours Nelson en tête*, saw his ghost, and destroyed their prizes in the most premature and shameful hurry.

That was about the size of it. A British convoy of merchant ships laden with sugar, rum and coffee had been in St John's harbour, waiting to join forces with convoys from the other islands before heading back to England. They had panicked at the sight of Villeneuve's fleet sailing past the harbour. Believing he was about to land 10,000 troops, they had sailed at once, without waiting for a proper escort. The schooner *Netley* was their only protection as they put to sea, but instead of escaping Villeneuve's fleet they sailed right into it. The merchant ships scattered, but by nightfall on 7 June their heavily laden craft had all been captured. Only the *Netley* escaped.

Yet Villeneuve's triumph was short-lived. Interrogation of his prisoners revealed the unwelcome information that Nelson and the Mediterranean fleet had arrived at Barbados on 4 June. The *Netley* was on her way to him now, to give him Villeneuve's position.

Villeneuve held a hasty council of war with Admiral Gravina. Clearing the British from the islands was out of the question now. His orders were to avoid battle with Nelson, in order to preserve his fleet for the invasion of England. He was supposed to remain in the West Indies until a set date, in case Ganteaume arrived from Brest, but the climate was unhealthy and yellow fever rife. If he waited, Nelson might find him and destroy his fleet. Villeneuve was for sailing back to Europe at once.

So was Gravina. His ships were in such a mess that they should never have left Cadiz. He backed Villeneuve all the way. To the disgust of many in the fleet, the two admirals decided to return to Europe without delay. Their decision was not well received by their junior officers.

'We have been masters of the sea for three weeks,' one complained, 'with a landing force of 7,000 to 8,000 men and have not been able to attack a single island.' His disillusion was widely shared. Villeneuve was fast losing the confidence of his men. They thought he was running away from a fight.

But his men hadn't seen Villeneuve's secret orders and didn't know that the invasion of England was their ultimate goal. They saw only an admiral apparently fleeing from Nelson. They didn't see an admiral luring Nelson to the tropics before doubling back to Europe with his fleet intact, ready for the biggest fight of all.

Villeneuve himself was no coward. He came from a martial family. A Villeneuve was said to have died with Roland at Roncesvaux in 778. Another had fought alongside England's Richard I during the Crusades. A third had been a friend of Bayard, the *chevalier sans peur* from whose helmet Napoleon had distributed the Légions d'honneur at Boulogne. Villeneuve was a good sailor and a skilled tactician. Unfortunately, he was also inordinately cautious and hesitant, particularly where Lord Nelson was concerned. After his experience at the Battle of the Nile, his mind seems to have gone to pieces whenever he thought of Nelson.

But his decision to return to Europe was sensible enough – that was where the real fight lay. According to Napoleon's plan, they were to go to Ferrol first, on the north-western tip of Spain. From there they would join forces with Ganteaume's Brest fleet for the attack on England. They only needed control of the English Channel for a day or two to get the Grand Army ashore and heading for London. Strength of numbers ought to do it, if Nelson was diverted elsewhere. Villeneuve gave the necessary orders on 10 June. The combined fleet sailed at once.

Nelson wasn't far behind. After several days' fruitless search of the islands, he received a definite sighting of the French on 13 June. The schooner *Netley* had spotted the entire fleet at sea, probably heading back to Europe. Nelson guessed they were aiming for Cadiz or Toulon, but it was a long way to go and they only had three days' start. He might still catch them if he tried. Nelson set off immediately.

CHAPTER 18

PREPARATIONS CONTINUE ON THE HOME FRONT

In Boulogne, meanwhile, the Grand Army had no idea what was happening anywhere else. Nobody had told them anything at all.

The army had been in Boulogne almost two years now, training constantly for the invasion of England. The men had endured another winter of inaction, huddling together in their huts while General Bonaparte bustled off to Paris to crown himself Emperor. They had been looking forward to the spring, with its promise of invasion, but nothing had happened in the spring and now it was almost summer again. The army could have been forgiven for wondering if it was going to be stuck in Boulogne for ever.

The soldiers had been there so long they were starting to put down roots. Babies were being born to them, attachments formed. They would lose their fighting edge if they stayed much longer. It was time to move on.

There were rumblings about Napoleon as well. The army had never been happy with the idea of a general as Emperor. Its men were citizen-soldiers, not subjects. They tolerated Napoleon's imperial ambition because he was an outstanding commander, but they did not like it. They liked it even less in his family – his sisters jockeying for position, his twenty-year-old brother Jerome styling himself 'Imperial Highness' and parading around in a hussar's uniform to which he was not entitled. And now from Milan had come the news that Napoleon had just appointed his stepson viceroy of Italy, a move that had prompted Marshal Joachim Murat to break his sword across his knee in anger. There seemed no end to the Bonaparte family and their pretensions.

On the waterfront at Boulogne, an enormous obelisk had been erected to the new Emperor. It proclaimed him the liberator of the seas and declared Boulogne the place from which the avenging thunderbolts would be launched. But there was precious little sign of it so far. The invasion barges were still in harbour, packed tightly side by side. The Royal Navy still patrolled outside, oppressing everyone with its presence. The regiments of the Grand Army had been issued with their new imperial eagles, which they referred to privately as cuckoos, but they had yet to carry them into battle anywhere. There had been no sign of avenging thunderbolts heading for England. The situation could not continue much longer like that before it began to fall apart.

Across the water, preparations for receiving the Grand Army continued apace. The fortifications in Kent and Sussex were still not ready, but there were more muskets now, more uniforms, greater organisation. Every day that passed saw the defences growing stronger and the populace better prepared. The Grand Army would not have an easy time of it when it came.

At Tilbury, just downriver from London, a row of blockships had been anchored across the Thames to defend the approaches to the city. The ships were armed with twenty-four-pounders capable of raking the entire river in a single broadside. Shore batteries on either side protected the approaches by land. New roads had been built from Tilbury to the military encampments at Warley Common in Essex and Coxheath in Kent, so that troops could be moved at short notice wherever they were needed. The men were properly equipped and well experienced at speed-marching. They had been training for it for months.

In London, too, the volunteer forces were increasingly well trained, becoming more military by the day. There had been a roar of derision when Prime Minister Addington first appeared in uniform at the House of Commons in 1803, but times had changed since then. They were all in uniform now. The Duke of Bedford had long been a private in the volunteers, the Lord Chancellor a corporal. Even Charles James Fox, fattest and least martial MP in the Commons, was a private in the Chertsey Association. The lawyers of the Temple were all volunteers together, drilling regularly in the Temple garden where the sides were said to have been chosen for the Wars of the Roses. The sight of so many lawyers in uniform had so appalled King George at a review in Hyde Park that he had dubbed them the Devil's Own – retained for the defence.

The rest of the country was in uniform as well, William Wordsworth drilling at Grasmere in Westmorland, Walter Scott slashing at turnip heads stuck on poles along the Musselburgh sands. All over the country, portly little bankers in snappy outfits were marching up and down and reading Henry V's Harfleur speech or Queen Elizabeth's Tilbury oration to bemused yokels who only wanted to get at the French. Nothing excited any of them more than the prospect of getting at the French.

But it was the Channel coast where the preparations were most urgent. The area nearest the sea had become an armed camp, row upon row of tents, guns and horse lines stretching from one field to the next. In every town and village the church towers had been converted into armouries, filled with pikes and muskets for drill after the service on Sundays. Every loft in every thatched cottage contained a tankful of water to extinguish the fires that the French were sure to start (a plumbing arrangement that continues to this day). Every farm cart within twenty miles of the coast had been listed for requisition as soon as the French landed, so that women and children could be evacuated inland. Benches for them to sit on had already been stored in farm buildings near the assembly points. All livestock was to go as well, herded away from the coast so that the Grand Army would have nothing to feed on. The evacuation was to be organised by the village constables and beadles, who were to see to it that everybody reported to the assembly points and nobody was left behind. As soon as the civilian population had moved off, the local clergy were to go round every parish making sure that all property had been destroyed and nothing remained for the French to take. If it was total war the French wanted when they came to England, total war they would have. The English would never surrender their liberty without a fight.

*

At the Admiralty, a new First Lord had been appointed. His name was Sir Charles Middleton and he was seventy-eight years old. It was a good choice, despite his age. Admiral Middleton had been in the navy all his adult life. He was a kinsman of Lord Melville and had worked closely with him at the Admiralty. Melville had trusted his judgement and relied heavily on him for advice.

Yet his appointment had been bitterly opposed by other members of the government. Former Prime Minister Addington had threatened to resign his Cabinet post if one of his own men didn't get the job instead. The king too was opposed to Middleton. But William Pitt had insisted on his choice. With the navy in a state of crisis, he needed a firm hand at the top. Middleton was the right man for the task.

He was not an MP, but needed to be answerable to Parliament. Pitt therefore arranged for him to be given a peerage so that he could take questions in the House of Lords. It was as Lord Barham that Middleton moved into the Admiralty in April and took up the reins where Melville had left off. Swallowing his own disappointment at not getting the job, a rival candidate gave the new lord his grudging approval:

> I was not aware that at his advanced age his health and faculties were equal to such a post. If they are he is indisputably the fittest man that could be chosen to occupy it at the time. His abilities were always considered great, his experience is consummate, and he has few equals in application and methods of business.

Barham's abilities were tested at once. Even as he was taking office, news reached London of Villeneuve's breakout from Toulon. Lord Mark Kerr aboard the *Fisgard* had passed the word to the *Melampus* off Finisterre and had sent a message to the Admiralty via the *Greyhound*, a Guernsey lugger bound for Plymouth. But even more disturbing news was to follow. The British had a spy in Paris who went by the name L'Ami. On 29 April, L'Ami informed London of Napoleon's strategy. L'Ami didn't know the precise details, but in general terms Napoleon was planning a feint, sending Villeneuve to the West Indies to lure the Royal Navy away from his real target and then striking when the navy's back was turned.

This was disturbing news indeed. Even if L'Ami didn't know the real target, it didn't take a genius to work out what was in Napoleon's mind. With so much movement towards the Channel, an invasion was clearly in the offing.

L'Ami's report reached Downing Street on the evening of 29 April. At 2.30 the next morning, William Pitt passed it to Barham with a covering note:

> On returning from the House, I have just found these papers; they are of the most pressing importance. I will not go to bed for a few hours, but will be ready to see you as soon as you please, as I think we must not lose a moment in taking measures to set afloat every ship that by any means of extraordinary exertion we can find means to man.

Barham agreed. If the spy was right, there was no time to waste. His first priority was to reinforce the Western Squadron, where the action was likely to take place. Barham issued orders for the three-decker *Prince George* to join the squadron at once and authorised the hire of half a dozen civilian ships to act as dispatch boats. He was desperately short of larger ships, but two seventy-four-gunners were nearing completion at Chatham. Barham sent Admiral Rowley down there to hurry the builders along and get the ships launched without delay. He also issued detailed instructions to the squadrons at sea, warning them to expect an invasion at any moment. The instructions varied for each squadron, but in essence the ships were to withdraw towards the English Channel the moment the enemy appeared, concentrating there at the point of greatest danger.

Barham knew that the approaches to the English Channel were the key to any invasion. Napoleon's strategy of luring the Royal Navy away from the Channel had never had any hope of succeeding. The navy was far too astute for that. Villeneuve had trailed his coat to the West Indies, but not a single ship from the home fleet had left station to follow him, or ever would. It was Nelson's job to follow Villeneuve with the Mediterranean fleet, while the rest of the navy stayed put, guarding the home shores. Napoleon's strategy had been doomed from the start. He must either fight the battle in the English Channel or abandon his invasion attempt altogether.

*

Across the parade ground from the Admiralty, William Pitt was working long hours in Downing Street to keep abreast of the situation. His letter to Barham at 2.30 a.m. was not unusual. It was perfectly routine for him to stay up almost until dawn, working by candlelight after a strenuous day at the House of Commons. The country needed it of him and Pitt was equal to the challenge.

But the strain was beginning to tell. He was not a well man. To the normal press of government business had been added an invasion threat more serious than any since William the Conqueror. On top of that, Pitt had to deal with a fractious House of Commons that seized every opportunity to make trouble for him. The censure of Lord Melville had been only one bruising encounter among many. The threat of ministerial resignations over his successor had been another. They were saying in the clubs that Pitt was not as good a war leader as his father had been. The opposition was determined to bring him down if it could – and it sometimes seemed to Pitt as if half the government wanted to bring him down as well. He would not have been human if his health hadn't suffered as a result.

His niece Hester Stanhope was very worried about him, as she later recalled:

What a life was his! Roused from sleep (for he was a good sleeper) with a dispatch from Lord Melville; then down to Windsor; then, if he had half an hour to spare, trying to swallow something; Mr Adams with a paper, Mr Long with another; then Mr Rose: then, with a little bottle of cordial confection in his pocket, off to the House until three or four in the morning; then home to a hot supper for two or three hours more, to talk over what was to be done next day – and wine, and wine. Scarcely up next morning, when 'tat-tat-tat', twenty or thirty people one after another, and the horses walking before the door from two till sunset, waiting for him. It was enough to kill a man – it was murder.

Lady Hester was more accurate than she knew. It was not quite murder, but Pitt was certainly dying from the strain. His health was deteriorating so rapidly that he only had a few more months to live.

*

At Windsor Castle, King George III was considering the case of Nicholas Lincoln, a seaman of the Royal Navy. He had been with the *Nemesis*, but had jumped ship and deserted. His recapture had been followed by a court martial at which Lincoln had been sentenced to death. The question now was whether the sentence should be carried out, or whether the king should exercise clemency.

The minutes of the case lay in front of him. They came from the new First Lord of the Admiralty:

> Your Majesty will perceive that the man is clearly a citizen of America, was pressed into your Majesty's service, and has not received your Majesty's bounty. Lord Barham therefore takes the liberty of submitting to your Majesty, whether, under all circumstances, it may not be advisable to grant him your Majesty's pardon.

A difficult one. Desertion was a capital offence and discipline had to be maintained in the Royal Navy, particularly at a time like this. But Lincoln was an American citizen and the Americans did not take kindly to the Royal Navy pressing their seamen, let alone hanging them from the yardarm. There might be political repercussions if the execution went ahead. And there might be more desertions if it did not.

Was he really American? US Federal law demanded a residence in America of at least five years for its citizens, and many sailors could not claim that. British law did not allow citizens to shed their obligations when they changed nationality. The US consul in London was notoriously corrupt, handing out bogus American citizenship to any British sailor who slipped him half a crown. There were all sorts of considerations to be taken into account before a sailor's claim to be American could be accepted. But Lord Barham seemed to think he was, and the king usually took the advice of his ministers in cases of this sort. His pen hovered uncertainly between life or death, while far away Nicholas Lincoln waited in his cell, wondering miserably what the mad old man's verdict was going to be.

CHAPTER 19

---•◆•---

VILLENEUVE RETURNS
TO EUROPE

At sea, Villeneuve was making good progress back to Europe. His fleet had sailed northwards at first, then turned starboard towards the Azores. By the end of June they were more than halfway home, with no sign of Lord Nelson on the horizon. They had the Atlantic all to themselves.

It was a difficult time for Villeneuve. He was not supposed to be in command on this leg of the operation – the plan had been for Admiral Ganteaume to assume overall command when their fleets combined at Martinique. It was Ganteaume who was supposed to be making all the difficult decisions, not Villeneuve. But Ganteaume was nowhere to be seen, probably still bottled up in Brest, and Missiessy had long since returned to Rochefort. Villeneuve was in sole charge, with the task of carrying out orders from Napoleon that seemed to change by the day.

He had received three different sets of orders from Napoleon while in the West Indies. They were contradictory and had arrived in the wrong sequence, which only added to the confusion. Villeneuve's aim now was to head for the northern coast of Spain in the belief that that was what the Emperor would want in the changed circumstances. It was difficult to tell, with Napoleon firing off instructions in all directions and expecting everything to proceed like clockwork.

Despite his successes so far, Villeneuve was not happy with the ships under his command. Jane Kerby had watched them in Antigua trying and failing to form a line of battle. Villeneuve had watched them too, doing his best to conceal his despair. His captains were courageous enough, but lacked the skill at manoeuvring that only came from years of experience at sea. His men were sick, going down in their hundreds with scurvy and dysentery. The Spanish were so feeble they should never have left Cadiz. Villeneuve had grave doubts about leading any of them into action against the Royal Navy.

His subordinates thought him timid, haunted by the Nile and *le souvenir d'Aboukir*. In fact, Villeneuve was simply a realist who knew what he was up against. Avoiding battle with Nelson was the sensible thing to do unless he could be sure of success. It was much more important to get his ships back to Ferrol in one piece, and thence to the English Channel. They had several days' start on Nelson – enough to get to Boulogne in reasonable time and see the Grand Army across to Dover before Nelson caught up. The operation was still feasible, albeit behind schedule. With a fair wind, it could still work out as planned.

Behind them, Nelson's men scoured the horizon every day, but never saw any sign of Villeneuve. His fleet remained as elusive as ever.

They crossed his wake on 17 June and two days later met an American ship, the *Sally*, which had sighted the French to the north. Two days after that, they spotted three wooden planks in the dark that might have come from the French. By Nelson's calculation, the two fleets were now about 240 miles apart. It was a big gap, but he could still close it before the French reached Cadiz or Toulon. Nelson used every inch of canvas to try.

Unfortunately for him, the French weren't going to Cadiz or Toulon. Ferrol was in northern Spain. The two fleets were on parallel tracks, heading for different destinations. With the French going north of the Azores and the British south, there was never any chance of Nelson catching Villeneuve before he got back to Europe. Nelson had miscalculated.

But he had insured against this by sending a frigate ahead to warn the British admiral blockading Ferrol that Villeneuve might be on his way. Another British ship, the *Curieux*, had actually spotted the French on a course that seemed to indicate the Bay of Biscay as its destination. Captain

George Bettesworth had debated whether to sail back to warn Nelson, or sail forward to warn the Admiralty. He had decided on the Admiralty, if England was about to be invaded, and was heading that way at full speed. It was a race now to see who would arrive first.

In Italy, King Napoleon had been busy since his coronation, dealing with the affairs of his new domain. To the dismay of his staff, he had appointed Josephine's twenty-five-year-old son Eugene as viceroy and had spent some time instructing him in the arts of kingship by proxy. He had also donated the little principalities of Lucca and Piombino to his sisters and annexed the whole of Liguria for France.

His activities had appalled the rest of Europe and Austria in particular, which now found itself sharing a border with the French Empire. Yet Napoleon took little notice. He was enjoying his new status. His wife had tried to restrain him a while back, sitting on his knee and begging him not to make himself king of France, but Napoleon hadn't listened. And where Josephine couldn't persuade him, no one else could either.

Soon after the coronation, he embarked on a grand tour of northern Italy, taking Josephine with him. They travelled in state from Brescia and Verona to Mantua, Bologna, Parma and other places, making a ceremonial entry into each in turn. Napoleon had 60,000 troops in Italy, scattered in different locations. He managed to review most of them at one place or another, meeting the local dignitaries at the same time and acknowledging the plaudits of the crowds. As an Italian of sorts, the new king had captured the popular imagination. Not everyone approved of him, but enough did to make his progress a triumph.

At Genoa, he stayed for a week, sleeping in Charles V's bed at the Palazzo Doria. His bedroom had a magnificent view of the sea, with a flotilla of boats in the bay laden with orange and lemon blossoms in his honour. The sun was scorching hot and he needed a mosquito net at night, but Napoleon was enjoying himself. His visit was a success and he had met an Italian girl whom he intended to see more of, without Josephine's knowledge.

During their tour, however, he never lost contact with Paris. Admiral Decrès was in charge of naval operations in his absence. Napoleon wrote to him almost every day with new plans and ideas for the invasion of Britain. Everything in his correspondence hinged on which admiral was where, with how many ships, and whether they would be somewhere else on a certain date. The constant bombardment of new orders was more than Decrès could bear. He preferred to work with Napoleon face to face, so that he could talk him out of his sillier ideas. Trying to put his schemes into practice from a distance was impossible. Decrès lost patience at length and wrote to the Emperor, imploring him to come home. Napoleon replied that there were few things more likely to mislead the British as to his real intentions than his continuing presence in Italy. 'Nothing is better calculated than my journey to hide my projects and fool the enemy.' Anyway, he *would* be home soon, but without the British knowing anything about it.

Villeneuve's fleet reached the Azores on 2 July, where they were rejoined by some frigates that had been following them from the West Indies. The fleet continued on its course until 4 July, when disaster struck. The wind began to drop and a squall approached from the north-east, impeding their progress. The fleet lost momentum and for several vital days lay almost becalmed, scarcely moving at all.

This was what Napoleon had never understood. Comfortably ensconced on land, playing chess games across a map of the Atlantic, he had never fully grasped that ships lay at the mercy of the weather, unable to move across the board as easily as infantry or cavalry. Villeneuve was powerless in the face of the elements. He knew full well that time was precious and every minute counted, but there was nothing he could do about it except pace the deck and pray for wind.

Nelson was in the same predicament to the south. He too lay becalmed for several days, fretting that Villeneuve was getting all the wind while he was not. He too realised that every minute was vital. Nelson put a brave face on it in public, but in the privacy of his cabin he was acutely concerned that the French were slipping away from him.

North of Villeneuve's fleet, it was a different story. The *Curieux*, heading for England under Captain Bettesworth, had a fair wind all the way, sailing into Plymouth on the afternoon of 7 July. Bettesworth leapt ashore at once and travelled through the night to warn the Admiralty in London that Villeneuve's twenty warships were almost certainly bound for the Bay of Biscay.

After thirty hours without a break, Bettesworth reached the Admiralty late the following evening. Lord Barham had already gone to bed. His officials stubbornly refused to wake him, despite Bettesworth's pleading. Invasion fleet or not, it would all just have to wait until tomorrow when Barham was up again.

The First Lord was furious when he found out. Still in his nightshirt next morning, he gave his officials a stiff reprimand for not waking him at once. Then he hurried to his desk to scribble some instructions for the British squadrons that lay in Villeneuve's path.

If the French were heading for the Bay of Biscay, the place to stop them was off Cape Finisterre. Vice-Admiral Sir Robert Calder's squadron was blockading Ferrol nearby. A few strokes of Barham's pen sent Calder racing westwards, with reinforcements from other squadrons, to patrol the area out to sea and await the enemy's arrival. At the same time, the Channel fleet under Admiral Sir William Cornwallis was ordered to cover the area between Finisterre and Ushant, at the approaches to the English Channel. Thanks to Captain Bettesworth's good sense, any chance of the invasion taking the British by surprise had been lost for ever.

CHAPTER 20

CALDER'S ACTION

As Barham sat in his nightshirt, Napoleon was stealing back to France. He left Turin secretly on 8 July, driving so fast that water had to be thrown onto the wheels at every relay stop to cool them down. Napoleon urged his postilions on, yelling at them not to waste time. He was determined to be back in Paris before anyone knew he had left Italy.

He travelled incognito, without his usual entourage. It was the 'Minister of the Interior' who passed through the Alps at Mont Cenis and took the road for Paris. The journey lasted four days without a break, covering almost ninety miles a day. Napoleon reached Fontainebleau late on the evening of 11 July and went exhausted to bed. He was up again after a few hours, letting his staff know he was back. A mountain of correspondence was waiting for him, including a report from Villeneuve. It detailed his progress in the West Indies, but gave no clue as to his present whereabouts. Villeneuve certainly wasn't at Boulogne, where he ought to be. Neither was anyone else.

Napoleon was livid. What was wrong with his admirals? Did they need a fire lit under them? Over the next few days, he dashed off letters to all and sundry, demanding to know what was happening. Minister of Marine Decrès bore the brunt of it, but Villeneuve was in the firing line as well, as were Ganteaume at Brest and Captain Zacharie Allemand at Rochefort, who had replaced Missiessy. All Napoleon wanted from any of them was control of the Channel for a few hours, enough for him to get his army across to the other side. He had set everything in motion, but nothing was happening as it was supposed to. What on earth was the point of hurrying back from Italy in great secrecy if the admirals had sat on their rear ends and done nothing in his absence?

His mood lightened a few days later when word reached him from Ganteaume that the British squadron blockading Brest appeared to be relaxing its grip. Napoleon clutched at this straw. If the British were withdrawing from Brest, it must surely mean that Villeneuve was in the vicinity. Napoleon replied to Ganteaume at once:

> When you receive this letter, I shall be already at Boulogne in person. All troops will be embarked, and the invasion fleet will be drawn up outside the anchorage. Thus, given control of the sea for three days, and with reasonable weather, I have no doubt whatever of our success. If the enemy has left his position in front of you, it means he thinks our offensive will come from Villeneuve. Confound his calculations by seizing the initiative yourself!

But the Royal Navy had already reappeared at Brest and Villeneuve himself was nowhere near the port. After two weeks of contrary weather, he was still out in the Atlantic. The Royal Navy squadrons from Ferrol and Rochefort had found him there and were about to bring him to battle.

The British were commanded by Sir Robert Calder. His squadron blockading Ferrol had been joined by Admiral Stirling's from Rochefort and further reinforcements from England. Their total force numbered fifteen ships of the line, against Villeneuve's twenty. Following Lord Barham's orders, they had sailed west of Finisterre, patrolling a wide area in search of Villeneuve. They found him shortly before noon on 22 July. A heavy sea mist lifted suddenly to reveal the French and Spanish coming towards them in three closely packed columns. As well as sail of the line, the French had seven frigates, two brigs and a captured galleon. All were rapidly bearing down on the British when the mist descended again, making it difficult for ships to signal each other or see what was happening.

These were not ideal conditions for a battle, but Calder did not flinch. He knew what was coming towards him – the invasion fleet his country had been expecting for so long. This was his moment and his duty was clear. Even though he was outnumbered, he had to stop the French and Spanish right there and prevent any further advance towards England.

Calder hoisted the signal for action at midday. An hour later, he ordered line of battle and signalled close order. The British were almost abeam of the enemy by then, about seven miles apart, but the two sides could barely see each other through the haze. Conditions were so bad that Calder had to rely on a frigate to keep him informed.

He aimed his fleet straight for the centre of the French, but passed them in the mist and found himself opposite the rearguard instead. Villeneuve's ships were already turning about to avoid being surrounded. Calder did the same, warily circling the French through visibility so poor that Villeneuve could not even tell if the British were to port or starboard.

About the middle of the afternoon, the two fleets came within range at last and began to fire sporadically at each other whenever a target presented itself. By 6 p.m., most of the Royal Navy ships had found something to shoot at, adding clouds of smoke to the all-pervading mist. Damage was done on both sides. Two dismasted Spanish ships were captured, but Calder's fleet took casualties as well. With night drawing on, and the fighting inconclusive, he was forced to give the signal to disengage at 8.25 p.m. Several ships failed to see it in the confusion and continued firing for some time. It wasn't until next morning that they were able to take stock of the situation and find out exactly what was happening.

The two fleets were seventeen miles apart by then, floating listlessly on a hazy sea with very little wind. The British had lost 198 men killed or wounded, the enemy 647 (the vast majority of them Spanish). Villeneuve had been unaware of the two Spanish ships captured by the British, but he saw them now, being towed away by their captors. With a Royal Navy ship dismasted as well, Calder was repositioning his fleet to protect the crippled vessels from the French.

Villeneuve misinterpreted this as a British withdrawal and decided to give chase. It took him the whole morning to form his fleet into a line of battle. He ordered his ships forward at 1.30 p.m. and by 3 p.m. the French and Spanish were advancing to the attack. Fifteen minutes later, the wind dropped once more and the attack petered out before it had even begun.

Without a breeze, there was no hope of engaging Calder before nightfall.

Next day, the wind shifted in favour of the British. Abandoning any further plans for attack, Villeneuve decided to break off the action and resume course for Ferrol. Calder considered pursuing him, but judged that he had already done enough. The French were in retreat, heading south, away from England and the Channel. Their attack had been blunted. Calder had done what he had been ordered to do. He turned away instead, heading back towards the Bay of Biscay with his prizes.

That evening, the weather turned nasty again. One of Villeneuve's Spanish ships lost its tiller, while others had their sails carried away. Worried that more ships would be dismasted, Villeneuve debated what to do. He was only a few hours from Ferrol, but the port lay the other side of Cape Finisterre and he doubted that his fleet could get round the headland in the weather. He decided to aim for Vigo instead.

Next day, he changed his mind again and altered course for Cadiz. He had hardly done so when the fleet ran into a storm. Villeneuve's own ship was struck by lightning and badly damaged. Others suffered damage as well. The wind had turned against them with a vengeance, making Cadiz an impossibility. Villeneuve was forced to change course several more times before turning eventually towards Vigo again. His fleet limped into the bay and dropped anchor on the evening of 27 July, fifty-two days after leaving the West Indies.

None of this was known to Nelson. He had reached Gibraltar on 19 July and set foot on land next morning for the first time in almost two years. He immediately began reprovisioning his ships and preparing them for sea again, ready for a quick turnaround when he got news of Villeneuve.

But no word came. Nelson waited three days without hearing anything. Villeneuve clearly wasn't returning to the Mediterranean, because he would have passed Gibraltar by now. Perhaps he was going to Cadiz instead?

By 22 July, Nelson could bear it no longer. Weighing anchor, he returned to sea and set course for Cadiz, scouring the horizon for any sign of Villeneuve's fleet. He soon got word that the French had been sighted far to the north, probably with the Channel as their ultimate destination. Nelson promptly followed, praying to God he would not arrive too late.

CHAPTER 21

---◆---

NAPOLEON RETURNS TO BOULOGNE

Unaware of what was happening at sea, yet certain everything was moving in the right direction, Napoleon went to Boulogne on 3 August to take command of the Grand Army for the invasion. Apart from a brief trip the previous November, he hadn't spent any time with his army since distributing the Légions d'honneur a year earlier.

He inspected his troops on 4 August. The line of men was nine miles long, presenting arms and cheering for the Emperor from Cape Gris-Nez all the way to Alprech Point. They carried knapsacks, tools, camping equipment and everything else they needed for a landing in England. Some were already living on board ship, ready for the crossing. They were in fine fettle, certain the invasion couldn't be more than a few days away now. Why else would Napoleon suddenly reappear among them, after such a long absence?

The army's numbers had changed since a year ago. There were now about 93,000 soldiers on the Channel coast, with the rest stationed inland – perhaps 167,000 in all. But the men who presented arms and looked Napoleon in the eye were still the finest army in Europe. A few hours' command of the Channel and they would be on their way to London, presenting the Emperor with the keys to the city as his Mamelukes trotted victoriously up the Mall.

Napoleon tested their skills soon after he arrived. He ordered a mass embarkation of troops aboard the invasion barges, to see how quickly they could put to sea. The men would have to be fast when it came to the real thing because the tide wouldn't wait and neither would the Royal Navy. Napoleon wanted to know how fast.

The embarkation had been rehearsed down to the last detail. Every soldier in every regiment knew exactly which barge was his, right down to the individual seat allocation. In traditional military fashion, it was all done by numbers. The first shot from the signal gun was for the men to fall in, the second for the staff officers to take their posts. The third gave the signal 'Prepare to embark' and the fourth 'Embark'. According to Marshal Ney, a force of 25,000 trained men could embark from the dockside in just over ten minutes flat. As for disembarking, the troops had practised invasion landings on nearby beaches and could be ashore, fully formed up for action, in just under thirteen minutes.

That was from the dockside. It took longer to get a whole corps afloat from the barrack huts strung out along the cliff tops. Napoleon had his staff time the operation, from the drummer boys beating the *Generale* in camp to the last man and horse safely aboard the barges two miles away. It took them just over an hour and a half, a creditable performance by any standard. Napoleon was impressed, but ordered the whole exercise to be repeated another day, just to make sure.

To save time, the men's rations for the voyage had already been stored aboard the flotilla, along with oats and hay for the horses. Fourteen million cartridges had been stored as well, along with 1,300,000 musket flints, 90,000 artillery rounds, 32,000 reserve muskets, 30,000 separate items of engineering equipment and 11,000 spare saddles and harnesses. It was a mammoth undertaking, the greatest amphibious operation ever contemplated. Napoleon's staff had been working for over two years to make sure everything proceeded with machinelike precision when the invasion finally went ahead.

While they waited for the moment to arrive, Napoleon summoned the Vaudeville Theatre to Boulogne to entertain the troops. The theatre put on a good show, packing them in nightly with rude sketches about William Pitt and the Royal Navy. The audience booed and hissed at every mention of Lord Nelson. The theatre company would be following them to London as soon as the English had surrendered.

Napoleon himself had little time for such frivolity. After reviewing his troops en masse, he also reviewed them in smaller formations, division by division, visiting different regiments every day and talking to them about the fighting that lay ahead. He inspected the flotilla crews as well, and spent long hours closeted with his staff, working on the final preparations for the invasion. His only relaxation was the Italian girl his brother-in-law had recommended in Genoa. Summoned to Boulogne, she duly presented herself at Napoleon's Pont-de-Briques headquarters. Like all such visitors, she was shown up to his bedroom with instructions to strip naked and wait for the Emperor. The Italian girl came to see him four or five times in his panelled room on the first floor of the chateau.

At one point, there had even been an Englishwoman who came to see Napoleon at Pont-de-Briques. She was very beautiful, a blue-eyed blonde of about twenty-five. She had no introduction but claimed to have a special message for the Emperor that she couldn't give to anyone else. Intrigued, Napoleon sent word for her to visit him next day at his other base, the wooden pavilion near the Tour d'Ordre. Meanwhile he had her investigated, sending people to make inquiries and examine her lodgings in Boulogne.

They reported that although the woman looked like a princess and claimed to be related to an ambassador, she was probably a British spy. They advised Napoleon against seeing her. But Napoleon overruled them, arguing that the British would laugh at him if they thought he was afraid of a woman. 'My head is to be taken from the Tour d'Ordre to the Tower of London and exhibited in a glass case,' he told them. He looked forward to the encounter with interest.

But it wasn't his head the woman was after when she advanced on him next day. Napoleon had positioned himself at his desk in the pavilion, with the door open so that his staff in the next room could hear everything. He defended himself with a map as the woman did her utmost to excite his interest. He was determined not to give in. Lesser men might succumb, but not Napoleon. He was a man of iron. If the English thought they could send a *coquette* to seduce him, they would have to think again. He would show *les rosbifs* what he was made of. There was triumph in Napoleon's voice as the woman abandoned the attempt at length and he called for an aide to show her out.

Yet women were a mere distraction for him at Boulogne. Most of his time was spent waiting for Villeneuve. Everything depended on Villeneuve. Napoleon had left orders for the errant admiral at various ports, instructing him to proceed to Boulogne immediately with all the ships he could muster. Villeneuve must have received the orders by now. He would surely appear at any moment, bringing a large armada with him. When he did, the Royal Navy would be forced to retreat and the way to England would be open at last.

Villeneuve was in Ferrol, nowhere near Boulogne. He had arrived there from Vigo on 31 July. His ships had already been dropping anchor when a rowing boat came alongside with Napoleon's orders. On no account was any ship to drop anchor. Instead, Villeneuve was to sail straight on to join forces with the Brest and Rochefort squadrons before proceeding up the Channel to 'make himself master of the Strait of Dover, if only for four or five days'.

Oh dear. The orders had been written before Villeneuve's brush with Calder. The situation was radically different now. The British knew the French were back from the West Indies. It would be madness to obey Napoleon's orders with the Royal Navy aware of their return and gunning for them on the open sea.

If only Villeneuve had managed to defeat Calder in the mist. If he had done that, he could have sailed on to liberate Admiral Ganteaume from Brest and then continued straight up the Channel without stopping for anything. It would all have been very different if only he had been able to beat Calder. Villeneuve said as much in a letter to Admiral Decrès:

All this should have happened – I do not say with a squadron of fine sailors – but even with very average vessels . . . We have bad sails, bad rigging, bad officers and bad seamen. The enemy have been warned, they have been reinforced, they have dared to attack us with numerically inferior forces, the weather favoured them. With little experience of fighting and battle tactics, each of our captains carried out one rule only in the fog, that of following the next ship ahead; and now we're the laughing stock of Europe.

Villeneuve's account was deliberately pessimistic, designed to help Decrès dissuade Napoleon from pressing ahead with his invasion plan. Both admirals considered it very ill-advised. Their view was shared by the Spanish government, which had secretly ordered Gravina to have nothing to do with any assault on England. He was to play along with the French as far as possible, but if push came to shove he was to refuse to take his ships even as far as Brest. Gravina was sitting on this information, hoping Villeneuve would decide for himself against Brest without forcing Gravina to reveal his hand.

To add to Villeneuve's troubles, scurvy and dysentery had left his crews desperately short-handed. Every ship in the Franco-Spanish fleet had at least sixty men sick after the Atlantic crossing, and some many more. The *Argonaute* had 150 men out of action, the *Achille* 200. Some of the ships were barely capable of putting to sea.

Nevertheless, Villeneuve knew his duty. His orders were put to sea, so to sea he would go. He wrote again to Decrès on 11 August:

I am about to set out, but I don't know what I shall do. Eight vessels are in view on the coast, a few leagues away. They will follow us, but I shan't be able to avoid them. Then they will go and join the other squadrons before Brest or Cadiz, according to which port I make for. I deeply regret to say that I am far from being in a position, on leaving this place with twenty-nine ships, to engage a similar number of the enemy. I'm not afraid to tell you, indeed, that I should be hard pressed to engage twenty.

The fleet sailed later that day, many of the ships bumping into each other as they struggled out of harbour. By 13 August, all twenty-nine had made it out to sea and were heading west past Corunna towards the Atlantic. That evening, they spotted some warlike sails on the horizon and shied away to avoid a fight. They saw more sails next day, one group of eight warships, another of fourteen. The ships flew no flags, so it was impossible to identify them as friend or foe.

This was a dilemma for Villeneuve. He had sent a frigate ahead to contact Captain Allemand's squadron, which had broken out of Rochefort, to arrange a rendezvous off Brest. It would complicate matters if he got into a fight along the way. He needed to arrive with his fleet intact, ready for the assault on England.

In fact, his frigate had been intercepted by the British and the message about a rendezvous had never reached Allemand. The sails spotted by Villeneuve almost certainly belonged to Allemand's squadron. Had they only known it, the nearest Royal Navy force of any strength lay 380 miles to the north. Villeneuve would have had command of the seas if either he or Allemand had been brave enough to hoist their colours and identify themselves to each other. As it was, neither did, and Villeneuve thought he had had a lucky escape from a hostile British fleet.

His view was confirmed on 15 August when he stopped a neutral Danish ship and was told that twenty-five British warships were in the vicinity, looking for him. Without a doubt, those must have been the sails he had seen on the horizon.

What Villeneuve didn't know, or the Dane either, was that the twenty-five warships were pure invention. Captain Edward Griffith of HMS *Dragon* had boarded the Danish ship a few hours earlier to interrogate the captain. Knowing how few navy ships were really in the area, he had casually let it slip that the *Dragon* was part of a fleet of twenty-five men-of-war, a piece of disinformation that was bound to disconcert the French if it came to their ears. Sure enough, Griffith later watched from a distance as one of Villeneuve's frigates stopped the Dane in turn and questioned the captain. The French had been sold a pup.

It had the desired effect on Villeneuve. He was badly shaken by the news. With twenty-five British warships lying in wait for him, it would be folly to sail north. His fleet would never make it to Brest, let alone the Channel. They would be heading for certain disaster.

Where should they go instead? Villeneuve's orders allowed for Cadiz in extremis. As it happened, the wind was blowing that way as well. He took it as an omen. On the evening of 15 August, he suddenly gave the order for his fleet to turn about. While the Grand Army waited impatiently for them at Boulogne, Villeneuve's dumbfounded crews hauled their ships around and reversed course, proceeding in precisely the opposite direction. By dawn next morning, they were all heading away from Boulogne as fast as their sails would carry them, aiming for Cadiz instead.

CHAPTER 22

LORD NELSON GOES HOME

As Villeneuve turned about, Lord Nelson's ships were making contact with the Royal Navy's Channel fleet at Brest. Twenty-seven miles off the isle of Ushant, the *Victory* hove to at 6 p.m. and fired a gun salute. Two hours later, after taking delivery of newspapers detailing Calder's action against Villeneuve, Nelson left his force with Admiral Cornwallis and sailed for England aboard the *Victory*.

He was due for sick leave at home. Long overdue, in fact, because his health had been deteriorating for months. 'The mind and body both wear out,' he had complained to his brother William. Nelson badly needed time ashore to rest from the strain and recover his strength for the coming fight.

Even so, he went reluctantly, nervous about what would happen in his absence. There was no immediate danger from the French, with Cornwallis's fleet now heavily reinforced and Villeneuve seen off by Calder, but Nelson hated the thought of missing any action. 'I would die ten thousand deaths rather than give up my command when the Enemy is expected every day.' Nelson was so exhausted that he feared the Admiralty would replace him while he was on leave. He was also worried about the reception he would receive in England. He was supposed to have blockaded Villeneuve in Toulon, but had ended up chasing him to the West Indies and back without ever catching him. It had not been a distinguished performance, with Villeneuve still at large somewhere, threatening the safety of the nation. Nelson was terrified the First Lord would sack him and give his command to someone else.

The *Victory* sighted Weymouth on 17 August and sailed on towards Portsmouth, anchoring at Spithead next day. Nelson was not allowed ashore at once because there was an outbreak of yellow fever in Spain and he had recently been in Gibraltar. It wasn't until the evening of 19 August that he persuaded the officials that no one aboard the *Victory* or the accompanying *Superb* was sick. Nelson went ashore immediately, longing to get home to his mistress and daughter at their farmhouse near London.

He found an enthusiastic crowd waiting for him at the dockside. For better or worse, Nelson was the most famous man in England, far more popular than the king or William Pitt. His face was familiar to the public from countless prints and plaster busts. They came to stare and stayed to cheer, applauding vigorously as the one-armed legend stepped ashore and made his way to the Commander-in-Chief Portsmouth for a brief courtesy call before taking a post chaise to London.

The post chaise left from the George, in the High Street. It was raining as they set out. The countryside beyond Portsmouth was full of tents and men in military uniform, volunteers and yeomanry preparing for the invasion. The whole country had rallied to the colours at the sighting of Villeneuve's fleet. With mass troop movements along the Boulogne coast, they knew it could mean only one thing: the French were coming at last. The British were going to stop them or die in the attempt.

Nelson travelled through the night and reached home at 6 a.m. next day. Merton lay in fifty-two acres on the London–Portsmouth road, an hour's drive from the Admiralty. It was a modest house by aristocratic standards, but it was where his heart lay, the place he always longed to be when not at sea.

He had sent word ahead that he was coming, but nobody was up when he arrived. Lady Hamilton soon surfaced, however, and flung herself into his arms. A blacksmith's daughter, stunningly beautiful in her youth, Emma Hamilton was in her forties now and putting on more weight than was prudent. But she adored Nelson and the slightly built admiral adored her in return. It was one of history's more bizarre love matches.

They hadn't seen each other for well over two years. 'What a day of rejoicing!' declared Emma. 'How happy he is to see us all.' She immediately sent invitations to his family to come and stay, inviting everyone except Nelson's wife.

For the rest of the day, Nelson did nothing except relax in his own home and reacquaint himself with his four-year-old daughter Horatia. Tomorrow he would go to London to report to the Admiralty and see the Prime Minister. But today belonged to his family. While he was away, Lady Hamilton had installed 'a large feather bed & bolsters fill'd with best goose feathers'. The passion they had for each other was 'as hot as ever', according to a family friend. Two years was a long time for a lover to be away at sea.

That same evening, at Montreuil near Étaples, Marshal Ney and his wife were giving a ball. The guest of honour was Napoleon's twenty-two-year-old stepdaughter Hortense. A military band was playing while the ladies and gentlemen danced the quadrille. Good-natured and popular, Hortense was enjoying the fun, dancing with a succession of young officers while the music continued late into the night.

The party went on almost until dawn, when it was suddenly interrupted by the appearance of a messenger from the Emperor. He brought astonishing news: the invasion was starting. Napoleon was embarking the troops at Boulogne. Everyone was to return to their unit at once.

They needed no urging. Hurriedly abandoning their partners, the officers called for their horses and headed at once for Boulogne, galloping through the darkness to rejoin their men. They couldn't believe this was happening. They were terrified they would arrive too late, to find everyone had gone without them.

Hortense followed, accompanied by an equerry. She was overcome with emotion at the momentousness of the event. 'I already imagined that, as I stood at the Tour d'Ordre, I was witnessing the naval battle and seeing our vessels plunge into the watery deep. I trembled at the thought.'

In the camps along the cliff tops, the troops had been roused in the middle of the night and ordered to parade outside with all their kit. Stumbling in the gloom, they assembled rapidly along the roads outside their huts, forming up in ranks for the march down to the port. By 5 a.m. on 21 August, tens of thousands of them had already moved off, heading in disciplined columns for the barges waiting to ferry them across the Channel. They were still half-asleep, but they sang as they marched, their hearts full of excitement. This was it, at last. They were on their way to England. The day had finally arrived.

As they reached the town, the people of Boulogne got up to see them off. Roused by the commotion, they came to their windows first, then to their doors to see what was happening. Some were fully dressed, others still in their nightclothes. All of them stood and watched as an endless procession of troops poured along the cobbled streets and made their way down to the port, halting there and numbering off in front of each barge, as they had practised so often before.

The port was frantically busy in the darkness. Artillery pieces were being loaded aboard the flotilla and supplies of gunpowder were being distributed from the powder ships anchored for safety in the middle of the river beyond the basin. Horses were whinnying as they were led down the gangplanks. Everywhere there was action and movement, flurries of men working flat out to get the army on to the barges and out on to the open sea. It was an operation they had rehearsed many times before. This time, though, it was for real.

As they waited to embark, many of the soldiers sold their watches on the quayside, trading their valuables for ready cash to spend in London. Some crossed themselves and a few prayed. Most just stood and cursed at the delay, longing to get on with it now that it was actually happening at last.

The operation was completed by 8 a.m. The men and horses were all aboard and the flotilla was ready for sea. The whole town came to see them off, thousands of spectators crowding the quays and cliff tops to watch the army go. The atmosphere was electric as Napoleon himself appeared. The men watched expectantly as the Emperor reviewed the flotilla and conferred with his staff officers. Not much longer now. A few more minutes and they would all be on their way to England.

But then Napoleon disappeared, heading back to Pont-de-Briques. A little later, a message arrived for the waiting troops. It was all off! No invasion today. No attack on England. The men were to disembark instead and return to camp at once.

It was an astonishing volte-face. The troops were visibly shaken as they did what they were told. Forming up again on the dockside, they shouldered their knapsacks unhappily for the march back to camp. Nobody sang as they went. They did not feel like singing any more. They simply shook their heads in disbelief.

They were told later it had all just been an exercise. In fact, though, the weather was right for a crossing and the invasion would almost certainly have been launched if Villeneuve's fleet had appeared with the daylight, as Napoleon had confidently expected it would. He had been waiting for the telegraph station to signal the fleet's arrival. But no signal had come, so he had abandoned the invasion for that day and returned his men to barracks instead.

It was the right decision, from a military point of view. For the ordinary soldiers, however, trudging angrily back to barracks without their watches, it simply confirmed what ordinary soldiers in every army know – that whoever is in charge doesn't have a clue what he is doing.

In Austria, meanwhile, the population was reluctantly preparing for war. It was inevitable now. Nobody wanted war, but the Austrians had little choice with Napoleon menacing them along their Italian border and across the waters of the Rhine. War was bound to come, sooner or later.

The previous November, the Austrian Emperor Francis II had signed a preliminary agreement with the Czar of Russia, pledging Austrian help if Napoleon displayed any further aggression towards Turkey, Naples or the states of north Germany. Now, on 9 August 1805, he followed this up by entering into a formal coalition with Russia and Great Britain, promising hundreds of thousands of troops for the war so long as the British could pay for them. The coalition was to remain secret for the time being, but its purpose was clear: Napoleon had to be stopped before he turned the whole of Europe upside down. The safety of everyone depended on it.

The Austrians had been quietly mobilising for some time, strengthening their southern borders with Italy and reinforcing their garrisons in the Tyrol. They assured Napoleon that they did not intend to fight and were only interested in defence, but he declined to believe them. On 12 August, he issued an ultimatum demanding withdrawal of Austrian troops from the Tyrol, a reduction of the Adriatic garrisons and a declaration to England of Austrian neutrality. Otherwise the French would have to take action. 'My heart bleeds at the thought of the evils that must follow,' he announced on 25 August. 'God knows, I am not to blame. But Austria is asking for war. She will get it sooner than she bargains for.' Napoleon meant what he said.

CHAPTER 23

VILLENEUVE RETREATS TO CADIZ

Villeneuve reached Cadiz on 22 August. All the way down the Iberian coast, his men muttered sullenly, outraged at what was happening. Those who hadn't already done so were fast losing confidence in their commanding officer.

The situation worsened when they arrived at Cadiz, because there was nothing for them there. With yellow fever still not eradicated, the port was in no state to accommodate the unexpected arrival of a large fleet. There were few naval stores and even less food. What did exist could not be released to the French without orders from Madrid. The Spanish were furious with the French. The two Spanish ships captured by Admiral Calder with great loss of life had come from Cadiz. It was widely believed that they had been abandoned by the French, who had sacrificed them in action to save their own skins. The Spanish authorities made their feelings plain by refusing to cooperate with Villeneuve in any way at all. They did their best to thwart him at every opportunity.

Villeneuve complained to the French ambassador in Madrid, but the Cadiz authorities still refused to help. They insisted on cash in advance for all transactions, rather than paper credit. Admiral Gravina travelled to Madrid and begged to resign his command, arguing that the loss of the two Spanish ships had compromised his honour. He was persuaded to stay, but advised to let the French bear the brunt of the fighting next time round. The Spanish were politically bound to France. They had to cooperate with Napoleon and his navy, whether they liked it or not.

But the Cadiz authorities were still difficult. The French were hated in the port. Eyewitness accounts of their cowardice in allowing the two Spanish ships to be captured were read out indignantly in tavernas and other public places. The French retorted that the Spanish only had themselves to blame for their own incompetence. Ordinary Cadiz citizens spat at French officers in the street. Relations had almost reached breaking point, as an Englishman in Cadiz reported to London:

> Our Admiral Gravina loudly accuses Villeneuve of treachery in the late action, and has solicited leave to resign. Between the sailors animosities have arisen to the highest pitch, and scarce a night passes but the dead bodies of assassinated Frenchmen are found in our streets.

So many were murdered that leave was cancelled and Frenchmen from the fleet were no longer allowed on shore.

Yet French officers too were critical of Villeneuve. They thought him pusillanimous, forgetting that his lack of confidence was based in part on their own shortcomings. He would have been much more adventurous if they had been capable of sailing their ships without bumping into each other. Villeneuve did not personally get on with Rear-Admirals de Magon and Pierre Dumanoir. He was a lonely man with no one to turn to, doing his best to carry out a plan of Napoleon's that had been fatally flawed from the outset.

Villeneuve was very worried about Napoleon. He feared the Emperor's wrath. What would Napoleon say when he learned that the French fleet was in Cadiz instead of bounding up the Channel towards Boulogne? He would undoubtedly be furious. Villeneuve was acutely aware that the whole invasion plan depended on him, that he had let everyone down. He waited miserably for a dispatch from France, wondering what Napoleon's reaction would be. But day after day no dispatches arrived. Villeneuve was left with nothing to do except busy himself with the fleet, repairing the damage and getting his ships ready for sea again.

It was no easy task. The ships were in a sorry state. Two were leaking badly, several had been damaged in collisions and many needed repairs of one kind or another. All the frigates were short of sails, and there was an acute shortage of manpower as well. Villeneuve had lost 311 men from desertion since leaving Toulon. The Spanish, with far fewer ships, had lost even more. A further 1,731 men lay sick in hospital, a substantial proportion of the total. The deficit was impossible to make up. Spanish press gangs regularly trawled the streets of Cadiz, but most trained seamen had either been pressed already or were dead of yellow fever. All that remained were beggars and herdsmen too slow or half-witted to escape when they saw the press gang coming. And for the French, prohibited by law from recruiting foreigners, it was a sign of their desperation that some crews had to be augmented with British sailors, Royal Navy deserters from Gibraltar.

Villeneuve did what he could, however. The ships must be repaired, the crews cobbled together somehow. The primary aim now was to be ready for sea again as soon as he heard from Napoleon. It was a long way from Cadiz to Boulogne and back by courier. Villeneuve set to work to regroup his fleet and have it ready for action the moment word came from the Emperor.

At Merton, Lord Nelson rose early on his first day at home and was on the road for London by 8.30 a.m. Emma Hamilton went with him, reluctant to let him out of her sight for a moment. They reached the Admiralty at 9.30. Emma left him there for his interview with the First Lord and went on in the carriage to her house in Clarges Street.

Nelson was not looking forward to his meeting with Lord Barham. They did not know each other and were men of different temperaments. Nelson was a vain attention-seeker, Barham irascible but shrewd. As soon as Nelson had landed in England, Barham had asked for his sea journals to be forwarded to the Admiralty so that he could look through them. It was an unusual request and Nelson had taken it personally. He suspected Barham was seeking an excuse to sack him.

In fact, Barham was deeply impressed by what he read. Whatever his opinion of Nelson's vanity, the man was a consummate sailor. His pursuit of the enemy had been everything it should have been. Barham decided that Nelson was an even better admiral than he had been led to believe. He duly informed the Cabinet that he had every confidence in Nelson to continue his operations against the French. Nelson's command was safe for the duration of the crisis. Indeed, Barham later recommended that it should be extended to include the blockade of Cadiz, not hitherto part of his brief.

Feeling considerably relieved, Nelson continued on his way. He had much to do in the next few days – people to see, business to conduct. One of his first calls was on the Prime Minister, who discussed the war with him and brought him up to date on the alliance with Russia and Austria. Two days later, he saw Lord Castlereagh, the Minister for War, and was equally well received. Far from being disappointed at his failure to catch Villeneuve, the politicians were full of praise for Nelson, convinced he was the man to beat the French. They seemed to think he could do no wrong, an attitude Nelson found distinctly unnerving. He said as much to a friend:

> I am now set up for a Conjuror. God knows they will very soon find out that I am far from being one. I was asked my opinion, against my inclination, for if I make one wrong guess the charm will be broken.

It wasn't only politicians who were impressed. Nelson was recognised at once in the street and mobbed wherever he went – hardly surprising, when every print shop in London carried pictures of him in the window. Ordinary people were thrilled to see him:

> When he enters a shop the door is thronged, till he comes out, when the air rings with huzzaz and the dark cloud of the populace again moves on and hangs upon his skirts. He is a great favourite with all descriptions of people.

Lady Elizabeth Foster agreed:

> Wherever he appears, he electrifies the cold English character. Rapture and applause follow all his steps. Sometimes a poor woman asks to touch his coat. The very children learn to bless him as he passes, and doors and windows are crowded.

Along the Strand, Nelson could hardly move for the crowd giving him repeated cheers. In Piccadilly, his friend Lord Minto observed, 'It is really quite affecting to see the wonder and admiration and love and respect of the whole world . . . the moment he is seen.'

Nelson enjoyed all the attention, but Merton was where he really wanted to be. He spent most of his leave there, relaxing among family and friends. One of the many who came to stay was his clergyman brother William, the heir to his title. Dull and untalented, William would have been a simple country parson if it wasn't for his brother's success. Instead, he had shamelessly used the Nelson name to become a prebendary at Canterbury Cathedral, with all the accompanying income. He was angling now to become dean.

Nelson was visited also by Captain Richard Keats, who had sailed home with him aboard the *Superb*. Walking in the grounds one day, the two men discussed the need to revise tactics for the inevitable battle with the French. Traditionally, opposing fleets were supposed to form line ahead and then lay alongside each other, a process that could take all day, as it had during Calder's action. But Nelson's new idea was to form his fleet into two or three lines instead, enabling his ships to reach the enemy much faster and attack in several different places at once. It was a thoroughly unorthodox notion for the time, but Nelson had every confidence that it would work. 'I think it will confound and surprise the enemy. They won't know what I am about. It will bring forward a pell-mell battle, and that is what I want.' Total annihilation of the French was Nelson's aim, rather than an indecisive action of the kind Calder and Villeneuve had fought off Finisterre.

But where *was* Villeneuve? To Napoleon, scanning the horizon with increasing irritation, it seemed as if the wretched man was never going to arrive. Day after day, the view to the south of Boulogne was distressingly free of French sails. Villeneuve had his orders and knew exactly what to do. Napoleon couldn't understand why he wasn't doing it.

The frustration was driving the Emperor mad. He had his army in front of him. He had England in the distance. All he needed was Villeneuve's fleet to clear the way, and everything would fall into place. It wasn't much to ask of an admiral with twenty-nine warships under his command.

Napoleon knew all about the business with Calder. As well as his own sources, he had read the English newspapers, which were full of it. The English had been highly critical of Calder for breaking off the action instead of seeing it through to the end. Some had even accused him of running away. That was music to Napoleon's ears – although of course he would never allow English newspapers to be so forthright once he had control of them. As in France, they would only print what Napoleon permitted them to print.

But if Calder had run away, why wasn't Villeneuve in Boulogne? What had happened to the man – and Ganteaume, and Allemand, for that matter? Why weren't any of them there, where they were supposed to be?

Napoleon had other worries as well. The news from Austria was not good: the Austrians were definitely mobilising. They clearly had no intention of complying with Napoleon's ultimatum. They were massing forces along their borders, pointing towards France. What if they attacked while Napoleon was in England? He would have to fight on two fronts at once, with a hostile stretch of water in between. It was not an acceptable prospect.

At Napoleon's Pont-de-Briques headquarters, the talk now was of the Austrian army rather than the Royal Navy. The maps of the English Channel had been put aside in favour of the road to Vienna. In low voices, Napoleon, Soult, Berthier and the rest weighed up their options if the Austrian army should decide to cross the River Inn. A few days' march would bring the Austrians to the French border along the Rhine. A few more days and they could be in Paris. It must never be allowed to happen.

Where was Villeneuve? What on earth was keeping him? How much longer before he arrived?

CHAPTER 24

———————•◆•———————

NAPOLEON POSTPONES
THE INVASION

Villeneuve was still in Cadiz. The British blockade there was so thinly stretched that Vice-Admiral Collingwood was desperately signalling to an imaginary fleet over the horizon in an attempt to frighten the French into remaining in harbour. But Villeneuve needed no urging. To the despair of his subordinates, he stubbornly refused to sail out and destroy Collingwood's four ships with his own enormous force. He remained in port instead, refitting his vessels and waiting for orders from Napoleon.

Villeneuve was expecting to be joined at Cadiz by Captain Allemand from Rochefort and a Spanish squadron from Cartagena. To this end, he had asked for the Cadiz lighthouse, which had not shone since Spain's entry into the war, to be lit every night. He also stationed some of his swifter vessels just inside the harbour mouth, ready to help the newcomers fight their way in when they arrived.

But Allemand was nowhere to be seen and neither were the Spanish from Cartagena. The only ships in sight were British. They knew where Villeneuve was now and they were determined to keep him there. A Royal Navy frigate had gone scudding back to England to warn the Admiralty that Villeneuve's fleet was in Cadiz. Other navy ships were hurrying down the coast to join Collingwood and plug the gaps in the blockade. Villeneuve's chances of escaping from Cadiz and arriving at Boulogne on time were looking more hopeless every day.

*

In fact, it was all too late anyway. Unknown to Villeneuve, Napoleon had given up on the invasion for the time being. After months of waiting for the navy, he had abandoned the idea in despair. His mind had turned to Austria instead. England was no longer uppermost in his thoughts.

On 25 August 1805, four days after they had rushed down to Boulogne to board the flotilla, the soldiers of the right-hand camp above the town were roused again and ordered to assemble on the parade ground. Napoleon wanted to see them all. He had something important to say to them. The men paraded reluctantly, wondering what was up. They had been frustrated so often by their commanders that they were beginning to lose faith. They wondered what they were going be told this time.

Napoleon had a proclamation to read to them. Printed copies were being distributed to all the invasion camps along the coast, but to the right-hand camp Napoleon announced it in person:

> Brave soldiers of the Boulogne camp.
> You are no longer going to England. English gold has seduced the Austrian Emperor, who has just declared war on France. His army has crossed the line. Bavaria has been invaded. Soldiers, fresh laurels await you beyond the Rhine! We march at once to beat the enemy we've already beaten before.

There was a moment of stunned silence after Napoleon had finished. The men stared open-mouthed at each other, wondering what to make of this. Then a great ripple of excitement spread through the ranks as the words sank in. The army's mood lightened visibly and their faces lit up as the men contemplated this new challenge. To Napoleon's valet, watching their change of mood, it seemed as if the men didn't really care who they fought, so long as they fought someone. England, Austria – what difference did it make?

They set out at once. Within a few hours of the proclamation, the first troops were already on their way, marching headlong across France to take the Austrians by surprise. The operation had been planned well in advance. Everything fell smoothly into place as the soldiers forgot all about London and shouldered their knapsacks for the long haul to the frontier. They were the Grand Army now, no longer the Army of England. They left Boulogne so fast that most didn't even have time to say goodbye to anyone, abandoning pet dogs and the girls of Happy Valley without a backward glance. Within two or three days, the bulk of the Grand Army was en route to the Rhine, leaving only 25,000 newly drafted conscripts behind to cover for the rest, giving the impression that the camps were still occupied and the invasion still on.

Napoleon himself lingered at Boulogne until 3 September to foster that illusion. Then he set off for Paris, intending to rejoin his army on the frontier. His plan was to defeat the Austrians in a lightning strike and then double back to the Channel to continue his unfinished business with England. He aimed to catch one enemy napping, and then the other. But the Austrians were the immediate target. Napoleon's first priority now was to crush them and destroy their army before it could join forces with the Russians.

While the French were moving out of Boulogne, the British frigate *Euryalus* was speeding up the Channel from Cadiz. The ship reached the Isle of Wight towards evening on 1 September. The telegraph from Portsmouth did not work in the dark, so the quickest way for the *Euryalus*'s captain to alert the Admiralty to Villeneuve's whereabouts was to go to London himself. Hurrying ashore, the Honourable Henry Blackwood hired a post chaise in Lymington and travelled to London through the night.

He arrived early next morning. On the way, he stopped off at Merton to brief Lord Nelson. It was 5 a.m. when his carriage swept up the drive, but Nelson was already up and dressed. One glance at Blackwood's face told him all he needed to know. 'I am sure you bring me news of the French and Spanish fleets. I think I shall yet have to beat them.' Nodding in confirmation, Blackwood told him Villeneuve's entire force was now refitting in Cadiz. He spent a few minutes giving Nelson the details, then got back in his carriage and resumed his journey to the Admiralty.

He was followed soon afterwards by Nelson himself. There was no time to waste now that Villeneuve had been found. Nelson hurried to London and went straight to see Lord Barham at the Admiralty.

The two men sat down to decide their strategy. They were determined to put an end to the invasion once and for all, but the task was formidable. According to the latest estimates, Villeneuve now had forty ships under command. Added to Allemand and Ganteaume's fleets, the total would come to sixty-five – a nightmare if they all sailed together. The Royal Navy would be hopelessly outnumbered in a battle.

The answer was to isolate Villeneuve's fleet and either sink or capture it. Nothing less would do. It was no good fighting inconclusive actions like Calder's, where the French survived to fight another day. The French must be annihilated for good, in Nelson's opinion. If they were to be annihilated, the Royal Navy would need every ship it could lay its hands on to make up the disparity in numbers.

Lord Barham agreed: Villeneuve's fleet must certainly be destroyed. The Cadiz blockade would be heavily reinforced as soon as ships could be found. Nelson would take command, with Vice-Admiral Collingwood under him. The telegraph station on the Admiralty roof was already sending the necessary signals – one of them to Portsmouth to recall the *Victory*, which had been ordered to sail to Brest without Nelson.

Handing Nelson a copy of the Navy List, Barham invited him to choose his own officers for the task. Nelson demurred. 'Choose yourself, my Lord. The same spirit actuates the whole profession. You cannot choose wrong.' But Barham told him to choose anyway and dictate the names to his secretary. He left the room while Nelson did so.

Back at Merton, Nelson's valet and steward packed his heavy bags and took them to Portsmouth on 5 September. Next day, Nelson was in London again to see the Prime Minister. On 7 September, he received a letter at Merton advising him that his orders were ready and drove at once to the Admiralty to collect them. He spent most of the following week at the Admiralty, finalising the details and making his official farewells. He saw William Pitt again and was escorted by the Prime Minister to his carriage at the end of their meeting, 'a compliment which I believe he would not have paid to a Prince of the Blood'.

He also went to see Lord Castlereagh, the Minister for War. Castlereagh was delayed at a Cabinet meeting when he arrived, so Nelson was left to wait in an anteroom until it was over. He fell into conversation with a youngish army officer who also wanted to see the minister. Sir Arthur Wellesley was a major-general of thirty-six, newly returned from India, but didn't look important to Nelson. Years later, the Duke of Wellington recalled their only meeting wryly:

> From his likeness to his pictures and the loss of an arm, I immediately recognised Lord Nelson. He could not know who I was, but he entered at once in conversation with me, if I can call it a conversation, for it was almost all on his side, and all about himself, and in a style so vain and silly as to surprise and almost disgust me. I suppose something that I happened to say may have made him guess that I was somebody, and he went out of the room for a moment, I have no doubt to ask the office-keeper who I was, for when he came back he was altogether a different man, both in manner and matter.
>
> All that I had thought a charlatan style had vanished, and he talked of the state of this country and the aspect and probabilities of affairs on the Continent with a good sense, and a knowledge of subjects both at home and abroad, that surprised me equally and more agreeably than the first part of our interview had done; in fact, he talked like an officer and a statesman.

The two men chatted for almost an hour. Wellington felt that he had never had a more interesting conversation and was glad Castlereagh had kept them waiting. Otherwise he would have thought Nelson 'light and trivial', as did others who didn't know him well.

Behind the mask, though, Nelson was intensely sombre during those last days in London. Years earlier, a gypsy fortune teller had been unable to predict any future for him beyond 1805 and Nelson had not forgotten it. 'Ah! Catty, Catty, that gypsy,' he had confided to his sister, when she asked him why he was so depressed. Nelson had a premonition that he was not going to survive his next trip to sea.

He already had his coffin prepared. It had been made from the timber of *L'Orient*, the French flagship blown up at the Nile, and presented to him by one of his captains. It was kept now at an upholsterer's shop in Brewer

Street. Nelson went to see it before he left London, admiring the cotton padding and silk lining that the upholsterers had installed. A notice pasted to the bottom certified that the wood came from *L'Orient*. Nelson asked for the words to be engraved on the lid as well, 'for I think it highly probable that I may want it on my return'.

The rest of the little time that remained to him was spent at Merton with Emma. They were both desolate at the prospect of Nelson's departure. It was impossible for them to marry, but they had held a private ceremony at which they took the sacrament together and exchanged gold rings 'to prove to the world that our friendship is most pure and innocent'. Emma longed more than anything to be Nelson's wife and live peacefully with him at Merton. She was distraught at losing him again so soon. 'Lady Hamilton was in tears all yesterday,' reported a house guest. 'Could not eat, and hardly drink, and near swooning, and all at table.' She had sensed Nelson's premonition that he was not going to return from the sea again.

He left Merton for the last time on the evening of 13 September. The mood at dinner that night was funereal. Afterwards, Nelson went up to Horatia's room and spent a while praying at the bedside of his only child. He looked in again four times before the rattle of wheels outside told him the coach had arrived. Nelson seemed like a condemned man as he tore himself away from his daughter and went downstairs. Emma was there to see him off, and his sister Catherine with her husband and son. 'Be a good boy till I come back again,' he told the stable lad holding the coach door for him. Choking with emotion, Emma gave him one last hug as he took his seat. Then the coach set off for Portsmouth and he vanished from her sight for ever.

At Liphook, the coach stopped for a change of horses. Nelson took advantage of the stop to record his feelings in his diary:

At half past ten, drove from dear, dear Merton, where I left all which I hold dear in this world, to go to serve my King and country. May the Great God whom I adore, enable me to fulfil the expectations of my country; and if it is His good pleasure that I should return, my thanks will never cease being offered up to the throne of His Mercy.

If it is His good Providence to cut short my days upon earth, I bow with the greatest submission, relying that He will protect those so dear to me, that I may leave behind. His will be done. Amen. Amen. Amen.

The coach reached Portsmouth at 6 a.m. the following morning. Nelson had breakfast at the George, then went to the dockyard to pay courtesy calls on Commissioner Saxton and other officials. After collecting copies of Sir Hume Popham's newly published *Telegraphic Signals* for use in the fleet, he was back at the hotel around mid-morning. He was joined there by George Canning, the new Treasurer of the Navy, and George Rose, the vice-president of the Board of Trade. Word of his arrival had spread by then and a crowd had formed outside the hotel, jostling to catch a glimpse of the great man. This was a crucial moment in the country's history and everyone knew it. They all wanted to see Nelson and touch his coat, be a part of the occasion. They knew he was sailing to defeat the French and save his country or die in the attempt. Their hopes and prayers went with him. Their fears, too.

The crowd was so large that Nelson couldn't leave the hotel by the main entrance again to join his ship. A party of soldiers tried to clear the way, but the High Street was so crowded that there was no chance of Nelson boarding his barge from the sally port at the end. He decided instead to embark from Southsea beach, where the funfair now stands.

Slipping out the back way, he headed down Penny Street into Pembroke Road. From there, he turned down past the King's Bastion and reached the beach through the narrow tunnel in the ramparts. He was followed every step of the way by an adoring crowd. 'Many were in tears and many knelt down before him and blessed him as he passed.' They were so excited by the time Nelson reached the beach that an army officer unwisely ordered his men to hold them back with bayonets. The crowd was not deterred. They simply pushed the bayonets aside and continued to pursue Nelson.

Benjamin Silliman, a Yale professor on his way back to America, happened to be in Portsmouth that day. Eager to see 'the man on whom the eyes of all Britain, and indeed of Europe and America, are at this moment fixed', he joined the throng watching Nelson's departure:

Some hundreds of people had collected in his train, pressing all around and pushing to get a little before him to obtain a sight of his face. I stood on one of the batteries near which he passed, and had a full view of his person. He was elegantly dressed, and his blue coat was splendidly illuminated with stars and ribbons. As the barge in which he embarked pushed away from the shore, the people gave him three cheers, which his lordship returned by waving his hat.

The *Victory* was anchored at St Helen's, off the eastern tip of the Isle of Wight. It was a long row from Southsea. Nelson was accompanied by the two government ministers and his flag-captain, Thomas Hardy. They reached the ship about noon and Nelson was ceremonially piped aboard. The White Ensign was hoisted at once to let the rest of the fleet know he was back.

That evening he entertained Rose and Canning at dinner while the *Victory* prepared for sea. She sailed next morning, accompanied by the *Euryalus*. Two days later, she was off Plymouth, where Nelson seized the opportunity to write a quick note to Emma:

> I sent, my own dearest Emma, a letter for you, last night in a Torbay boat, and gave the man a guinea to put it in the post-office. We have a nasty blowing night, and it looks very dirty. I am now signalizing the ships at Plymouth [*Ajax* and *Thunderer*] to join me; but I rather doubt their ability to get to sea. However, I have got clear of Portland, and have Cawsand Bay and Torbay under the lee. I intreat, my dear Emma, that you will cheer up; and we will look forward to many, many happy years, and be surrounded by our children's children. God Almighty can, when he pleases, remove the impediment. My heart and soul is with you and Horatia.

It took another two days for the *Ajax* and *Thunderer* to join Nelson. They finally reached him on 19 September. Without further ado, the four British ships turned their backs on England and hoisted full sail for Cadiz.

CHAPTER 25

THE GRAND ARMY CROSSES FRANCE

In Austria, Emperor Francis had decided not to wait for his Russian allies now the war had started, but to advance into Bavaria at once. Austrian troops crossed the River Inn on 8 September, six weeks ahead of the agreed timetable. They struck north from the Tyrol, aiming for the fortress city of Ulm on the Danube, 100 miles from the French border. Field Marshal Karl von Mack intended to establish his base there until the Russians arrived.

By Mack's calculation, the French army would be unable to reach the Danube before 10 November at the earliest. That would allow him ample time to set up a defensive position along the River Iller, which joined the Danube at Ulm. The Austrian army was cumbersome, ill-suited to forced marches and rapid manoeuvres. It was much better at defending a fortified position. With the Iller in front of him and fortress Ulm on his right, Mack was confident nothing could dislodge him before his Russian allies arrived.

But he had reckoned without Napoleon. The French would reach the Danube long before 10 November – they would be there seven weeks earlier, by Napoleon's calculation. He had been very thorough in his preparations, poring over the map with a pair of dividers, estimating to the nearest mile how far his men could march each day, and for how many days they could keep up the pace. His dividers had been no use to him when determining Villeneuve's progress across the sea, but they worked perfectly on land. Napoleon knew what he was doing on land.

Napoleon lingered in Paris to allay suspicion while his troops rushed to the frontier. There were 200,000 of them in total, advancing in seven different columns. They came from Holland and Hanover as well as the Channel, converging on Bavaria at the rate of fourteen miles a day. They followed different routes, so as not to get in each other's way, but they were always within a day or two's march of each other, so that they could join forces if necessary. The staff work to keep so many men on the move was brilliant. It had never been attempted on such a scale before.

Even so, the staff had plenty of logistical worries, as Corporal Blaise of the 108th Regiment recalled:

The speed of our march made it impossible for supplies to keep pace with us. We were often short of bread in spite of all the efforts of our commanding general, Marshal Davout . . . Fortunately, it was the height of the potato season, and they were plentiful in our sector. How many times did we ruin the hopes of the villagers! We pillaged from them the fruits of an entire year's work.

Private Jean-Roch Coignet of the Grenadiers remembered the weariness rather than the lack of food:

Never was there such a terrible march. We didn't have a moment for sleep, marching by platoons all day and night, and at last clinging on to each other to avoid falling. Those who did fall could not be roused. Some fell into ditches. Hitting them with the flat of a sabre had no effect. The bands played and the drums beat, but nothing could stop them sleeping.

The nights were dreadful. I was on the section's right. About midnight one night, I tumbled down the bank at the side of the road. I went rolling down and didn't stop until I reached an open field. I kept hold of my musket, but I rolled into another world. My brave captain sent a man down to look after me. I was badly bruised. He took my knapsack and musket for me, but I was wide awake after that.

The march was even worse for the thousands of women following in the army's wake, grumbling constantly as they struggled to keep up. The men were setting an outrageous pace, in their opinion, without a thought for the camp followers trailing along behind. Some of them had to give birth under trees by the roadside before gathering up their babies and continuing the onward march. What kind of army was it that moved so fast and never seemed to stop?

Even for the men, the pace was often too much. Those who couldn't keep up had to be thrown into horse-drawn carts to follow the rest. Nothing was allowed to delay the army. It pushed forward relentlessly, hurrying across Europe at terrifying speed. Men, horses and artillery never stopped moving, the long columns snaking forward as far as the eye could see. Nothing like it had ever been known before. Marlborough had covered this ground with 40,000 men. Turenne had sworn it couldn't be done with more than 50,000. Yet Napoleon was advancing with four times as many, stopping for nothing in his headlong dash for the Rhine and the Danube beyond. The advance was unparalleled in military history. So many men, so many horses and guns. So many boats for the river crossing, all moving like clockwork, all in the right place at the right time, all proceeding exactly according to plan. It was just what Napoleon had intended for England.

He himself remained in Paris until the last week of September. It was not until the 26th that he rejoined his army at Strasbourg, on the French side of the Rhine. Before leaving, he sent Villeneuve a fresh set of instructions, the orders Villeneuve had been expecting for so long.

Napoleon had lost all patience with Villeneuve. The retreat to Cadiz had been the last straw. Napoleon had complained bitterly about it to Decrès, heaping abuse on Villeneuve for everything that had gone wrong:

He is a wretch who ought to be cashiered in disgrace. He has no plan, no courage, no insight; he would sacrifice everything to save his own skin. Until you find something plausible to say, I beg you will not speak to me of an affair so humiliating, nor remind me of a person so cowardly.

Yet Napoleon still needed the man, for the time being at least. The invasion of England might have been postponed, but there was trouble now in the Mediterranean. British troops in Malta were poised to join forces with the Russians to attack Napoleon's army in Italy, thus relieving the pressure on their Austrian allies to the north. The quickest way for Napoleon to forestall them would be to send Villeneuve to Italy with the troops aboard his fleet. They had been expecting to go to England, but they could just as easily go to Italy instead. Villeneuve would take them.

Napoleon dictated the orders with care. Villeneuve was to leave Cadiz at once, taking the whole Spanish fleet with him. He was to head past Gibraltar, collect the Spanish squadron at Cartagena and proceed to Naples, where he would land his 4,000 troops to reinforce General Laurent St Cyr's army at Taranto. He was then to return to Toulon and await further instructions from Paris.

There was no mention in the orders of Villeneuve's feebleness in running for Cadiz instead of Boulogne. Napoleon didn't discuss it at all. Admiral Decrès had borne the brunt of his wrath on the subject. Napoleon had been all for hanging Villeneuve on the spot, but Decrès had shielded his old shipmate from the worst of it. He had tactfully put it to Napoleon that Villeneuve's task had never been as easy as it looked, arguing that it would have been suicide for Villeneuve to sail for Boulogne as planned. He had pointed out that the Royal Navy was simply too strong for the French in the Channel.

Napoleon had not been mollified, but he had calmed down by the time he composed Villeneuve's new orders. What mattered now was to regain the initiative in Italy. 'Audacity and lots of action,' he emphasised to his recalcitrant admiral. 'Attack wherever you outnumber the enemy. Attack without hesitation. Make a decisive job of it.'

Napoleon signed the orders in hope rather than expectation. They went off at once and reached Cadiz on 28 September. They arrived the same day as Lord Nelson.

CHAPTER 26

—•◆•—

NELSON ARRIVES OFF CADIZ

As soon as he had seen Napoleon's new orders, Admiral Gravina rowed across to the *Bucentaure* to discuss them with Villeneuve.

Relations between the two were not good. Gravina was a proud man, deeply ashamed at having lost two of his ships in the fight with Calder. He blamed the French for the debacle and shared the general lack of confidence in Villeneuve. If it had been up to him, Gravina would have handled things very differently over the past few months. But it was not up to him while Villeneuve was in overall command. As a professional officer, Gravina had little option but to swallow his pride and make the best of it.

Aboard the *Bucentaure*, he and Villeneuve conferred quietly. Between them, they now had forty warships under command, but crews for only thirty-three. They could sail at once if necessary, although Gravina would have preferred more time in port to train his new men and get them ready for sea. The numbers had been made up with landlubbers, many of whom had only just come aboard. Few of them knew one end of a ship from the other.

Both men realised that once at sea, a battle with the British was all but inevitable. Collingwood's little squadron had now been massively reinforced and was spoiling for a fight. Even as the two admirals sat talking, the blockade was being joined by three new ships from England. One of them was a three-decker, according to Villeneuve's lookouts. This was the *Victory*, although he did not yet realise it.

The fight would come as soon as they left harbour, in Villeneuve's opinion. 'From the position and strength of the enemy outside this port, an engagement must take place the very same day that the fleet puts to sea,' he wrote to Decrès. But he was optimistic about the outcome:

The fleet will see with satisfaction the opportunity offered to it to display that resolution and daring which will ensure its success, avenge the insults to its flag, and lay low the tyrannical domination of the English upon the seas.

Our allies will fight at our side, under the walls of Cadiz and in sight of their fellow citizens. The Emperor's gaze is fixed upon us.

Gravina did not share Villeneuve's optimism, but felt obliged to pledge his support. His fourteen ships would sail with the French. They could not leave at once because the 4,000 French troops were still ashore, recuperating on dry land. Villeneuve gave orders for the men to re-embark immediately. Once they were aboard, the fleet would move to the harbour mouth to wait for a fair wind. After that, it would set course for Gibraltar, forcing a way through the Royal Navy if it had to, and avenging all the insults to its flag.

While Gravina and Villeneuve were conferring, Nelson was arriving unheralded to take command of the blockade. At his insistence, there was no gun salute or hoisting of signals when the *Victory* appeared. He had sent the *Euryalus* ahead to ensure that no one took any notice of his arrival. He didn't want Villeneuve to know he was there, in case it frightened him into remaining in port.

But everyone on the British side knew Nelson had arrived. The word had spread as soon as the *Victory* had been sighted. Few of the many thousands aboard the British fleet had ever set eyes on the admiral, but they all knew him by reputation. He was a legend throughout the navy. A brilliant sailor, whose skill in battle was unmatched. A fearless commander, who always led from the front and had lost an arm and an eye in the process. A good and decent man, whose kindness to officers and men alike was legendary. Nelson was that rarest of beings in British history, a commander who enjoyed the full confidence of the people serving under him. Just to know he was there made them all feel better. 'Lord Nelson is arrived,' wrote one officer to his wife. 'A sort of general joy has been the consequence, and many good effects will shortly arise from our change of system.' The officer spoke for the whole fleet.

The *Victory* anchored on the evening of 28 September. At seven next morning, Vice-Admiral Collingwood came aboard to pay his respects. He and Nelson were old friends who had known each other for most of their careers. Cuthbert Collingwood was eight years older than Nelson, a veteran of the American War of Independence. He had fought at Bunker Hill with a party of sailors attached to the British army. Thereafter, he and Nelson had often served side by side, learning to value each other highly. Collingwood resented Nelson's appointment over his head, but was far too good an officer to show it. He was a fine sailor and a safe pair of hands. Now fifty-five, he had already spent forty-four years in the navy, all but six of them at sea. His hobby was gardening.

'Tell me,' he once wrote to his wife in Northumberland. 'How do the trees which I planted thrive? Is there shade under the three oaks for a comfortable summer seat? Do the poplars grow at the walk, and does the wall of the terrace stand firm?' It was Collingwood's habit on his rare home leaves to scatter acorns around the countryside, to provide oak for future Royal Navy ships.

Aboard the *Victory*, he quickly briefed Nelson on the situation in Cadiz. The town was in trouble as a result of the navy's blockade. It was suffering food shortages, exacerbated by the presence of so many extra mouths aboard the French and Spanish fleets. The betting was that Villeneuve would have to put to sea sooner rather than later to relieve the situation on land. Collingwood's strategy had been for a show of strength outside the harbour mouth to keep the French in port for as long as possible, while he waited for British reinforcements to arrive.

Nelson decided to reverse this policy as soon as the British vessels were all in place. He planned to withdraw his ships altogether, presenting Villeneuve with an apparently empty horizon. He knew the only way to destroy Villeneuve was to lure him out to sea. He knew too that autumn gales were approaching, bringing westerly winds that might blow Nelson's unwieldy three-deckers off course and force them past Gibraltar into the Mediterranean. By withdrawing his fleet fifty miles to the west of Cadiz, Nelson would have much more room to manoeuvre in the teeth of a gale. He would also be better placed to attack the French when they did finally venture out of harbour.

As Collingwood and Nelson talked, other ships' captains were rowing across to the *Victory* to meet their new commander. Carrying swords and in their best uniforms, they came aboard one by one and made their way aft to Nelson's cabin. Only eight of them had previously served with him. The rest knew Nelson solely by reputation and were eager to meet him in the flesh.

Passing through the dining cabin, the captains gave their names and were announced at the door to Nelson's day cabin. It lay at the stern of the ship, comfortably furnished with tables and leather armchairs. The captains shook Nelson's left hand and wished him many happy returns, because he was forty-seven that day. John Cooke of the *Bellerophon* was among the new arrivals, as was Israel Pellew of the *Conqueror*. So too were Rear-Admiral the Earl of Northesk, himself a newcomer at Cadiz, Edward Codrington of the *Orion* and Thomas Fremantle of the *Neptune*. Nelson had a particular word for these last two.

'Would you have a girl or a boy?' Nelson asked Fremantle, whose wife was expecting a baby.

'A girl,' Fremantle replied.

'Be satisfied.' Nelson gave him a letter announcing the safe delivery of a daughter. He had another letter for Codrington, who hadn't heard from his wife for some time. 'He received me in an easy, polite manner,' Codrington later told her, 'and on giving me your letter said that being entrusted with it by a lady, he made a point of delivering it himself.'

Pleasantries over, the conversation swiftly turned to business. Nelson outlined his strategy for bringing the French to battle. It was well received, as he later reported in a letter to Emma:

> I believe my arrival was most welcome, not only to the Commander of the Fleet, but also to every individual in it; and, when I came to explain to them the 'Nelson touch', it was like an electric shock. Some shed tears, all approved – 'It was new – it was singular – it was

simple!'; and, from Admirals downwards, it was repeated – 'It must succeed, if ever they will allow us to get at them! You are, my Lord, surrounded by friends whom you inspire with confidence.' Some may be Judases; but the majority are certainly much pleased with my commanding them.

Once the discussion was over, the steward poured drinks and the captains relaxed. Nelson invited the fifteen most senior officers to stay on for his birthday lunch and told the rest to come back for lunch next day. They were delighted to do so, because Nelson was a convivial host, unlike dour old Collingwood. Earnest and pious, Collingwood kept a dismal table, although he was perfectly cheerful in private life. He discouraged frivolity and had forbidden his officers to make social visits between ships. They considered him a bore as a result and were pleased Nelson was now in command. The 'Nelson touch' was much lighter.

But there was one officer unhappy at Nelson's arrival. The *Victory* had brought newspapers from home, highly critical of Sir Robert Calder's action against the French. He should have pursued Villeneuve's fleet to destruction, according to the papers, instead of breaking off the action and running north with his prizes. He should have displayed more courage and daring, instead of concentrating on profit. Calder had let the Royal Navy down, in the press's opinion, and his country, too.

Reading the papers aboard his flagship, Calder was outraged. He had done everything that could reasonably have been expected off Finisterre. He had attacked a much larger French fleet, forced it to a halt and come away with a couple of prizes as well. It was the French and Spanish who had done an about-turn at the end of the encounter. Calder had placed his ships between Villeneuve and the invasion of England and stopped it there and then. He had not expected to be vilified for his actions. How many newspapermen, fighting the battle from the safety of their desks, would have done better?

To make matters worse, Calder had been ordered home by the Admiralty to explain his conduct. After thinking about it overnight, he decided the only way to clear his name was to ask for an official court of inquiry. The facts could be properly assessed at an inquiry and his conduct examined by people who knew what they were talking about. With public opinion against him at home, it was all he could do to save his career.

Calder wrote to the Admiralty at once, demanding a formal investigation. He had 'learnt with astonishment yesterday by the ships just arrived, and by letters from friends in England, that there has been a most unjust and wicked endeavour to prejudice the public mind against me as an officer'. He wanted the facts examined immediately.

Nelson was sympathetic. Calder was an old enemy, but Nelson shared his view that he had been unfairly treated. The newspapers were saying that Nelson would have handled the action better, but he wasn't so sure. 'I should have fought the Enemy, so did my friend Calder; but who can say that he will be more successful than another?' War at sea was never as simple as the newspapers imagined.

Calder's flagship was the ninety-gun *Prince of Wales*. He had been ordered to transfer to a frigate for the journey home, but was loath to give up the prestige of his own ship. He asked permission to sail home in the *Prince of Wales* – a considerable dilemma for Nelson, who could ill afford to lose so many guns at such a critical juncture. Calder also wanted to take several captains with him, to testify in his defence. He asked for the captains of the *Ajax*, *Thunderer* and *Defiance* to leave their ships and return to Britain to help save his career. It was a great deal to ask, with a battle imminent off Cadiz. A bigger man than Calder would have balked at the idea.

But Nelson sided with Calder. His need to be liked overcame his better judgement. He gave Calder permission to sail home in the *Prince of Wales*, taking the captains with him. In the event, though, only two of them went. The third, Philip Durham of the *Defiance*, asked to see the Admiralty order, which said they did not have to go if they were unwilling. Durham chose to remain with the fleet instead.

'I trust that I shall be considered to have done right as a man, and to a Brother Officer in affliction,' Nelson wrote to Lord Barham. 'My heart could not stand it, and so the thing must rest.' But he had not behaved responsibly. He was well aware that he could not spare the *Prince of Wales* at such a time. It was a very unwise decision, with the French and Spanish poised to emerge from Cadiz at any moment.

CHAPTER 27

VILLENEUVE HOLDS A
COUNCIL OF WAR

While Nelson celebrated his birthday, General Sir John Moore was 5,000 yards off Boulogne, studying the port's defences from the deck of the *Antelope*. He was weighing up the chances of a military raid on the town to seize the invasion barges in the inner harbour and destroy them once and for all.

The Grand Army's departure from the coast had not gone unnoticed by the British. Despite Napoleon's best efforts, word had crossed the Channel almost at once. The *Hythe Gazette* had reported the story as early as 6 September: 'All idea of invasion is now at an end. We learn that the camp at Boulogne has been broken up.' The bulk of the army had certainly gone, but thousands of troops still remained. The question for Sir John was whether a British landing near the town was either feasible or desirable.

The *Antelope* had surveyed the coastline from Ambleteuse to Étaples, examining the defences and looking for a potential landing place. At Boulogne, her arrival the day before had been greeted by thirty-two French ships that emerged from the harbour and formed a defensive line off the pier. After dark that night, as the *Antelope* lay at anchor, a small boat approached from the shore and nosed up alongside. It contained six French soldiers, deserters from the Grand Army. They wanted to come aboard and surrender to the Royal Navy.

Unbelievably, one of the deserters was a Corsican wagoner who had served with the British in Egypt. He recognised Sir John at once and was delighted to see him. He had tried both armies, he told him, and he preferred working for the British. Morale was poor among the soldiers left behind at Boulogne. They hadn't been paid for a long time and feelings were running high, particularly among the Italians. There was great discontent in the camps.

Sir John thought it best not to mention that the crew of the *Antelope* hadn't been paid for eighteen months either. The deserters seemed impressed with the Royal Navy, so much so that one of them wanted to go back ashore to fetch his friend. It appeared that the Italians in the French army might desert en masse with a little encouragement. Most of the rearguard at Boulogne were recent conscripts, according to the deserters, little more than boys. They weren't seasoned fighting men.

Sir John got a glimpse of them next day when some 5–6,000 soldiers assembled outside the huts of the right-hand camp and fired a *feu de joie* into the air. Seasoned or not, there were more than enough of them to make a landing impossible east of Boulogne. A British force would have to land west of the town, if it was to land at all.

Sir John himself was against the whole idea of a landing. He thought it far too difficult. He had never really believed that Napoleon would succeed in invading England because the problems were insurmountable, in his opinion. And what was difficult for the French one way would be just as difficult for the British the other. Previous British attacks on Boulogne had all been costly failures – 'breaking the windows of the good citizens of Boulogne with English guineas', as Napoleon had put it. Sir John saw no need for another attack now, when the Grand Army was no longer an immediate threat.

Back in Kent on 1 October, he penned a report to that effect for the Duke of York:

I have not a doubt, if proper measures are adopted, and if secrecy is observed, that at present a landing, in spite of the Batteries, may be effected to the westward of Boulogne; but I cannot say whether, when landed, the troops will be able to advance to carry the enemy's lines and take up a position from whence they can destroy the Flotilla in the Harbour, and afterwards secure their own re-embarkation. This will depend upon the nature of the country, which from the sea cannot be observed, the force which can speedily be assembled against them, and other circumstances of which I have no means of information.

I have no hesitation to say that no attempt should be made on Boulogne but with a considerable force, and it must be recollected that on that coast, with certain winds, the ships cannot hold their anchorage, and at all events troops cannot be re-embarked from it in bad weather. There will therefore always be a risk, even should troops gain possession of the harbour and destroy the Flotilla, that if by any circumstance of weather their re-embarkation was retarded, they would have to contend with such superiority of numbers as to prevent the possibility of their getting off.

In short, a raid on Boulogne was a bad idea. Sealing his report, Sir John sent it at once to the duke's headquarters in London. Then he called for his horse and rode the fourteen miles from Shorncliffe to Walmer Castle to deliver the same message to the Prime Minister. He was worried that William Pitt might approve of another attack on Boulogne. He wanted to see him in person to kill the idea before it ever got off the ground.

Pitt was looking ill when he arrived – coughing badly and wearing one shoe larger than the other to ease his gout. He was studying the latest dispatches from Vienna and Berlin. They did not make good reading. Prussia was refusing to join the fight against Napoleon, for fear of provoking a French invasion. The Elector of Bavaria had initially pledged his support to Austria, but had now withdrawn his troops without warning. Everything in Europe seemed to be going Napoleon's way.

To Sir John's relief, however, Pitt listened carefully to his report and agreed with his conclusions. There was little point in a land assault on Boulogne harbour. As Sir John said, it was far too risky. The Prime Minister would not give the idea his support.

In truth, Pitt was always inclined to favour smaller and cheaper operations, rather than lavish ventures involving thousands of troops. He was still listening to Robert Fulton, the American inventor whose torpedoes had performed so dismally at Boulogne a year ago. Techniques had been much improved since then, according to Fulton. He was negotiating to blow up a brig off Deal, to show Pitt just how effective his torpedoes could be if they were handled properly.

But torpedoes weren't Sir John Moore's concern. After seeing the Prime Minister, he paid his compliments to Lady Hester Stanhope – they were popularly supposed to be in love – and set off back to Shorncliffe. He was a happy man as he went. He had achieved his aim in talking Pitt out of an attack on Boulogne, and he had seen with his own eyes that a French invasion of England was no longer an immediate threat. The situation was looking a great deal better than it had a year ago.

While Sir John was riding home, the French soldiers in Cadiz were busy re-embarking aboard Villeneuve's fleet for their return to sea.

Most of the men were infantry, although there were also two troops of Chasseurs without horses. Some were Swiss mercenaries, distinguished by their red coats. A few were foot artillery, complete with field guns and limbers. And some were proud. The two battalions of the 67th Regiment could trace their history of sea service back to Cardinal Richelieu, who had raised the regiment specifically to serve as musketeers in the navy. Their task in a sea battle was to line the shrouds and upper decks as soon as they came within musket range of the enemy, pouring fire into the British as the opposing ships converged.

The bulk of the troops were French, but there were Spanish soldiers aboard the fleet as well. They too had a long history. Just as there had been a *Victory* among the English ships that defeated the Spanish Armada of 1588, so also some of the Spanish regiments aboard Gravina's ships had served with the Armada. The forebears of the Regimiento de Africa had been captured by Sir Francis Drake off Torbay. Three thousand men of the Regimiento de Soria had drowned off the Irish coast while trying to flee back to Spain. These were not the happiest of precedents for the battle that lay ahead.

By the evening of 2 October, all the troops were aboard again and the fleet was ready for sea. But then the weather intervened, as it had so often before. The wind freshened and blew from the west, making it impossible to leave harbour. There was always bad weather off the Andalusian coast at this time of year. Even if the weather improved for a moment, Admiral Gravina and the other Spanish officers were against sailing at once. Far better to wait, they argued, until the two Spanish three-deckers, the *Rayo* and *Santa Ana*, were ready to sail. Why not delay for a couple of weeks until their new crew members had settled in, since the weather was unlikely to be favourable anyway? To the Spanish officers, familiar with the conditions along this stretch of coast, it made perfect sense to wait for a while, rather than set out at once.

But they didn't have Napoleon for an Emperor. Villeneuve was determined to sail as soon as the wind changed. He was adamant that the fleet must put to sea at the first opportunity. He knew he would be answerable to Napoleon if it did not.

It was 7 October before the wind finally obliged. It shifted round to the east that morning and blew steadily out to sea. Villeneuve immediately ran up the signal to weigh anchor. Even as he did so, though, the wind changed its mind again and returned to the west. His ships never even left their anchorage.

Frustrated beyond measure, Villeneuve resigned himself to a few more days in harbour. He took advantage of the delay to hold a meeting with his senior officers, giving them a chance to discuss the situation and air their grievances. They were all aware that the fleet was in bad shape – short of men and poorly equipped. They wanted to put their complaints on record before they left Cadiz.

The council of war took place aboard the *Bucentaure* on 8 October. Thirteen very unhappy officers filed into Villeneuve's cabin and sat around the table. The Spanish had met beforehand to agree a line among themselves. The French were bitterly divided. Rear-Admiral Magon had been so appalled by the French performance against Calder that he had foamed at the mouth and thrown his wig and telescope at Villeneuve's ship as it passed. Rear-Admiral Dumanoir hadn't been impressed either.

Villeneuve opened the proceedings with a summary of his orders from Napoleon. Their combined fleet was to put to sea at the first opportunity and 'wherever the enemy should be encountered in inferior strength they must be attacked without hesitation in order to force them to a decisive action'. The enemy, they now knew, was commanded by Lord Nelson. He had between thirty-one and thirty-three ships of the line under his command, according to their estimates. How should the French and Spanish react to this threat?

Most of the French were keen to sail at once. They thought they could fight off the British and have an easy run of it to Naples. The Spanish were more cautious. Two of their biggest ships were not yet ready for sea and there was a period of stormy weather ahead. The British could not remain on station much longer without running short of food and water. The storms would break their fleet up, if nothing else did. Why not wait in harbour and let the weather do their work for them, instead of risking their inadequate fleet against a navy that had been continuously at sea since 1793?

Rear-Admiral Antonio de Escano, the Spanish chief of staff, pointed out that some of the Spanish sailors hadn't been to sea in eight years and would be no match for the British – 'Superior orders cannot bind us to attempt the impossible.' Disaster would be inevitable, in his view, if they left harbour now.

Rear-Admiral Magon, for the French, didn't bother to conceal his contempt for such talk. The Spanish weren't equal to the challenge, in his opinion. Commodore Alcala Galiano leapt to his feet at that and insisted that Magon retract. Magon refused to do anything of the sort. Hands flew to sword hilts and Latin blood boiled. The honour of France was at stake. And of Spain.

Order was hastily restored before Galiano could challenge Magon to a duel. But the Spanish were so touchy by now that a chance remark by Villeneuve triggered another confrontation. Admiral Gravina, normally an even-tempered man, told Villeneuve that only a madman would think of sailing at the moment. 'Do you not see, sir, that the barometer is falling?'

'It is not the glass that is falling,' Villeneuve replied, 'but the courage of certain persons.'

Stung, Gravina retorted that the Spanish had been in the forefront against Calder and were ready to sail tomorrow, if necessary. But the technically minded Commodore Cosma de Churruca pointed out that the barometer was indeed falling, which confirmed the imminent arrival of the October gales. It was only common sense to let the gales scatter the British. In Churruca's view, the Spanish would be better off altogether without the French. 'Did we not see at Finisterre, the French fleet standing idly by, doing nothing as the *San Rafael* and *Firme* were captured? Making no attempt to rescue them?'

More blood boiled. The French took a while to calm down. When discussions were finally resumed, a compromise was reached. The fleet would not sail at once, but would move down to the harbour mouth, ready to leave as soon as the weather improved. They would wait for the British to divide their forces – as they would have to when their supplies ran low – and then sail immediately. In the meantime, the officers wanted it placed on record 'that the vessels of both nations are for the most part badly equipped, that a portion of the crews have never been trained at sea, and that, in short, the fleet is in no state to carry out the duties allotted to it'.

After that, the council of war broke up. The Spanish bowed stiffly to Villeneuve as they left, departing with the air of men who knew they were doomed. Villeneuve himself wrote to Decrès that the Spanish were 'quite incapable of meeting the enemy', but would put to sea anyway, as ordered. So would the French. Under Villeneuve's command, thirty-three ships of the line would begin moving down to the harbour mouth next day to wait for a favourable wind.

CHAPTER 28

NELSON'S MEMORANDUM

The Spanish were right about the weather. It deteriorated sharply on 10 October and remained intermittently bad for another week. There was no chance of the fleet putting to sea for the time being. All they could do was sit at anchor and wait.

Outside the harbour, Nelson continued his preparations for their reception. His own force was not yet fully assembled because new ships were arriving every day. They came in ones and twos, rather than a great forest of sails, so that the French lookouts would notice nothing untoward. Nelson did not have as many ships as Villeneuve imagined. He was only too aware that the odds would be stacked against him when the French did finally come out to fight. On 8 October, he calculated that:

> I have thirty-six sail of the line looking me in the face. Unfortunately, there is a strip of land between us, but it is believed they will come to sea in a few days. The sooner the better. I don't like to have these things upon my mind; and if I see my way through the fiery ordeal, I shall go home and rest for the winter.

Later that day, Nelson penned a memorandum outlining his strategy for the fight. He based his figures on the hope that the British fleet would have been considerably reinforced before it took place:

> Thinking it almost impossible to bring a Fleet of forty Sail of the Line into a Line of Battle in variable winds, thick weather and other

circumstances which must occur, without such a loss of time that the opportunity would probably be lost of bringing the Enemy to Battle in such a manner as to make the business decisive.

I have therefore made up my mind to keep the fleet in that position of sailing . . . placing the fleet in two Lines of Sixteen Ships each with an advanced Squadron of Eight . . . which will always make if wanted a Line of Twenty-four Sail, on which ever Line the Commander in Chief may direct . . .

This was the strategy Nelson had discussed with Captain Keats in the garden at Merton: a two-pronged attack, flexible as required, driving straight at the enemy's centre and cutting Villeneuve's line into three, each isolated from the others. If Villeneuve was in the middle section, he would be rapidly overwhelmed. The rearguard too would be destroyed before the leading ships could return to help. By the time the leading French ships had managed to turn round, the British would be ready to deal with them as well, annihilating the whole enemy fleet at a stroke. It was a brilliant idea, very radical for its time, and very dangerous too. Nothing of the kind had ever been attempted before, but it would be wonderful if it worked.

The memorandum ran to several pages, with a copy for every captain in the British fleet. Nelson's secretary laboured far into the night to ensure that they all went out next day. The French and Spanish were 'all but out of the harbour', according to British lookouts. Nelson's captains needed time to study the plan before the enemy put to sea.

Nelson had two frigates watching Cadiz, ready to warn him the moment the enemy emerged. His own ship was fifty miles away, out of Villeneuve's sight. A string of signal ships kept Nelson in touch with events on shore. They had orders to fire guns at three-minute intervals as soon as Villeneuve emerged, or rockets from the masthead at night. Speedy frigates were best for such work, but the British were so short of frigates that Nelson was using ships of the line as well. By his own calculation, he needed at least eight frigates and three brigs to serve his fleet properly. At the moment he only had two such vessels.

Otherwise, though, Nelson was as ready for battle as he could be. He had ordered those ships that had not already done so to paint their lower masts yellow, to distinguish them from the enemy's black ones in the fog and smoke. He had earlier painted three parallel yellow strakes along the *Victory*'s hull as well, level with the gunports. The port hatches were painted black, giving a chequerboard effect when they were closed. Other captains had been doing the same, at their own expense, to emulate the *Victory*. It made their ships look stylish and smart, boosting everyone's morale.

Nelson's main concern, as he waited for Villeneuve, was to keep his fleet properly fed and watered. The Spanish had been right in predicting that resupply would be a problem. The British fleet needed a minimum of 800 bullocks every month, which could only come from the Moroccan port of Tetuan, across the Strait from Gibraltar. They needed fresh water and vegetables as well, in prodigious quantities. One of Nelson's first actions on joining the fleet had been to detach a substantial number of ships under Rear-Admiral Thomas Louis to fetch more water from Gibraltar. With a battle in the offing, however, Louis was loath to reduce Nelson's fighting strength at such a crucial time.

'You are sending us away, my Lord. The enemy will come out, and we shall have no share in the battle.'

'My dear Louis,' Nelson soothed him, 'I have no other means of keeping my Fleet complete in provisions and water, but by sending them in detachments to Gibraltar. The enemy will come out, and we shall fight them; but there will be time for you to get back first. I look upon *Canopus* as my right hand, and I send you first to ensure your being here to help beat them.'

Louis wished he could believe it. So did his flag-captain, Frank Austen, whose sister Jane later mentioned the *Canopus* in her novel *Mansfield Park*. Austen had sailed all the way to the West Indies and back in pursuit of Villeneuve. He didn't want to miss the dénouement now, as he told his fiancée:

> Having borne our share in a tedious chace [sic] and anxious blockade, it would be mortifying indeed to find ourselves at last thrown out of any credit or emolument which would result from an action. Such, I hope, will not be our lot.

Like Captain Wentworth in *Persuasion*, Frank Austen needed prize money to get married. He was hoping to make his fortune when Villeneuve came out of harbour. He knew he was never going to make it on a dull supply run to Gibraltar.

A thousand miles away, Napoleon's troops had long since crossed the Rhine and were pushing deep into Bavaria, heading for Ulm. One column had advanced into the Black Forest, prompting Field Marshal Mack to send Austrian troops forward to meet them. The rest of Napoleon's army had rapidly bypassed the forest and was advancing on Ulm from the north and east, threatening the Austrians' rear. They reached the Danube on 7 October, two days ahead of schedule. Crossing the river in pouring rain, they pressed on southwards, hurrying to close the gap and encircle the Austrians before Field Marshal Mack realised what was happening.

Mack enjoyed a fine reputation in Austria, but he was not a distinguished commander. 'Let not General Mack be employed, for I know him to be a rascal, a scoundrel and a coward,' Lord Nelson had warned two months earlier. He knew Mack from Naples, where he had once witnessed an exercise in which Mack managed to surround his own troops instead of the enemy.

Napoleon was not impressed by Mack either. He had met him when the Austrian was a prisoner of war in 1800:

> Mack is one of the most mediocre men I have ever come across. He is presumptuous, conceited, and considers himself equal to anything. I hope one day he will find himself up against one of our good generals. That would open his eyes. He is one of the least able of men, and unlucky as well.

Mack thought the main French thrust was coming through the Black Forest. He hadn't expected Napoleon to cross the river in his rear. He had sent to the Tyrol for reinforcements, but they had been intercepted by the French. With the net rapidly closing, Mack faced a stark choice. He could counter-attack in an attempt to wrest the initiative back from the enemy. He could stand his ground, holding the defences at Ulm until the Russians arrived. Or he could retreat to the Tyrol, leading his army back to the safety of the mountains before it was annihilated by Napoleon.

He was considering these options when word reached him from behind enemy lines – a spy had overheard French troops discussing a British invasion of Boulogne. There was trouble in Paris as well, apparently, where people were rioting in protest at the cost of the war. It was all just hearsay, but Mack was happy to believe it. If the British were in Boulogne, Napoleon would be forced to retreat at once to protect his own rear. His troops would have to pass Ulm on their way home. Mack decided to stand his ground there, ready to harry the French as they went by and pursue them relentlessly back to their own borders.

At Merton, Emma Hamilton was missing Nelson. The house seemed empty without him. She couldn't bear it on her own, with only her mother and daughter for company. A few days after Nelson's departure, Emma left, too, and went to stay with William Nelson and his family at Canterbury.

Emma and William were hardly boon companions. He was a stuffy clergyman, concerned with the proprieties and his own advancement. She was his brother's mistress, with an illegitimate daughter and a racy past. But it suited both to see each other. Emma wanted to replace Lady Nelson in the family's affections. William Nelson wanted to inherit his brother's title, which he would so long as his brother remained with Emma, who could not bear him legitimate children. To that end, William was happy to keep in with Emma and invite her to stay with his family in the precincts of Canterbury Cathedral.

Canterbury itself was a dull town as a rule, but livelier than usual at the moment. It had been a haven for refugees from Dover during the invasion scare. Now it was full of soldiers, officers from smart regiments adding tone to the town's social life. The Royal Horse Guards had been stationed at Canterbury for a while (it was troopers from the Blues who had given Lady Hester Stanhope such a fright at Ramsgate). There were officers from all the Foot Guards regiments as well, and volunteers from the local gentry. Among them was Edward Austen, another of Jane Austen's brothers, who commanded the volunteers on his Godmersham estate. Jane herself was staying with him that September and had attended balls in Canterbury during Race Week.

The Austen family and the Nelsons had acquaintances in common, but moved in different circles. William Nelson lived with his wife and children in a pretty house beside the cathedral, known today as Linacre. It was there that Emma Hamilton arrived at the end of September, for a stay with her lover's family. She felt the need for moral support at a difficult time. She wanted to be with Nelson's flesh and blood as they all fretted together about what was happening at sea.

It was not Emma's first visit to Canterbury. She had sung a duet in the cathedral on a previous occasion and embarrassed William by drinking all the champagne in the house. This time, though, her behaviour was more muted. She prayed in the cathedral every morning and received a stream of visitors in the Nelsons' drawing room. People dropped in every day to pay their respects and enquire discreetly after the events at sea. Emma's information came straight from Lord Nelson, better than anything they could read in the newspapers.

Her own letters to Nelson were full of love and admiration, and chat about their daughter Horatia, who thought Nelson was her godfather:

My dearest life, we are just come from church, for I am so fond of the Church Service and the cannons [sic] are so civil, we have every day a fine anthem for me. Yesterday Mr, Mrs & Miss Harrison, Mrs Bridges, Marquis of Douglas and General Thornton and Mr Baker the Member dined with us. The Dr gave a good dinner and Mariana dressed the macaroni and curry, so all went off well . . .

My dear girl writes every day in Miss Conner's letter & I am so pleased with her. My heart is broke away from her but I have now had her so long at Merton that my heart cannot bear to be without her. You will be even fonder of her when you return. She says 'I love my dear dear godpapa, but Mrs Gibson told me he kill'd all the people, and I was afraid'. Dearest angel she is! Oh, Nelson, how I love her, but how do I idolize you – the dearest husband of my heart you are all in this world to your Emma – may God send you victory and home soon to your *Emma*, *Horatia* and *Paradise Merton* for when you are there it will be Paradise. My own Nelson may God prosper you and preserve you for the sake of your affectionate Emma.

In Deal, fifteen miles down the road, the American inventor Robert Fulton was putting the finishing touches to his latest batch of torpedoes. He was sure they would work better now than they had at Boulogne, and he had obtained permission to blow up a captured brig to show how effective they could be if they were handled properly.

The demonstration was scheduled for 15 October. Fulton spent the previous day rehearsing two boat crews, each towing a torpedo underwater. The torpedoes were joined by an eighty-foot rope that was supposed to wrap itself around the target ship's anchor cable. The tide would then carry the torpedoes under the target's hull. A few minutes later, if the firing mechanism worked, the torpedoes would explode and the *Dorothea* would sink to the bottom.

A large and sceptical audience gathered on the beach between Deal and Walmer to watch the demonstration. Fulton had been hoping the Prime Minister would be there, but Pitt had been called back to London on business. Some very senior naval officers attended instead, most of them convinced the experiment would fail. One announced that he would feel perfectly safe having dinner aboard the *Dorothea* with Fulton's torpedoes coming towards him.

But his cynicism was misplaced, as Fulton happily recorded:

At forty minutes past four, the boats rowed towards the brig, and the Torpedoes were thrown into the water; the tide carried them, as before described, under the bottom of the brig, where, at the expiration of eighteen minutes, the explosion seemed to raise her bodily about six feet; she separated in the middle, and the two ends went down; in twenty seconds nothing was to be seen of her except floating fragments; the pumps and foremast were blown out of her; the fore-topsail-yard was thrown up to the crosstrees; the fore chain plates, with their bolts, were torn from her sides; the mizen-chainplates and shrouds being stronger than those of the foremast, or the shock being more forward than aft, the mizenmast was broke off in two places; these discoveries were made by means of the pieces which were found afloat.

It was a brilliant performance, a great triumph for Fulton. The experiment had worked perfectly. He could hardly have wished for a more exhilarating result.

But the admirals were horrified. Torpedoes were all very well if they were used against the French, but they could also be turned against the British – 'a mode of war which they who commanded the seas did not want, and which if successful would deprive them of it'. The admirals were worried about the wider implications of Fulton's dreadful machines. In the sinking of the *Dorothea*, they had seen the future of naval warfare. They did not like it one bit.

CHAPTER 29

———◆·◆·◆———

WAITING FOR THE ENEMY

Down in Cadiz, the Spanish too were unhappy. Ill fed, unpaid, cooped up on board ship, they had been kept awake night after night, waiting sleeplessly at their guns for a British attack that never came. Most of them had been forced into the navy against their will and knew they were going to be massacred as soon as they set sail. They were growing more restless every day.

There had already been a mutiny aboard the *San Juan*. The soldiers had refused to obey their orders and threatened to shoot their officers. The situation had only just been saved by Commodore Churruca, who had made a personal appeal to the mutineers' loyalty. A few had been swayed by his oratory, but most had stood firm against him. Churruca had promptly had the ringleaders arrested at gunpoint. They had been taken ashore in chains, but Churruca had used his influence to save them from the death penalty. The other mutineers had been separated and reassigned to different ships.

It had been a narrow escape, nevertheless. They could not afford any more trouble. The whole fleet needed to sail as soon as possible, to take the men's minds off their grievances. All this waiting around in harbour was doing nobody any good.

No one realised it more than Villeneuve. He had more reason than most to put to sea, because Napoleon was about to dismiss him. Vice-Admiral François Rosily was on his way to Cadiz, bearing dispatches from the Emperor. Rosily's orders were to remove Villeneuve and take command of the fleet himself. Villeneuve had a shrewd suspicion that something of the sort was about to happen because his friend Denis Decrès had given him a broad hint to put to sea at the first opportunity. The sooner he put to sea, the lesser his chance of being humiliatingly relieved of his command on the eve of battle. Villeneuve was all for sailing at once.

Offshore, the two English frigates watching for him had now been joined by three more frigates, a brig and a schooner. To the west, the seventy-four-gun *Defence* was a speck on the horizon, ready to signal Villeneuve's escape to the *Agamemnon*, and thence via the *Colossus* and the *Mars* to Lord Nelson on the *Victory*, fifty miles out to sea. 'I am confident you will not let these gentry slip through our fingers,' Nelson had told one of the frigate captains. 'We shall give a good account of them, although they may be very superior in numbers.' Nelson was relying on the frigates to warn him the moment the enemy left harbour.

The *Agamemnon* had only just joined his fleet from England. On her way south, she had been intercepted by Captain Allemand's Rochefort squadron, still prowling the waters off Finisterre. The French had chased the *Agamemnon* for seventy miles and would have caught her if the British hadn't jettisoned equipment and drinking water to increase their speed. The French had also chased the accompanying frigate *L'Aimable*, as a twelve-year-old midshipman cheerfully recounted to his mother:

I hope you are all well at home and I am sure will be very glad to hear from me, but you were very near losing me on the 10th of this month, for we were chased by the French Squadron and were very near being come up with, but we cut away two of our boats and one anchor and hove two or three hundred shot overboard . . . We were so deep we could not sail until we staved in nine butts of water and pumped it out, and cut the boats adrift. Besides all, there was a very heavy squall came, and we had all sails set and were very near going down. She laid down on her beam ends for several minutes . . . Do not fret about me, for if you cared no more for the French than I, you would care very little about them. Give my love to father, brothers and sisters. Success to William and his rabbits . . . Your ever affectionate son, Charles.

But Allemand's force was too small to do any real damage to the British. The only real damage would come from Villeneuve, still biding his time in Cadiz. Nelson's frigates cruised past the harbour mouth every day, looking for signs of movement from the enemy fleet. They sailed so close inshore that they could smell the land and count the French and Spanish ships one by one. But there was no sign of the ships preparing to depart. The wind remained westerly and their masts devoid of sails. There was nothing the British could do about it except sit and wait for events to develop, as develop they surely must.

The waiting was the worst part. They all knew what to do when the enemy appeared; they had rehearsed the drill ad infinitum. But the waiting was difficult to bear, day after day of nothing happening, when all they wanted to do was have the fight and get it over with. No one on the British side was enjoying the waiting.

The men were kept busy from morning till night to take their minds off their worries. They had plenty of music aboard the fleet and were encouraged to dance the hornpipe regularly, to keep themselves fit. The *Victory* had an amateur-dramatic group as well, as did most ships on the blockade. The officers of the *Britannia* managed to stage three different plays that October. *Columbus, or A World Discovered* was performed on 9 October, with elaborate sets made by the ship's carpenter. *Catherine and Petruchio* followed a few days later, accompanied by a short piece, *The Village*, written by 2nd Lieutenant Halloran of the Marines. The stage was Lord Northesk's fore-cabin, with the partitions removed so that the audience on the main deck could enjoy the show. The girls were played by midshipmen with rouged cheeks and wigs made from teased-out rope ends. The crew stared open-mouthed, trying to remember what a woman looked like. It gave them something to think about while they waited for the enemy to emerge from harbour.

But the enemy showed no sign of moving. The wind remained stubbornly in the west, leaving Villeneuve with little prospect of putting to sea. His plan was to slip out on the first easterly breeze and sail far into the Atlantic. He would then turn round and allow the October gales to blow his fleet past Gibraltar into the Mediterranean. He would have liked to escape under cover of darkness, but there was no moon at the moment and his crews couldn't find their way out of harbour without a moon. So he would have to leave in daylight, in full view of the English frigates waiting for him outside.

The wind continued from the west for ten days without a break. It did not begin to change until the evening of 17 October. Even then it remained variable, reducing in strength and blowing in every direction until the afternoon of 18 October. Then it shifted and blew steadily from the east for a spell, the first time since Villeneuve's council of war that the French and Spanish had had any realistic chance of getting their ships out of harbour.

As if to confirm that this was the moment, Villeneuve had received a message that day from the Spanish in Algeciras, across the bay from Gibraltar. Rear-Admiral Louis' detachment of six British warships had been spotted sailing through the Straits into the Mediterranean. If Nelson was short of six ships, this was clearly the right time for Villeneuve's fleet to put to sea. There was never going to be any time better.

Villeneuve consulted Gravina, who declared the Spanish ready to sail that afternoon. Signals were hoisted for all personnel ashore to rejoin their ships at once. They did so with alacrity, according to a French officer, even the ones who were sick: 'Our invalids, soldiers and sailors, forsook the hospitals; they rushed to the quay in crowds to embark.' No one wanted to be left behind if they were going into action at last.

The plan was for Rear-Admiral Magon to sail first, with an advance force of seven ships of the line. They were to drive the English frigates away and reconnoitre out to sea, looking for the rest of Nelson's fleet. While Magon was doing that, the remainder of Villeneuve's force would work its way out of harbour. The operation would be complex and time-consuming, with a total of thirty-three capital ships and little room to manoeuvre.

Villeneuve intended to sail that afternoon, in the hope of being out by dark. To everyone's frustration, though, the wind dropped again at 4 p.m. and remained erratic throughout the night. It did not pick up again until early next morning, 19 October. Then, at last, Villeneuve was able to give the signal they had all been waiting for: 'Make sail and proceed.'

Magon weighed anchor at once and broke out his topsails. Others followed suit, slipping their moorings in the dawn light and moving one by one towards the harbour mouth. The wind wasn't as strong as they had

Above: While the Royal Navy watches from a distance, Napoleon addresses his invasion troops at Boulogne, 16 August 1804. *Museo Napoleonico, Rome/www.bridgeman.co.uk*

Below: The same view today. The site of Napoleon's throne is marked by a small obelisk. *Author's collection*

Above: In July 2004, descendants of
the Grand Army celebrated the
bicentenary of Napoleon's review at
Boulogne. Napoleon's column stands
in the background. *Paul Chalmin
Association/NORDMAG*

Above: The obelisk marks the site of Napoleon's throne at Boulogne, from where he addressed his invasion army on 16 August 1804. His troops later erected the column on the skyline in his honour. *Author's collection*

Below: The ancestors of these men stood ready to invade England in 1804. *Paul Chalmin Association/NORDMAG*

Above: Walmer Castle's cannon are still trained on the beach where Julius Caesar landed and the French were hourly awaited. *Author's collection*

Right: Weather permitting, news of a French landing would have reached the Admiralty from Deal's beachfront telegraph station in less than ten minutes. *Author's collection*

Below: Walmer Castle. While waiting for the French to arrive, Lady Hester Stanhope busied herself reorganising the castle garden. *Author's collection*

Above: The French coast from Dover Castle. In 1804, the cliffs were white with the encampments of Napoleon's army. *Author's collection*

Left: As soon as the French landed, a chain of signal beacons like this one at Dover would have alerted the country from one hilltop to the next. *Author's collection*

Opposite: Trafalgar was Lord Nelson's finest hour, but he was hit early on and actually saw very little of the battle. *Royal Naval Museum, Portsmouth/ www.bridgeman.co.uk*

Right: Although wounded, Vice-
Admiral Collingwood took command
of the British fleet after Nelson's death
and saw it through the four-day storm
that followed the battle. *The Crown
Estate/www.bridgeman.co.uk*

Above left: Captain Jean Lucas was one of the few French commanders to emerge with credit from the battle. *Getty Images*

Above right: Admiral Federico Gravina, the Spanish commander. He fought honourably at Trafalgar, but later died of his wounds. *Mary Evans Picture Library*

Right: Vice-Admiral Pierre Villeneuve commanded the combined fleets of France and Spain. He was a good officer, but no match for Nelson. *Bibliotheque Nationale, Paris/www.bridgeman.co.uk*

Right: A contemporary copy of the portrait of Emma, Lady Hamilton, which hung in Nelson's cabin on the morning of Trafalgar. 'Take care of my Guardian Angel', he told the sailor who removed it before the battle. *Great Cabin, HMS Victory/ www.bridgeman.co.uk*

Below left: Pressed into the Royal Navy against his will, John Roome hoisted the flags for Nelson's last signal: 'England expects that every man will do his duty'. *Private Collection*

Below right: As a teenage midshipman, John Pollard was credited with killing the French sharpshooter who killed Nelson. *Private Collection*

Above: The British fleet advances towards the enemy in two columns, with Cape Trafalgar in the distance. *National Maritime Museum*

Left: 'England expects...' Nelson's last signal is hoisted as HMS *Victory* races towards the enemy. *National Maritime Museum*

Opposite: Copy of a plan of the battle of Trafalgar drawn by Captain Jean Magendie on 28 October 1805, while a prisoner aboard the *Neptune*. Nelson's strategy was to divide the enemy fleet into three and destroy it piecemeal. *The Stapleton Collection/ www.bridgeman.co.uk*

First Position of the English Fleet at Daylight 21st October 1805

2d Position at 9 o'Clock...

Third Position at 12 o'Clock Noon

English ... Red
French ... Blue
Spaniards. Yellow

Defiance
Thunderer
Defence
Dreadnought
Prince
Devasture
Revenge
Polyphemus
Achille
Bellerophon
Tonnant
Mars
Belisle
R. Soverign
Adm. Collingwood

Spartiate
Minotaur
Orion
Ajax
Agamemnon
Conquerer
Leviathan
Lord Northesk
Neptune
Temeraire
Victory
Lord Nelson

Phœbe
Naiad
Sirius
Leviathan
Euryalus

Intrepranand
Cutter

Africa

Pickle Shooner

Position of the Combined Fleets of France and Spain, at the Commencement of the
Battle on the 21st October 1805. with Lord Nelson

Certifie Veritable Le Capitaine de Vaisseau
Officier de la Legion d'honneur Command de
Le Bucentaure J. Magendie

Copy

Above: The battle begins in earnest as the British smash through the enemy line. *Bonhams, London/ www.bridgeman.co.uk*

Below: The *Victory*'s gun decks were so full of noise and smoke during the battle that the crews compared them to Hell. *2SL Photographic*

Right: Many years after the battle, HMS *Victory* was still capable of firing a gun salute. *Royal Naval Museum*

Above: As HMS *Victory* runs alongside the *Redoutable*, Nelson is hit by a musket shot from the French mizentop. *National Maritime Museum*

Below: Nelson lived long enough to hear of the victory, but was dead before the end of the battle. *National Maritime Museum*

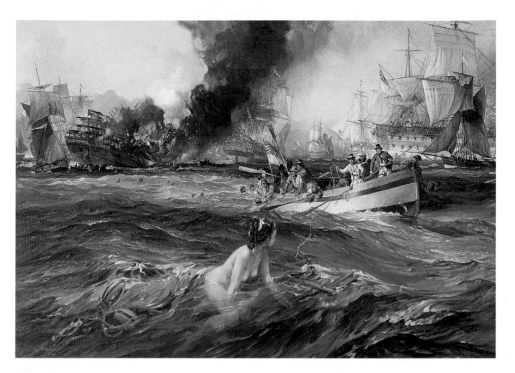

Above: After escaping from the *Achille*, Jeanette Caunant is rescued by the ship's boat from HMS *Naiad*. *L. A. Wilcox RI, RSMA (1904-1982)/ www.bridgeman.co.uk*

Below: The *Bellerophon* in Plymouth Sound, August 1815. Napoleon stands at the gangway, surrounded by boatloads of British admirers. *National Maritime Museum*

After his defeat at Waterloo, Napoleon
was brought to England aboard HMS
Bellerophon. This portrait of him was
painted by an eyewitness. *National
Maritime Museum*

hoped. Several ships were forced to lower rowing boats to tow them out to sea. There was confusion too as to whether Villeneuve's signal applied only to Magon's ships or the whole fleet. Some ships weighed anchor, others remained where they were. Without a stronger wind, most of them could not move anyway.

But enough ships were moving to alert the British. The frigate *Sirius* was closest inshore. Captain William Prowse was watching the enemy through his telescope. Shortly after 6 a.m., he sent a message to Captain Blackwood, further out on the *Euryalus*: 'Enemy have their topsails hoisted.' A little later, as soon as he was certain what was happening, Prowse signalled again. He sent signal number 370, one of the most compelling in the book: 'The Enemy's ships are coming out of port, or are getting under sail.'

Blackwood responded at once. With three spare frigates at his disposal, he ordered the *Phoebe* and *Naiad* westwards, to serve as relay stations between his own ship and the *Defence* on the horizon. Then he told the *Weazle* to sail immediately for Gibraltar, to warn Admiral Louis' six ships that Villeneuve was at sea. 'Make all possible sail,' he ordered the *Weazle*'s captain, 'with safety to the masts.'

The frigates scattered obediently. The *Phoebe* headed west, firing a gun every three minutes to alert the *Defence* on the horizon. She was already flying the three flags of signal 370 from her masthead. They were soon identified by the *Defence* and transmitted in turn to the *Agamemnon*, *Colossus* and *Mars*. From there, the signal was seen shortly after 9 a.m. by Lieutenant William Cumby of the *Bellerophon*:

> I immediately reported this to Captain Cooke and asked his permission to repeat it. The *Mars* at that time was so far from us that her topgallant-masts alone were visible above the horizon; consequently the distance was so great for the discovery of the *colours* of the flags that Captain Cooke said he was unwilling to repeat a signal of so much importance unless he could clearly distinguish the flags himself, which on looking through his glass he declared himself unable to do.
>
> The very circumstances of the importance of the signal, added to my own perfect conviction of the correctness of my statement

founded on long and frequent experience of the strength of my own sight, induced me again to urge Captain Cooke to repeat it, when he said if any other person of the many whose glasses were now fixed on the *Mars* would confirm my opinion he would repeat it. None of the officers or signalmen, however, were bold enough to assent positively, as I did, that the flags were number 370, and I had the mortification to be disappointed in my anxious wish that the *Bellerophon* should be the first to repeat such delightful intelligence to the Admiral.

Even as Cumby fretted, the *Mars* hauled the flags down again. He guessed what would happen next. 'Now she will make the distant signal 370,' he announced. Distant signals were used when flags were too far away for the colours to be distinguished. The distant signal for 370 comprised a flag, ball and pendant flown from different mastheads. Sure enough, a flag, ball and pendant appeared on the *Mars* and Cumby was proved right. The enemy were putting to sea.

The *Bellerophon* moved at once to repeat the signal, but was beaten to it by the *Victory*, which had also spotted the ball and pendant. Lord Nelson promptly followed it up with two signals of his own. Addressed to the entire British fleet, the first said simply: 'General chase, south-east.' The second said: 'Prepare for battle.'

CHAPTER 30

LAST LETTERS HOME

With one accord, the British turned and set their sails. They were aiming for the Straits of Gibraltar. It was the obvious place to intercept the French before they could slip through and escape into the Mediterranean.

There was very little wind as they set out. The battle was unlikely to happen that day. It would take the fleets all day just to catch sight of each other, let alone come to quarters. There would be no actual fighting until next morning at the earliest.

Nelson understood this as well as anyone. He remained on deck for a while, chatting to the other officers while the fleet got under way. Then he left them to it and went below to spend some time alone in his cabin, composing himself for the ordeal that lay ahead.

At his writing desk, he sat down and wrote to Emma. It would be his last chance before the battle:

Victory, October 19th, 1805, Noon, Cadiz, ESE 16 leagues.
My dearest beloved Emma, the dear friend of my bosom. The Signal has been made that the Enemy's Combined Fleet are coming out of Port. We have very little Wind, so that I have no hopes of seeing them before tomorrow. May the God of Battles crown my endeavours with success. At all events, I will take care that my name shall ever be most dear to you and Horatia, both of whom I love as much as my own life. And as my last writing before the Battle will be to you, so I hope in God that I shall live to finish my letter after the Battle. May Heaven bless you prays your
Nelson & Bronte

Having signed the letter with his full title, Nelson wrote another to Horatia, acknowledging her as his daughter for the first time:

My dearest Angel,
I was made happy by the pleasure of receiving your letter of September 19th, and I rejoice to hear that you are so very good a girl, and love my dear Lady Hamilton, who most dearly loves you. Give her a kiss for me. The Combined Fleets of the Enemy are now reported to be coming out of Cadiz, and therefore I answer your letter, my dearest Horatia, to mark to you that you are ever uppermost in my thoughts. I shall be sure of your prayers for my safety, conquest, and speedy return to dear Merton, and our dearest good Lady Hamilton. Be a good girl, mind what Miss Connor says to you. Receive, my dearest Horatia, the affectionate parental blessings of your Father,
Nelson & Bronte

Others were writing, too. Aboard the *Euryalus*, much closer to the enemy, Captain Henry Blackwood took advantage of the drop in the wind to pen a quick note to his wife Harriet:

What think you, my own dearest love? At this moment the enemy are coming out, and as if determined to have a fair fight; all night they have been making signals, and the morning shewed them to us getting under sail. They have thirty-four sail of the Line and five frigates. Lord Nelson has but twenty-seven sail of the Line with him; the rest are at Gibraltar, getting water. Not that he has not enough to bring them to close action; but I want him to have so many as to make this the most decisive battle that was ever fought, and which may bring us lasting peace and all its blessings.

Within two hours, though our fleet was sixteen leagues off, I have let Lord Nelson know of their coming out, and have been enabled to send a vessel to Gibraltar, which will bring Admiral Louis and the ships there.

At this moment (happy sight) we are within four miles of the enemy, and talking to Lord Nelson by means of Sir H. Popham's signals, though so distant, but reached along by the rest of the frigates of the Squadron.

You see dearest, I have time to write to you, and to assure you that to the latest moment of my breath, I shall be as much attached to you as man can be. It is odd how I have been dreaming all night of carrying home dispatches. God send me such good luck. The day is fine, and the sight magnificently beautiful. I expect before this hour tomorrow to carry General Decrès on board the *Victory* in my barge, which I have just painted nicely for him.

Like many in the British fleet, Blackwood had been reading the newspapers from home, which claimed Villeneuve had been dismissed. His replacement was assumed to be Admiral Decrès. Blackwood was rather hoping so, because he knew and liked Decrès, who had been his prisoner in 1802. In truth, though, Villeneuve was still in command, and still in Cadiz. By midday on 19 October, only nine of his ships had managed to clear the harbour. The tide was too strong for the rest and the wind had dropped to nothing. It was not the swift exit he needed so badly.

His own ship still lay at anchor, as did Admiral Gravina's. Some of the lighter vessels were being towed towards the harbour mouth, their crews straining at the oars as they struggled to make headway. The ships could only leave one at a time, which did nothing to aid the fleet's progress. There were reefs outside the harbour and dangerous cross-currents. The ships already out had made little attempt to chase away the watching British frigates. It was as much as they could do to keep station while they waited for the remainder to emerge. Only two of them were from Rear-Admiral Magon's advance force. The rest were miscellaneous vessels that had managed to slip out one way or another.

By mid-afternoon, Villeneuve was forced to abandon any hope of getting his fleet out before dusk. His strategy now was to tow or warp as many ships as possible towards the harbour mouth, ready for another attempt next morning. The breeze came off the land in the early morning. If the ships were in the right place, they could catch it and sail on the tide before the wind dropped again. Villeneuve worked his men long into the evening to get the fleet into position, ready for a quick start next day.

Dawn on 20 October brought thick clouds that blotted out the sun. The wind was coming mostly from the south. Villeneuve gave the order to sail at 6 a.m. An hour later he told his fleet to prepare for battle. By 8 a.m., all the ships were under canvas except the *Rayo*, which was having trouble raising anchor. Outside the harbour, the nine ships under Rear-Admiral Magon had lost formation during the night but were hurriedly re-establishing contact in the daylight.

All of Cadiz turned out to watch the fleet go. The quays and harbour walls were thronged with spectators, anxiously wishing them well. It was a Sunday, and the churches were crowded all day with distraught families praying for the safe return of their menfolk. At the sailors' church, the Iglesia del Carmen, the crowds were so great that they could only be admitted in relays. At the Oratorio de San Felipe Neri, the archbishop himself spent much of the day on his knees before the high altar. The fleet's departure was a time of high emotion for the people of Cadiz. They were under no illusion as to what would happen when the Royal Navy caught up with it. They could only pray that the men in their own family would be spared, whatever might happen to anyone else.

The ships were a fine sight as they inched out of harbour. Pride of place went to the *Santissima Trinidad*, at four decks and 140 guns the biggest warship in the world. Her sides were painted with four long red lines and thin ribbons of white. The *Santa Ana* and *Principe de Asturias* carried 112 guns each, and the *Rayo* 100. They were complemented by another twenty-nine ships of the line, five frigates and two brigs – a total of forty vessels in all. It was the largest formation of warships to sail out of Cadiz since the days of the Spanish Armada.

Of Nelson's fleet there was no sign. The only British ships in sight were Blackwood's frigates, which had withdrawn to a safe distance as soon as the enemy emerged. The French lookouts scanned every quarter, searching nervously for a host of British sails, but saw none. Wherever the British were, they were keeping a low profile as their enemies put to sea.

The weather worsened as the morning drew on. The wind veered to the south-west, bringing squalls and drizzle. It was a baptism of fire for the untrained seamen, struggling with unwieldy sails 150 feet above the tossing sea. The *Bucentaure* promptly lost a man overboard and was lucky to see him recovered by the *Redoutable*, sailing next-astern. Other crews floundered as well. The wind was against them for Gibraltar. They were forced to steer west-north-west instead, as close to the wind as they could manage.

The last ship cleared the harbour at noon. An hour later, the wind shifted to the west, enabling the whole fleet to go about. Villeneuve signalled the battle squadron to form three columns on the starboard tack, with flagships in the centre of their divisions. They spent the rest of the afternoon trying to do what he said, but without much success. By 6 p.m., ships were milling about in all directions, their officers quietly cursing as the unskilled sailors struggled to bring the vessels under control.

Shortly before 7 p.m., Captain Jean Lucas of the *Redoutable* caught his first glimpse of Nelson's fleet to starboard:

The sea was still rough, with a swell setting in from the south-west. The fleet was now steering to the south-south-west. I signalled to the admiral that I could make out a fleet or squadron of the enemy to windward. They did not, to me, seem very far away.

An hour later, Lucas's sighting was confirmed to Villeneuve by the brig *Argus*, which came alongside with a message from Admiral Gravina. The *Achille* had counted eighteen sail of the line to the south-south-west. The message was followed by another from the *Themis*, which reckoned the figure was twenty. Whatever the exact total, it was clearly the British fleet, on course for a confrontation with the French.

It was dark by this time. The British frigates shadowing the combined fleet had orders to signal Villeneuve's position to Nelson every hour. Two blue lights burning close together meant the French were heading south towards Gibraltar. Three guns fired in rapid succession meant the French were heading west. The British also had orders not to sail too close to the enemy, for fear of scaring them back to Cadiz. But Admiral Gravina, aboard the *Principe de Asturias*, did not know that:

We began to observe, at no great distance, glimmers of light. They could only be from the enemy's frigates, which were positioned midway between the two fleets. At nine o'clock the English squadron made gun signals. From the interval between the flash and bang, they must have been about two miles away from us.

To Gravina, it looked as if the British were about to attack. He immediately signalled Villeneuve by lantern, urging him to form the fleet into line of battle. There was no time to waste if the British were coming after them.

Villeneuve was appalled. *Two miles!* Surely the British were not going to attack in the dark? And yet . . . and yet . . . they had done exactly that at Aboukir, during the Battle of the Nile, and from the landward side. The British seemed capable of anything, with Lord Nelson in command.

Villeneuve didn't hesitate. Gravina was right. The whole fleet must form line of battle at once, the three columns merging into one to repel an imminent attack. Villeneuve promptly gave the order, flashed from ship to ship. He followed it immediately with a second order: '*Branle-bas de combat.*' The command was acknowledged from every ship and the drummers moved swiftly to beat the *Generale*, the signal for the crews to clear the decks for action.

CHAPTER 31

VICTORY AT ULM

Far away in Bavaria, Napoleon was enjoying one of the most glorious days of his life. Ulm had fallen, with hardly a shot fired. Austrian troops had surrendered in tens of thousands, laying down their arms without a struggle.

It had been a whirlwind campaign. The Austrians had been wrong-footed from the start and had never recovered. The French had run rings round them – literally. They had encircled Ulm and laid siege to the fortress city while Field Marshal Mack dithered, not knowing what to do. He had tried to fight but had been forced to surrender, outwitted on every front by French speed and cunning.

Napoleon had been in the thick of it, leading from the front. He had marched ceaselessly among his men, pushing forward with them through mud, rain and snow. He had advanced so rapidly that for eight days in a row he had never once taken off his boots. One night he had shared his quarters with a wounded drummer boy, protecting the child from cold. At the approaches to Ulm, he had stood on a hill exposed to enemy fire and surveyed the city below him. And now the fortress was his, surrendered after a bombardment of less than an hour.

The negotiations had been completed on 17 October. Field Marshal Mack had secured an eight-day armistice, to give his Russian allies time to come to his aid. Napoleon had consented, knowing the Russians were too far away to be any help (this was not the moment to remind Mack of the twelve-day difference between the old and new calendars, something the Austrians had overlooked in their planning). Mack had agreed to surrender on 25 October if no Russians appeared. In the event, Austrian morale was so low that he was forced to raise the white flag on 19 October, six days early. The formal surrender took place next morning, at the foot of the Michelsberg Heights outside the city.

Napoleon waited to receive the surrender at the head of his Guards. The Grand Army formed up behind him in a giant semicircle, with fifty cannon trained on the town. Private Coignet of the Grenadiers was standing near the Emperor when the enemy appeared:

Suddenly we saw an endless column file out of the town and march up towards the Emperor on a plain at the foot of the mountain. All the soldiers had hung their cartridge boxes on their knapsacks, ready to remove them when they reached the disarmament point. They threw their weapons and cartridge boxes on to a pile as they passed. General Mack came at their head to surrender his sword to the Emperor. The Emperor refused to accept it, allowing all the officers to keep their swords and knapsacks. He spent a long time talking to the more senior officers.

The surrender took well over four hours, as 25,000 men and 2,000 cavalry filed past shamefacedly to lay down their arms. Some were glad it was all over, but most were angry and humiliated at giving up without a fight. They felt badly let down by their leaders. Captain de l'Ort of the Austrian army spoke for many:

The shame which overwhelms us, the mire which covers us, can never be wiped out. While the battalions were marching past and laying down their arms, Napoleon, in the plainest of uniforms, stood in the centre of a group of his gorgeously arrayed marshals, chatting with Mack and several of our generals, whom he sent for after they had marched past. The Emperor himself was dressed like an ordinary private in a grey overcoat, singed in front and at the elbows, a hat without any distinguishing mark pulled down on his head, his arms behind his back, warming himself at the camp fire. He was talking animatedly and appeared to be in a good mood.

Napoleon was in more than a good mood. He was ecstatic. He had won the victory every general dreams about. In three brilliant weeks, he had outmanoeuvred the enemy and forced them into submission without even fighting a battle. Napoleon had every reason to feel pleased with himself as Mack's dejected troops shuffled past.

'I have destroyed the Austrian army simply by keeping them marching,' he boasted to Josephine. 'I have taken 60,000 prisoners, captured 120 pieces of cannon, more than ninety flags, and more than thirty generals.' It was a magnificent achievement, one of the most spectacular triumphs of his career. It was everything Napoleon could have wished for, everything he had ever wanted, except in one crucial particular. It wasn't London.

While Napoleon savoured his victory and the Grand Army found shelter in Ulm, the French and Spanish fleets were moving hurriedly to form a line of battle in the dark. The manoeuvre was difficult at the best of times. In the dark, it was almost impossible.

The ships blundered to and fro, the two windward columns of the battle squadron dropping to leeward to form on the third column, trying to squeeze in wherever they could find a space. There was no moon and the stars were obscured by cloud. French and Spanish ships hailed each other constantly to identify friend or foe. Captain Lucas of the *Redoutable*, a highly professional French officer, did not enjoy it one bit:

We were all widely scattered. The ships of the battle squadron and those of the squadron of observation were all mixed up. Another cause of confusion was this. Nearly all the ships had answered the admiral's signals with flares, which made it impossible to tell which was the flagship. All I could do was follow the other vessels near me, which were closing on some ships to leeward.

Towards eleven I found myself close to Admiral Gravina who, with four or five ships, was beginning to form his own line of battle. I was challenged and our name demanded, whereupon the Spanish admiral ordered me to take post in his line. I asked permission to lead it and he assented, after which I stood in to station.

The French and Spanish ships showed a light at each masthead, to indicate their positions. To the British frigates, shadowing them now at a distance of half a gunshot, they looked 'like a well lit up street', nine miles long. The seventy-four-gun *Defence* took advantage of the dark to have a closer look:

> We came very near the Combined Fleet without their being able to discern us. While we concealed every light, they continued to exhibit such profusions of theirs, and to make night signals in such abundance, that we seemed at times in the jaws of a mighty host ready to swallow us up. We, however, felt no alarm, being confident that we could fight our way or fly, as occasion required. The former was certainly more congenial to our feelings.

The French were still heading south, towards Gibraltar. This came as a relief to Lord Nelson, who had feared they might try to steal back to Cadiz under cover of darkness. But they were fully at sea now, committed to their course. The British would have them next day and a battle would ensue.

Nelson was looking forward to it, convinced the British would capture twenty ships at least. 'Tomorrow I will do that which will give you young gentlemen something to talk and think about for the rest of your lives,' he promised his junior officers. But his optimism was tempered with pessimism as to his own chances. 'I shall not live to know about it myself.' Nelson was sure he would be killed in the battle. The fortune teller's prophesy had filled him with foreboding.

Others did not have time for premonitions. Aboard the frigate *Euryalus*, midway between the two fleets, Henry Blackwood's crew had run themselves ragged over the last forty-eight hours, keeping Villeneuve's ships in sight and reporting their every move to Nelson. It was exhausting for everyone, as Midshipman Hercules Robinson recalled:

> For two days there was not a movement that we did not communicate, till I thought that Blackwood who gave the orders, and Bruce our signal mid, and Soper our signalman, who executed them, must have died of it; and when we had brought the two fleets fairly

together, we took our place between the two lines of lights, as a cab might in Regent Street, the watch was called, and Blackwood turned in quietly to wait for the morning.

Thousands of others followed Blackwood's example, conserving their strength and getting some rest while they still could. Most fell asleep at once, but many lay awake all night, wondering anxiously what the morning would bring. It was a time of last letters home, for those who could write, of silent prayers for some and private moments of reflection for others. They harboured no illusions as to how it would be when the opposing fleets met next day. Casualties would be high and many of them would be killed. It was the price they had to pay to put a stop to the French. But the hope of every man in the fleet was that it would be someone else who paid, not them. They all wanted to be alive when the battle was over, and still in one piece, if it was humanly possible.

CHAPTER 32

---·:·●·:·---

ENEMY SAILS OFF
TRAFALGAR

So it came to the morning of 21 October 1805, a day that would live for ever in the minds of those who were there. A day that lives still, in the annals of the Royal Navy.

There was very little wind as the sky began to lighten. The mist was lifting and the day was promising to be bright. The coast of Spain was a dark mass in the distance, the sun just beginning to reveal itself over a low range of hills that the Moors had named Tarif-al-Ghar. A few miles off the coast, the French and Spanish were still heading southwards, desperate to slip through the Straits of Gibraltar and scatter into the Mediterranean before the British could catch them. They were not in line of battle, as Villeneuve had ordered. They were in no formation at all, just a random collection of ships scurrying south on a heavy swell, looking to avoid a fight if they possibly could.

Further out to sea, about nine or ten miles away, the British were determined not to let them escape. They had sailed parallel to the French during the night, keeping a good distance between the two fleets so as not to panic the enemy into a retreat. Now, as the sky brightened, they had turned north and were searching the horizon for a first sight of the French, straining for a glimpse of the enemy's sails against the rays of the rising sun.

William Robinson, a seaman aboard the *Revenge*, remembered the moment vividly:

As the day began to dawn, a man at the topmast-head called out, 'A sail on the starboard bow,' and in two or three minutes more he gave another call, that there was more than one sail, for indeed they looked like a forest of masts rising from the ocean, and as the morning got light we could plainly discern them from the deck, and were satisfied it was the enemy.

Midshipman William Badcock of the *Neptune* agreed:

It was my morning watch, I was midshipman of the forecastle, and at the first dawn of day a forest of strange masts was seen to leeward. I ran aft and informed the officer of the watch. The Captain was on deck in a moment, and ere it was well light the signals were flying through the fleet to bear up and form the order of sailing in two columns.

To Lieutenant Paul Nicolas of the *Belleisle*, the horizon appeared covered with ships:

The whole force of the enemy was discovered standing to the southward, distant about nine miles, between us and the coast near Trafalgar. I was awakened by the cheers of the crew and by their rushing up the hatchways to get a glimpse of the hostile fleet. The delight manifested exceeded anything I ever witnessed, surpassing even those gratulations when our native cliffs are descried after a long period of distant service.

Aboard the *Royal Sovereign*, Vice-Admiral Collingwood's servant

. . . entered the Admiral's cabin, about daylight, and found him already up and dressing. He asked me if I had seen the French fleet; and on my replying that I had not, he told me to look out at them, adding that, in a very short time, we should see a great deal more of them. I then observed a crowd of ships to leeward; but I could not help looking with still greater interest at the Admiral, who, during all this time, was shaving himself with a composure that quite astonished me.

Collingwood dressed with particular care that morning, wearing shoes and stockings for the battle instead of his normal leather boots. Later, seeing Lieutenant John Clavell in boots, he advised him to do the same. 'You had better put on silk stockings, as I have done. If one should get a shot in the leg, they would be so much more manageable for the surgeon.'

On the deck of the *Victory*, Nelson too was dressed in silk stockings, with his blue undress coat and four replica decorations on the left breast. Unusually, though, he had not put on his sword for the fight, but had left it behind in his cabin. Shortly before 6 a.m. he gave the order for the fleet to form two columns, preparatory to attacking the enemy. One column of thirteen ships was to be led by Collingwood aboard the *Royal Sovereign,* the other, of fourteen ships, by Nelson himself. He was in a good mood as he went up to the poop to watch the operation. He told Hardy, his flag-captain, that he would not be satisfied if they captured fewer than twenty of the enemy's capital ships before the day was out.

Nelson watched as his fleet formed itself into two columns, just under a mile apart, and turned east towards the French and Spanish. The wind was so light that it would be several hours before they reached them. At 6.40 a.m., he ordered his flag-lieutenant, John Pasco, to hoist the signal 'Prepare for battle.' A minute later, the flags had been run up and bosuns' mates all over the fleet were sounding the call on their pipes, summoning the crews to clear for action.

It was the order they had all been waiting for. Every man went at once to his allotted task. For the landsmen and others without specialist skills, the first job was to clear away the bulkheads, either securing them to the deckhead above or carrying them down to the hold. The next task was to remove the furniture from the officers' cabins, and the men's mess tables and benches. Much of it had been removed the night before, but the remainder was taken away now, either carried down to the hold or thrown overboard if there was no alternative. Everything else followed, that wasn't needed for the battle. In a few minutes, every deck on every ship had been stripped of unnecessary clutter, leaving a clear view from one end of the vessel to the other. All that remained were the guns, the equipment to serve them and whatever else was required for the fight that lay ahead.

The skilled men too went to their tasks. In the powder magazines below the waterline, gunners in leather slippers that struck no sparks checked their cartridge bags and prepared them for distribution to the young boys who would carry them up to the gun decks. The powder monkeys were sometimes as young as ten, assisted by women if there were any on the ship. Their job was dangerous because loose gunpowder could easily be ignited by a spark. The fire engines were primed and ready for action, and seamen were positioning leather fire buckets in the centre of every deck, supplemented by water casks at strategic intervals. Nearer the time, they would sluice the decks as well, making sure the woodwork was damp when the action started.

In the ships' cockpits, the surgeons laid out their instruments while their assistants cleared the tables, ready for the crude operations that would be performed when the wounded were brought in. The wounded would be left to lie on anchor cables covered with spare sails until their turn came. Without anaesthetics, those due for amputation would be held down by loblolly men while the operation was performed. Afterwards, their 'wings and limbs' would be thrown into the large wooden tubs now being hauled into place for the purpose.

In the carpenters' storerooms, the carpenters' mates took down their shot plugs – conical pieces of wood covered in oakum and tallow that would be used to plug cannon-holes in the ships' sides. Larger holes would be covered with sheets of lead and hide, nailed firmly into place until proper repairs could be made. It was the carpenters' job also to mend the ship's wheel and repair the tiller if it was smashed in action.

On the gun decks, the gun captains stood to their weapons and made sure the ammunition racks were full of shot. Extra rounds were brought up from below and stored in a thick coil of rope behind each gun. The cannon were fired by flintlocks, which would not be distributed until just before the action, but there was time now for the gunners to examine the rest of their equipment – sponge, rammer, handspikes, breeching – and satisfy themselves that all was in order.

On the main-deck, the ships' bosuns distributed axes and grappling irons and rehearsed their men in the procedure for repairing rigging in a hurry. French tactics were to shoot at a ship's masts to try to bring them down, so the bosuns sent their men aloft to reinforce the yards with extra chains, to prevent any spars from crashing to the deck. They hung splinter nets between the masts as well, because almost half the casualties in the coming action would be caused by flying wooden splinters.

Everyone understood the danger of infection from such wounds. It was for this reason that Admiral Collingwood had dressed with such care, putting on his cleanest clothes for the battle. Many of the ordinary sailors preferred to fight naked from the waist up, to reduce the risk of septicaemia from dirty clothing. 'Take off that shirt, my boy,' Nelson had advised a powder monkey on the *Victory*, 'or you will be in trouble later in the day.' The sailors were under no illusions about the dangers ahead. Second-Lieutenant Ellis, a Marine officer on the *Ajax*, was impressed by their thoroughness as they prepared for the fight:

I was sent below with orders, and was much struck with the preparations made by the bluejackets, the majority of whom were stripped to the waist; a handkerchief was tightly bound round their heads and over the ears, to deaden the noise of the cannon, many men being deaf for days after an action. The men were variously occupied; some were sharpening their cutlasses, others polishing the guns, as though an inspection were about to take place instead of a mortal combat, whilst three or four, as if in mere bravado, were dancing a hornpipe; but all seemed deeply anxious to come to close-quarters with the enemy. Occasionally they would look out of the ports, and speculate as to the various ships of the enemy, many of which had been on former occasions engaged by our vessels.

On the *Revenge*, William Robinson was struck by 'the different dispositions of the British sailor':

Some would be offering a guinea for a glass of grog, whilst others were making a sort of mutual verbal will, such as: 'If one of Johnnie

Crapeau's shots (a term given to the French) knocks my head off, you will take all my effects; and if you are killed and I am not, why I will have all yours'; and this was generally agreed on.

Aboard the *Tonnant*, Able Seaman John Cash found the mood less reflective:

Our good Captain called all hands and said: 'My lads, this will be a glorious day for us, and the groundwork of a speedy return to our homes for all.' He then ordered bread and cheese and butter and beer for every man at the guns. I was one of them, and, believe me, we ate and drank, and were as cheerful as ever we had been over a pot of beer.

On the *Minotaur*, Captain Charles Mansfield assembled every available man on the quarterdeck after they had cleared for action. He spoke earnestly to them about what lay ahead:

We are now in the sight of the enemy. I trust that this day, or tomorrow, will prove the most glorious our country ever saw.
　　I shall say nothing to you of courage: our country never produced a coward . . . I have only to recommend silence and a strict attention to the orders of your officers. Be careful to take good aim, for it is to no purpose to throw shot away. You will now, every man, repair to your respective stations, and depend, I will bring the ship into action as soon as possible. God save the King!

On the *Bellerophon*, Captain Cooke took his second-in-command Lieutenant Cumby aside after breakfast and showed him the Nelson memorandum, the admiral's strategy for the battle. Cooke wanted Cumby to see it in case he was 'bowl'd out' during the fighting and Cumby had to take command. But Cumby thought someone else should see it too:

I observed that it was very possible that the same shot which disposed of him might have an equally tranquilizing effect upon me

and under that idea I submitted to him the expediency of the Master
(as being the only officer who in such case would remain on the
Quarter deck) being also apprised of the Admiral's instructions.

Cooke took the point and showed the memorandum to Ship's Master
Edward Overton as well.

All the ships prepared for action in their different ways – even the little
ones, the repeating frigates and attendant vessels whose function was to
carry the admiral's signals rather than attack the enemy. Almost the
smallest of all was the *Pickle*, only fifty-six feet from stem to stern at the
waterline. Midshipman Hercules Robinson had a good view of her from
the deck of the *Euryalus*:

> Even the saucy little schooner *Pickle* – a tiny thing, too small except
> to make herself useful to Blackwood's frigates – tried to look fierce
> and threatening, with a confident assumption ridiculous to witness.
> She took post between the stately lines of the towering three- and
> two-deckers, cleared for action fore and aft in ludicrous imitation of
> them, with her small boarding-nettings triced up, and her four-
> pounder popguns – about as large and formidable as two pairs of
> jack-boots – double-shotted and run out.

A few miles away, similar preparations were taking place among the
French and Spanish. Whatever doubts there may have been about their
seamanship, there were none as to their courage. They too were eagerly
preparing for the fight, now that it could not be avoided.

They first spotted the British at 6.30 a.m. Thirty minutes later, Villeneuve
gave the order to clear for action. Once again, the drummers on the French
ships beat the *Generale* and the crews hurried to their tasks. Much noisier
than the British, the French shouted and cheered as they went, crying 'Vive
l'Empereur' and 'Vive le Commandant.' They were as keen as Villeneuve to
redeem themselves after the embarrassment of Calder's action. Now was
their chance, with the British fleet in plain view, forming up against them.

Peering at the British through his telescope, Villeneuve tried to read
Lord Nelson's mind.

The enemy's fleet, which was counted as twenty-seven ships of the line, seemed to be heading en masse for my rear squadron; with the double object, apparently, of engaging it with greatly superior force and cutting our whole fleet off from Cadiz. I therefore signalled the fleet to turn about and form line of battle in reverse order. My chief aim was to prevent the rear squadron from being overpowered by the enemy.

It was a necessary gamble. All night long, the French and Spanish had been hurrying southwards, desperate to get past Gibraltar and escape into the Mediterranean. But the Mediterranean was beyond their grasp in the faint breeze. The British would almost certainly cut them off before they passed Gibraltar. Villeneuve knew they could not afford to be cut off from Cadiz as well. They needed the port for their crippled ships if there was going to be a battle.

So he gave the order to turn round and head north again. Cadiz was just twenty-five miles away, the nearest haven for his fleet. It was not an easy decision to take, with the British so close, but Villeneuve could see no realistic alternative. The nearer his fleet was to Cadiz, if battle was unavoidable, the safer he would feel.

Slowly, awkwardly, the forty ships of the combined fleet acknowledged Villeneuve's signal and began to turn about. More than one captain had grave misgivings, but it was too late to argue now. The ships did what they were told and struggled to haul round, back the way they had come. It was 8 a.m. when Villeneuve gave the command, but another two hours before they had managed to complete the manoeuvre, and then only approximately. As they faced towards the north again, the ships were still not in line, although the order of battle had been completely reversed. Vessels that had been in the rear of the fleet, following everyone else, now found themselves in the lead. The advance squadron, headed by Admiral Gravina, was now trailing behind. Villeneuve himself remained in the middle, observing operations from the poop of the *Bucentaure*.

Captain Jean Lucas was doing his best to keep up with the others:

In this new order, the *Redoutable*'s place was third ship astern of the flagship *Bucentaure*. I at once made every effort to take station in the wake of the flagship, leaving room between her and myself for the two in front of me. One ship was not very far out of line, but the other showed no sign of trying to get into position. That ship was some way to leeward of the line now beginning to form ahead of the admiral.

Elsewhere the French and Spanish were bunched side by side, two or three ships together, clumsily attempting to fall in behind each other. The entire fleet was sailing now in a vast crescent formation rather than a straight line. It was all too much for Commodore Cosma de Churruca, watching in despair from what was now the rear of the line. 'The fleet is doomed,' he told his second-in-command. 'The French admiral does not understand his business. He has compromised us all.'

The enemy's movements were watched closely by Lord Nelson. He had guessed that Villeneuve would turn back for Cadiz, but was not happy about it. The coastal waters between Cape Trafalgar and Cadiz were shallow and treacherous, a death trap for ships disabled in battle, particularly with a heavy swell presaging a storm in the west. Nelson would have much preferred to fight the battle off Gibraltar, the only port available to the British.

But the choice was not his to make. Trafalgar it would be, although not for some time yet. The wind was still light and the enemy several miles away. On the poop of the *Victory*, Nelson spent some time chatting to Henry Blackwood, captain of the *Euryalus*, who had come aboard with the other frigate captains in case Nelson had any last-minute orders for the fleet that couldn't be sent by signal. Then he left them and went down to his cabin to spend some time alone before the battle.

Nelson's chairs had already been cleared away for action, as had the portrait of Lady Hamilton that hung in his cabin ('Take care of my Guardian Angel,' he had told the men removing it). But his writing table remained. Kneeling down, Nelson made a note of the enemy fleet's movements in his diary, then added a short prayer of his own composition:

May the great GOD whom I worship grant to my Country, and for the benefit of Europe in general, a great and glorious Victory, and may no misconduct in any one tarnish it, and may humanity after Victory be the predominant feature in the British Fleet! For myself individually, I commit my life to Him who made me, and may His blessing alight on my endeavours for serving my Country faithfully! To Him I resign myself, and the just cause which is entrusted to me to defend. Amen, Amen, Amen.

Nelson was still on his knees when Lieutenant John Pasco arrived with a message. Pasco was the senior lieutenant on the *Victory*, but had been ordered to act as signals officer for the battle, a job normally allocated to someone more junior. The appointment would affect his chances of promotion, so he had been waiting for a chance to complain about it to Nelson. But now was clearly not a good time:

On entering the cabin, I discovered his Lordship on his knees writing. He was then penning that beautiful prayer. I waited until he rose and communicated what I had to report, but could not at such a moment disturb his mind with any grievances of mine.

Pasco left again and Nelson took a sheet of paper to add a codicil to his will. He was worried about Emma and his daughter – he would not be able to provide for them if he was killed in the battle. Years earlier, Emma had done good work in Naples as the British ambassador's wife, obtaining supplies for Nelson's fleet in 1798 and intercepting a letter giving advance warning of Spain's intention to declare war. Nelson wanted to arrange a government pension for her.

Could I have rewarded these services I would not now call upon my Country; but as that has not been in my power, I leave Emma Lady Hamilton, therefore, a Legacy to my King and Country, that they will give her an ample provision to maintain her rank in life. I also leave to the beneficence of my Country my adopted daughter, Horatia Nelson Thompson; and I desire she will use in future the name of Nelson only. These are the only favours I ask of my King and Country at this moment when I am going to fight their Battle. May God bless my King and Country, and all those I hold dear. My relations it is needless to mention; they will of course be amply provided for.

As soon as he had completed the codicil – actually little more than an appeal for help – Nelson called for Captains Hardy and Blackwood to witness his signature. Then he returned to the main-deck. It was time for the crew to take up their battle stations. At Hardy's order, the drummer beat to quarters and the bosun's pipe shrilled again. Seconds later, men all over the *Victory* were running to their posts, some to other tasks but the vast majority to man the ship's 104 guns and carronades. There were 821 men aboard the *Victory* and well over 600 of them served the guns. Even so, the crews were short-handed, alternately operating the cannon on both sides of the ship because there weren't enough people to go round.

Once at their guns, the men went automatically to work, preparing the weapons for action. Two men removed the tampion plugging each cannon's mouth while others hauled on ropes to open the port lids and let some daylight into the ship. The powder monkey handed a cartridge to the loader to shove down the gun barrel. The sponger rammed it home and followed it with the shot. Then the guns were run out until their muzzles protruded through the ports. The gun captains primed them with powder and fuse, before standing back smartly and reporting to the officer that they were ready to fire.

Similar preparations were taking place all over the ship. In the galley, the fire in the great iron stove was doused, and would not be relit until after the battle. At the gunners' store, a queue of sailors waited to collect their small arms – pistols, pikes, cutlasses, axes, muskets – for close combat with the enemy. On the quarterdeck, red-coated Marines formed up with bayonets and muskets. At the fore and aft hatches, other Marines were posted as sentries, standing guard over the hatches to make sure no one used them without authorisation. Once the crew were at their posts, only officers, midshipmen and powder monkeys could use the hatches. Anyone else would be regarded as a deserter, and might be shot.

Nelson toured the ship, rallying the men as they prepared for action. He spoke to each gun deck in turn, urging them not to waste a single round. 'My noble lads,' he told them, 'this will be a glorious day for England, whoever lives to see it. I shan't be satisfied with twelve ships this day, as I took at the Nile.' At one gunport, he found an Irishman carving a notch on a gun carriage, next to a row of other notches, each representing a British victory. The Irishman explained that he was carving the latest one now, in case he was killed in the battle. 'You'll make notches enough in the enemy's ships,' Nelson assured him.

On deck again, he was an arresting sight in an admiral's hat, with four glittering orders on his left breast. The *Victory* would be the first ship of the column to reach the enemy line. It was obvious to his officers that Nelson would be a prime target for the enemy's sharpshooters. Blackwood had already implored him to transfer his flag to the *Euryalus* and direct the action more safely from there, but Nelson would have none of it. His place was on the *Victory*, setting a good example. Blackwood had had better luck persuading him that the *Téméraire*, *Neptune* and *Leviathan* should take the lead instead, allowing Nelson a chance to stand back and observe the developing battle. The *Téméraire* had been ordered to go ahead if she could, and was now sailing alongside the *Victory*, doing her best to push in front. Nelson's response had been to cram all sail on the *Victory* to prevent any other ship from taking the lead.

The column was aiming for the head of the enemy line. Nearly a mile to the south, Collingwood's column was sailing parallel and slightly in front. Nelson was approaching the enemy at right angles, but Collingwood was advancing obliquely into the curve of the crescent. Both columns were advancing at the magnificent speed of one and a half miles per hour. There were 17,000 people aboard the British fleet, including hundreds of young boys and an unknown number of women. All of them were ready for what they had to do, and all were looking to Nelson for direction. Their lives were in his hands, their faith in him absolute. He was the man, if anybody was, to lead them to victory.

It was just after 11.30 a.m. Ahead of them, the French and Spanish would soon be within range. The sun was shining and the weather was calm. On many ships a band was playing. The tunes were the familiar, reassuring ones of old England – 'God Save the King', 'Hearts of Oak', 'Britons, Strike Home'. But there was one tune above all others that everyone recognised as they heard it, either aboard their own ship or from others across the water. Very few of the men could remember the words, but all of them were achingly familiar with the chorus:

Rule, Britannia; Britannia rule the waves!
Britons never, never, never shall be slaves!

The fleet sailed on. The enemy were so close now that their cannon could clearly be seen above the waterline, like rows of iron teeth. In a few minutes, the battle would begin and they would all be fighting for their lives. There was just time for Nelson to send one last message before the holocaust engulfed them all. Turning to Henry Blackwood, he said, 'I'll now amuse the fleet with a signal.' Then he looked round the poop for Lieutenant Pasco, his reluctant signals officer.

CHAPTER 33

ENGLAND EXPECTS

By Pasco's reckoning, it was 11.45 a.m. when Nelson spoke to him, although others put it earlier.

> His Lordship came to me on the poop, and about a quarter to noon said, 'Mr Pasco, I want to say to the fleet, "ENGLAND CONFIDES THAT EVERY MAN WILL DO HIS DUTY." You must be quick, for I have one more to add, which is for close action.'
>
> I replied, 'If your Lordship will permit me to substitute *expects* for *confides*, the signal will sooner be completed, because the word *expects* is in the Signal Book, and *confides* must be spelt.' His Lordship replied in haste, and in seeming satisfaction, 'That will do, Pasco: make it directly.'

Lieutenant George Brown, who was with Pasco, remembered it slightly differently:

> I was on the poop and quarter-deck whilst preparations for the fight were going on, and saw Lord Nelson, Captain Blackwood, and some other Captains of the frigates, in earnest conversation together, and a slip of paper in the hand of the former (which Captain Blackwood had looked at), yet I have no recollection that I ever saw it pass through other hands till it was given to Pasco, who, after referring to the telegraph signal book, took it back to his Lordship, and it was then that, I believe, the substitution of the words took place. I think

(though not sure), the substitution was 'expects' for the word 'confides', the latter word not being in the telegraph book, and I think the word 'England' had been previously substituted for 'Nelson' for the same reason, at the suggestion of Captain Blackwood.

Whatever the truth, it still took thirty-one flags to spell out the message. They were hoisted by John Roome, a former barge hand who had been press-ganged in 1803. Without seagoing skills, he had been classed as a landsman on joining the *Victory*, but had been promoted to signaller because of his smartness and intelligence. Roome hauled the flags up as soon as he was told, but the wind was so light that they hung limply from the yardarm and were difficult for the rest of the fleet to read. It was some time before the other ships succeeded in deciphering Nelson's message.

Initial reaction was mixed, when at length they understood it. 'What *is* Nelson signalling about?' demanded Collingwood. 'We all know what we have to do.'

The *Ajax* shared his view, as Second Lieutenant Ellis discovered when he read out Nelson's words to the men on the main-deck.

I delivered with becoming dignity the sentence, rather anticipating that the effect on the men would be to awe them by its grandeur. Jack, however, did not appreciate it, for there were murmurs from some, whilst others in an audible whisper murmured, 'Do our duty! Of course we'll do our duty! I've always done mine, haven't you? Let us come alongside of 'em, and we'll soon show whether we'll do our duty.' Still, the men cheered vociferously – more, I believe, from love and admiration of their Admiral and leader than from a full appreciation of this well-known signal.

On the *Euryalus*, they took little notice of the message at all, beyond transmitting it to other ships and recording it in the log. Reading about it in the papers later, Midshipman Hercules Robinson was puzzled to learn that the message had been received with rapture throughout the fleet. 'Why, it was noted in the signal-book and in the log, and that was all about it in our ship till we heard of our alleged transports on our return to England.'

But most ships reacted more positively. The *Britannia*, *Neptune*, *Belleisle*, *Polyphemus* and *Dreadnought* all gave three hearty cheers, outdoing each other from ship to ship. The men of the *Prince* cheered as well, as did the crew of the *Bellerophon*, chalking 'Victory or Death!' on their guns for good measure. On the *Victory* herself, as Surgeon William Beatty remembered, they were particularly enthusiastic:

> It is impossible adequately to describe by any language the lively emotions excited in the crew of the *Victory* when this propitious communication was made known to them: confidence and resolution were strongly portrayed in the countenance of all, and the sentiment generally expressed to each other was that they would prove to their Country that day how well British Seamen could 'do their duty' when led to battle by their revered Admiral.

What the seventy-one foreigners aboard the *Victory* made of it, Beatty did not record. Hans Yaule, for instance, was Swiss, press-ganged from a merchant ship after incautiously stepping ashore at the Thames. Men like Yaule had little personal interest in the outcome of a battle between the English and the French, beyond hoping they would still be alive to see it. Nor had Lamberd Myers from Hamburg or Dominick Dubine from Italy or Samuel Lovitt from America, all similarly forced into the Royal Navy against their will. For them, the approaching battle was simply part of a nightmare that had begun when the press gang laid hold of them, a nightmare that showed no sign of coming to an end. If they fought for a British victory, it was in the hope of receiving their discharge and being released from bondage, rather than any great love for England.

Others had even more mixed feelings. 'John Packet' was one of four Frenchmen aboard the *Victory* and at forty-seven one of the older members of the crew. Originally from Le Havre, he had been taken by the press gang and was now an able seaman, about to bear arms against his own people. So too were Jean Baptish and Jean Dupuis of Nantes – Dupuis had actually volunteered for the Royal Navy, though not necessarily to fight his fellow countrymen.

From Philadelphia, Richard Collins had been pressed into fighting for the British, but William Thompson had taken the king's bounty and was a volunteer. Ironically, Collins had been promoted to able seaman while Thompson, seven years his senior, was still only an ordinary seaman. From New York, William Sweet too was an ordinary seaman. Of the twenty-two Americans aboard the *Victory*, two were classed as landsmen and the rest as able or ordinary seamen, apart from Tom Bailey, who enjoyed the rank of gunner's mate.

From Canada, John Graham and master's mate Sam Spencer. From India, John Thomas and John Callaghan (it was the navy's habit to anglicise unpronounceable names). From Africa, George Ryan, and from the West Indies, John Summers, John François, George Ogilvie and Jonathan Hardy. From Norway, Malta, Portugal and Holland, from Brazil, Sweden, Sicily and Denmark, all sorts and conditions of men lay aboard the *Victory*, preparing for battle and wondering what on earth they had got themselves into. This wasn't their fight. They had no quarrel with the French. Why, they must have asked themselves, was this happening to them?

On the other side, the British sailors in the French and Spanish fleets viewed the approaching battle with equally mixed feelings. Some had been pressed into enemy service, but quite a few were deserters from the Royal Navy, as out of place in the combined fleet as the French and Americans were in Nelson's. Villeneuve alone had eighteen Royal Navy deserters aboard his ship, who had fled from Gibraltar and ended up in Cadiz. They had been kept together on the *Bucentaure* and served two of the guns on the lower deck. They could hardly have been looking forward to the fight. If they weren't killed outright, they stood a good chance of being taken prisoner by their own countrymen. They would be shown no mercy if they were captured. It would be the yardarm for them, with no chance of reprieve.

There were also plenty of Irish on the enemy side, who loathed the English for reasons of their own. Chief among them was Captain Henry Macdonnell, who commanded the 100-gun *Rayo*. He had left Ireland at sixteen to join the European coalition against the British during the American war. He had served in the Regimiento de Hibernia at the siege of

Gibraltar, later transferring to the Spanish navy. Macdonnell was officially retired, but had returned to service because the Spanish were desperately short of officers. He was the most senior of the Irish in the Spanish fleet, all of them fighting for the same ideal as the English – the right of small islands to run their own affairs without interference from a bullying neighbour.

The Irish remembered particularly the words of Robert Emmet, executed in 1803 for leading a rebellion against British rule. 'Let no man write my epitaph,' he had announced at his trial. 'When my country takes her place among the nations of the earth, then, and not till then, let my epitaph be written.' Emmet had been publicly beheaded next day, his blood lapped up by dogs. It was for his epitaph that the Irish in the Spanish fleet were preparing now to fight the English.

The fight would not be long delayed. From his position at the very rear of the line, Commodore Churruca surveyed the oncoming British with dismay. They were advancing exactly as Nelson had planned, two columns aiming straight for the enemy to cut their fleet into three sections, each of which could then be destroyed piecemeal, denied support from the other two. It was a very daring manoeuvre, only attempted because the British understood the enemy's weaknesses and had full confidence in their own ships and men. It would be a disaster for the French and Spanish if it was allowed to succeed.

To Churruca, the solution was obvious. The leading ten ships of the combined fleet were already clear of the British, pressing on towards Cadiz. Villeneuve should long ago have ordered them to wear round, returning under full sail to attack the British in the flank. He should have sent the signal hours ago. But no signal had been forthcoming.

'The French admiral does not, will not, grasp it,' complained Churruca. 'He has only to act boldly, only to order the van ships to wear round at once and double on the rear squadron. That will place the enemy themselves between two fires.'

In gloom and rage, muttering *'Perdidos'* to himself, Churruca summoned his crew on deck for a pep talk before the battle. He held a short service first, the men baring their heads while the padre gave them absolution. Then Churruca addressed them from the quarterdeck:

My sons, in the name of the God of Battles I promise eternal happiness to all those who fall today doing their duty. On the other hand, if I see any man shirking I will have him shot on the spot. If the scoundrel escapes my eye, or that of the gallant officers I have the honour to command, be assured of this, that bitter remorse will dog the wretch for the rest of his days, for so long as he crawls through whatever remains of his miserable and dishonoured existence.

Churruca concluded by calling three cheers for the king.

Among the French, there was less talk of cowardice as the British approached, more of patriotism. The Spanish ships each had a large wooden cross hanging over the taffrail, but the French put more faith in the Imperial eagles given to every ship after Napoleon's coronation. On the *Bucentaure*, the eagle was in the charge of two midshipmen who were to guard it throughout the battle. Villeneuve paraded it around the deck first, followed by his officers, as Captain Jean Magendie remembered:

It is impossible to display greater enthusiasm and eagerness for the fray than was shown and evinced by all the officers, sailors and soldiers of the *Bucentaure*, each one of us putting our hands between the Admiral's and renewing our oath upon the Eagle entrusted to us by the Emperor, to fight to the last gasp; and shouts of '*Vive l'Empereur, vive l'Amiral Villeneuve*' were raised once more.

The men then returned to their posts as the British bore down. The eagle was given a place of honour at the foot of the mainmast.

The battle was just a few minutes away now. Among the British, telescopes were out on every ship, scanning the enemy line for a sight of Villeneuve's flag. It was important to identify the enemy's command vessel, but there was nothing in the anonymous array of French and Spanish ships to indicate which one was Villeneuve's. He would raise his flag in due course, but he hadn't done so yet. Observing the four-deck *Santissima Trinidad* in the middle of the line, Nelson guessed that the French admiral would be in one of the three ships sailing immediately astern. He gave the order to steer that way, using the *Santissima*'s bow as an aiming marker.

It was a race now to see which of the two British columns would reach the enemy first. At the moment, it was looking like Collingwood, well ahead of the rest in the *Royal Sovereign*. But there were ships in both columns that sailed badly, forcing the leaders to hold back. Some were leaky, others long overdue for a refit. Unlike the new ships just out from England, their hulls were encrusted with seaweed and barnacles, severely reducing their speed through the water. Even with studding sails out – extensions to the yards to catch every last breath of wind – they were making slower progress than they wished.

But they were still advancing steadily, so close to the enemy now that the shooting could not long be delayed. Aboard the *Orion*, Captain Codrington finished the turkey leg he had been eating and turned his full attention towards the French. On the *Bellerophon*, Captain Cooke, Lieutenant Cumby and the other officers completed the lunch of cold meat they had been enjoying on the rudder head – their tables and chairs had been cleared away – and did the same. On the *Victory*, the men swallowed the last of the raw pork that had been issued to them and took a final swig of wine, bracing themselves for the fight. Aboard the *Conqueror*, Captain Israel Pellew sent his red-coated Marines below, to keep them out of harm's way until they were needed. One or two newly arrived ships were even completing the painting of the lower masts that Nelson had ordered long ago, hurriedly whitewashing them to distinguish them from the black-hooped masts of the enemy.

Ahead, the race to reach the enemy was going to be won by Collingwood's ship. All eyes were on the *Royal Sovereign* as she pushed forward alone. British, French and Spanish alike, no one could tear their eyes away. Nearer the enemy line and nearer, almost within range now, almost within killing distance, the *Royal Sovereign* billowed on – while deep in her belly at least one young man tensed miserably, wishing he was back on the farm in Hampshire, safely at home with his plough.

It was getting on for noon now, just a few minutes short of the hour. The clock had still not reached 12 by most accounts when a sudden ripple of flashes twinkled prettily from the French ship *Fougueux*. It was followed moments later by a corresponding roll of thunder across the water. The British watched fascinated as the sea around the *Royal Sovereign* suddenly erupted into fountains of spray and spume. The first shots had been fired from the enemy line. The Battle of Trafalgar had begun.

CHAPTER 34

———•◆•———

BATTLE IS JOINED

Undaunted, the *Royal Sovereign* pressed on, oblivious to the French broadside, oblivious to anything except the urge to get in among the enemy and break their line as soon as possible. Fresh out from England, her copper bottom free of barnacles, she sliced through the water 'like a frigate', speeding forward as quickly as the wind would allow. The *Sovereign* was at her most vulnerable now, within range of the enemy guns, yet unable to return fire while sailing directly towards them. She was several hundred yards ahead of the next British ship, attacking the combined fleet all on her own. It was do or die for the *Royal Sovereign*, steering a solitary course while the rest of Collingwood's column struggled to catch up.

In the other column, Admirals Nelson and Northesk followed Collingwood's example and raised their flags immediately the shooting started. So did the French and Spanish admirals, with the exception of Villeneuve, whose flag appears to have become tangled up. They all watched intently as the *Royal Sovereign* continued towards the enemy, aiming for the gap between the *Santa Ana* and the *Fougueux*. Several ships were firing at her, beginning to score hits. The *Sovereign* pushed on regardless, her men lying flat on the deck as shot tore through the rigging. By some accounts, she was nearly a mile ahead of the next British ship as she reached the enemy line, a feat without parallel in naval history.

'Steer straight for the Frenchman and take his bowsprit,' was Collingwood's only command as the gap closed. He was determined to break the enemy line or die in the attempt.

The *Fougueux* had been moving forward to close the gap between herself and the *Santa Ana*, but changed her mind as the *Royal Sovereign* bore down. Seeing that the British intended to smash through regardless, she backed her sails at the last minute to avoid a collision. The *Royal Sovereign* carried straight on and just squeezed through, almost shaving the *Santa Ana*'s stern in the process. It was the moment the *Royal Sovereign*'s gunners had been waiting for.

Each gun fired in turn, straight into the unprotected stern of the *Santa Ana*, raking the length of the Spanish ship from a distance of only a few yards. The guns were double- or treble-shotted, primed for maximum damage at close range. The havoc they wrought was devastating. When the last gun had fired and the *Royal Sovereign* was safely through the enemy line, the *Santa Ana*'s stern had been shattered and scores of her men lay dead or wounded. Fourteen of her guns had been disabled as well, with just one broadside.

'See how that noble fellow Collingwood carries his ship into action!' observed Nelson delightedly from the other column.

'What would Nelson give to be here!' Collingwood told his flag-captain, equally delightedly.

But they hadn't finished yet. Turning hard aport, the *Royal Sovereign* quickly drew alongside the *Santa Ana*, so close that their yardarms touched across the water. The *Sovereign*'s gunners hurriedly reloaded while the *Santa Ana*'s struggled across to the other side of their ship, pushing through a mass of torn and mangled bodies to reinforce the men on the starboard guns. It was a race to see which ship could fire first. With almost fifty guns already loaded and still working on the starboard side, the Spanish won.

The *Royal Sovereign* reeled under the impact, heeling 'two strakes out of the water' as the shots thudded home. The Spanish had been badly hurt, but they were nowhere near beaten. There was still plenty of fight left in them.

Other ships were coming to their rescue. The *Fougueux*, *Indomptable*, *San Leandro* and *San Justo* all closed in on the *Royal Sovereign*, subjecting her to a withering fire from different directions. The crossfire was so heavy that French and Spanish cannon balls smacked into each other above the

British sailors' heads. British ships were approaching too, peering anxiously into the smoke to see if Collingwood's flag was still flying among so many hostile ships.

Through it all, Collingwood remained unperturbed, 'pacing up and down on the poop munching an apple' as shots flew all around. His ship was a mess now, with halyards dropping away and a top-gallant studding-sail hanging down over the gangway hammocks. Collingwood called Lieutenant Clavell to help him clear it out of the way. The two men carefully rolled the sail up and stowed it in one of the ship's boats. Practical as ever, Collingwood told Clavell they would need the sail some other day. He was a reassuring presence in a battle, soothing everyone around him with his unruffled manner as the fighting raged.

'Dear old Cuddie,' one midshipman recalled, 'walking the break of the poop, with his little triangular gold-laced cocked hat, tights, silk stockings, and buckles, musing over the progress of the fight and munching an apple.'

His servant Smith was impressed by his calmness:

The Admiral spoke to me about the middle of the action, and again for five minutes immediately after its close; and on neither occasion could I observe the slightest change from his ordinary manner . . . I wondered how a person whose mind was occupied by such a variety of most important concerns could, with the utmost ease and equanimity, enquire kindly after my welfare, and talk of common matters as if nothing of any consequence were taking place.

Collingwood had plenty to think about. The *Royal Sovereign* was muzzle to muzzle with the *Santa Ana*, the two ships firing straight into each other's portholes, desperate to put each other out of action. Overexposed on the poop, Collingwood dropped down to the quarterdeck to watch the fighting. He was a gunnery expert who had trained the crew of his previous ship to fire three broadsides in three and a half minutes – an achievement rarely emulated, even in the Royal Navy. Ignoring the enemy fire, he strode down the line of guns, looking along every one to make sure it was properly aimed, then stood beside a black seaman as he pumped ten rounds directly into the *Santa Ana*.

The Spanish were hard pressed, but still fighting. The *Fougueux* was coming to their aid, so close to the *Royal Sovereign* at one point that the ships almost touched. There was little wind to carry the smoke away, so they could hardly see each other in the confusion. It was a question now of holding their nerve and keeping up the pressure until somebody gave in and struck their colours. Collingwood's flag-captain had already shaken the admiral's hand and congratulated him on defeating the *Santa Ana*, but he had been premature. A few Spaniards had taken refuge on the outside of the *Santa Ana*, the side furthest away from Collingwood's guns, but most were still fighting. With the *Royal Sovereign* surrounded by hostile ships, anything could happen yet.

Almost a mile to the north, the *Victory* was still short of the enemy line, only just coming into range. The enemy ships in her path included the *Santissima Trinidad*, the *Redoutable* and the *Bucentaure*, Villeneuve's flagship. To Midshipman Badcock, watching from two ships behind the *Victory*, the scene was one he would never forget.

> It was a beautiful sight when their line was completed, their broadsides turned towards us, showing their iron teeth, and now and then trying the range of a shot to ascertain the distance, that they might, the moment we came within point blank (about 600 yards), open their fire upon our van ships – no doubt with the hope of dismasting some of our leading vessels before they could close and break their line.
>
> Some of the enemy's ships were painted like ourselves – with double yellow sides, some with a broad single red or yellow streak, others all black, and the noble *Santissima Trinidad* with four distinct lines of red, with a white ribbon between them, made her seem to be a superb man-of-war, which indeed she was.

Badcock's ship had already tried to push ahead of the *Victory* and lead the dash towards the enemy line, only to be pulled up short by the admiral. 'Poor Lord Nelson himself hailed us from the stern-walk of the *Victory* and said, "*Neptune*, take in your stun'sls and drop astern; I shall break the line myself.'" The *Téméraire* was still attempting to overtake the *Victory*, as ordered, but Nelson would not allow it. As the *Téméraire* moved up, only a few yards away across the water, Nelson raised his speaking trumpet and hailed the *Téméraire*'s captain. 'I'll thank you, Captain Harvey, to keep in your proper station, which is *astern* of the *Victory*.' Eliab Harvey fell back reluctantly, leaving Nelson's ship in the lead as they continued towards the enemy.

The admiral's starry appearance was still worrying his officers. If he wouldn't remove his decorations (actually just sequin facsimiles), then at the very least he should cover them with a handkerchief to make himself less conspicuous. William Beatty, the ship's surgeon, wanted to tell him so, but was advised against it by Nelson's secretary, John Scott. 'Take care, Doctor, what you are about. I would not be the man to mention such a matter to him.' The surgeon persisted nevertheless, waiting around the quarterdeck for an opportunity to make his daily sick report to Nelson and urge him at the same time to cover his decorations. But Beatty was ordered below when the *Royal Sovereign* came under fire and never got a chance to talk to Nelson.

Twenty minutes after the *Sovereign* went into action, the first shot was fired at the *Victory*. It came from the *Héros* and fell short. The *Victory* was still about 1,000 yards from the enemy, not yet in proper range. The French waited a couple of minutes and fired again. That shot fell alongside. A third went over the ship, as did the next two or three. At length, one tore a hole through the *Victory*'s main top-gallant sail, the first visible proof to the enemy that they were on target. For a minute or two nothing happened. Then seven or eight French and Spanish ships opened up together, all firing at the *Victory* in unison. Their purpose was to dismast the British flagship and put her out of action before she came anywhere near their line.

It could not have happened at a worse moment for the *Victory*. The wind had dropped away to nothing, leaving the ship to be carried forward by the swell alone. She was helpless on the ocean, a sitting target for her opponents. All she could do was proceed at a snail's pace, taking hits all over the ship and praying that none of them would disable her before she reached the battle line. It was not an enviable position to be in. More than one officer in Nelson's column was secretly relieved that it was the *Victory* bearing the brunt of the onslaught and not his own vessel. On the *Britannia*, three ships behind, Admiral Lord Northesk openly ordered his flag-captain to reduce sail as they approached the enemy and was later held to have 'behaved notoriously ill in the Trafalgar action'. At the rear of both columns, other ships also appeared in no great hurry to join the action.

On the *Victory*, at least two of the frigate captains were still aboard, waiting in case Nelson had any final orders for the fleet. When the first shots whistled overhead, he summoned Prowse of the *Sirius* and Blackwood of the *Euryalus* and told them to instruct the other captains in his column to get into the action any way they could if his own plan proved impractical. Prowse and Blackwood then dispersed to their own ships, Prowse stopping on the way to say goodbye to his nephew Charles Adair, captain of the *Victory*'s Marines.

Henry Blackwood shook Nelson's hand before going over the side. 'I trust, my Lord, that on my return to the *Victory*, which will be as soon as possible, I shall find your Lordship well, and in possession of twenty prizes.'

'God bless you, Blackwood.' Nelson was full of foreboding. 'I shall never speak to you again.'

Blackwood pulled away from the *Victory* and was rowed back to his own ship. Nelson remained on the quarterdeck, enduring the enemy's fire as the *Victory* inched forward. With almost 200 guns trained on her, it was only a matter of time before disaster struck. Six hundred yards short of the enemy line, the *Victory*'s mizen topmast was shot away. A few yards further on, her wheel was smashed as well, blown to pieces by a lucky shot. Her foremast was riddled and her foresail collapsed in tatters across the fo'c'sle. Other sails were pockmarked with holes. But still the *Victory* pressed on, steered now by an emergency arrangement of rope and tackle, forty sailors hauling on the tiller in response to commands shouted down from above. Although under fire herself, she had yet to return fire. Her gunners were huddled below, grimly waiting for their moment. It would come, but it hadn't come yet.

On deck, Nelson's secretary John Scott was talking to Captain Hardy when a cannon ball spun him round and laid him dead at Hardy's feet.

Captain Adair of the Marines and a seaman hurried to remove the corpse. 'Is that poor Scott that is gone?' asked Nelson. Adair nodded. 'Poor fellow,' said Nelson, as they threw him overboard.

He and Hardy were walking on the quarterdeck when a single shot killed eight Marines on the poop. Nelson promptly told Adair to disperse the rest around the ship. Another Marine lost an arm and an Irish able seaman was scalped by a splinter. Other splinters ricocheted between Nelson and Hardy, bruising Hardy's foot and tearing the buckle from his shoe. Both men stopped and examined each other all over, wondering which of them was hurt. 'This is too warm work to last long,' Nelson told Hardy. He added that in all his career he had never seen such 'cool courage' as the men of the *Victory* were displaying that day.

Already twenty of them were dead and another thirty wounded. The remainder were still at their posts, holding steady as the *Victory* neared the enemy line. The French and Spanish were packed so tightly that it would be impossible to break right through them. They would have to go alongside one of the enemy ships first. Captain Hardy said as much to Nelson.

'I cannot help it.' Nelson shrugged. 'It does not signify which we run on board of. Go on board which you please. Take your choice.'

The *Santissima Trinidad* was the preferred target, but the gap between her and the *Bucentaure*, immediately astern, was too narrow for the *Victory* to force a passage. Hardy decided to go for the *Bucentaure*'s stern instead, punching a hole between her and the bow of the *Redoutable*, next in the enemy line. He gave the order and heard it shouted down to the gun deck, where the sailors hauled on the tiller. The *Victory* swung round and steered for the *Bucentaure*, with the rest of the British column following closely behind.

From the *Redoutable*'s poop, Captain Jean Lucas had guessed what was about to happen and was already moving up to close the remaining gap between his own ship and the *Bucentaure*. If the British were going to attack the *Bucentaure*, Lucas intended to be there too. At all costs, he was determined to protect Villeneuve's ship from capture and see to it that the admiral's flag was not taken by the British.

The *Redoutable* moved up so close that her bowsprit bumped against the *Bucentaure's* taffrail several times. But Lucas was unabashed. A remarkable little man, only four foot nine, he was full of enthusiasm for the fight.

I laid the *Redoutable's* bowsprit against the *Bucentaure's* stern, fully resolved to sacrifice my ship in defence of the admiral's flag. I told my officers and men, who greeted my decision with cries of '*Vive l'Empereur! Vive l'Amiral! Vive le Commandant!*' repeated a thousand times.

Preceded by the drums and fifes, I paraded at the head of my officers round the decks. Everywhere I found gallant lads burning with impatience to get at the enemy, many of them saying to me, 'Captain, don't forget to board them!'

Lucas was a highly professional officer who had spent months training his crew for this moment. As the *Victory* loomed towards them, he sent some of his best men into the rigging, armed with muskets, bayonets and grenades to rain down destruction on to the enemy. Others were equipped with pistols, cutlasses and grappling irons, ready to board the *Victory* as soon as they came alongside. After endless weeks of sword drill and dummy grenade throwing, they were itching to try the real thing. For all his lack of height, the bellicose Lucas enjoyed the full confidence of the men towering over him. He knew his business and he had seen to it that they knew theirs, too.

Ahead of them, the *Santissima Trinidad* lay just in front of the *Bucentaure*, scarcely moving at all through the water. All three ships were bunched so close together that a collision seemed inevitable as the *Victory* bore down. By Villeneuve's account, the *Victory* was almost within 'half pistol shot' when she suddenly veered towards the *Bucentaure's* stern. By another French account, Villeneuve immediately seized the Imperial eagle from the foot of the *Bucentaure's* mainmast and brandished it in front of his men.

'My friends,' he told them. 'I am going to throw this aboard the English ship.' He gestured towards the *Victory*, now seconds away from a clash. 'We will go and fetch it back – or we will die!'

CHAPTER 35

NELSON HIT

Both British columns had now reached the enemy. From his position near the head of the French line, Rear-Admiral Pierre Dumanoir watched the *Victory* bearing down on the *Bucentaure* and wondered if he should turn the leading squadron round and hurry back to attack Nelson's column in the flank. It was the logical thing to do, but there had been no orders from Villeneuve – none that Dumanoir had seen, at any rate. Should he use his own initiative and turn back anyway? Or should he carry on towards Cadiz, leading the French and Spanish back to safety? Dumanoir couldn't make up his mind.

There was very little he could do in the short term. Even if he gave the order now, it would take at least an hour to turn his squadron round, and the fight might well have been decided by then. His ships might arrive in time to save the day, or they might arrive in time to be destroyed in their turn. If they continued towards Cadiz, they would escape the carnage and live to fight another time. That was what Villeneuve had done at the Nile, quietly distancing himself from the action when he saw that further resistance was useless. Should Dumanoir do it now?

A more resolute man would have said no. With the *Victory* about to ram the *Bucentaure*, Dumanoir's duty was clear. He should have turned round at once and sailed back towards the sound of the guns. But Dumanoir had no stomach for the fight and judged it wiser not to get involved. He sailed on instead, turning his back on the battle behind him, apparently pretending to himself that it wasn't happening. His squadron followed unhappily in his wake.

*

At the other end of the line, about half a mile south of Villeneuve, Admiral Gravina could see both Collingwood and Nelson attacking the combined fleet but could do nothing about it. A solid wall of French and Spanish ships stood between him and the British, preventing his squadron from bringing their guns to bear. All Gravina could do was pace the deck and curse, watching helplessly as other ships engaged the enemy while his own squadron looked on, idle and useless.

It was Gravina's own fault. He commanded the observer squadron, sailing independently of the main body. He was supposed to be to windward, nearer the British, in order to strengthen the centre of Villeneuve's line if necessary. But Gravina had ignored Villeneuve's orders when the fleet turned about that morning. He had attached his squadron to the rear of the line instead, ending up parallel to the rear squadron but on the side away from the enemy. Gravina may have been positioning himself to attack the British when they broke through, but it was not what Villeneuve had asked of him. If Gravina's squadron had been in the centre of the line, to windward, it would have been ideally placed to break up both Collingwood and Nelson's columns before they could reach the combined fleet. Gravina had been given some of the fleet's best fighting ships for that very purpose. The situation would be looking radically different now if he had only done what he was told – and no one can have realised it more than Gravina.

But it was too late now. In the middle of the line, the men of the *Bucentaure* were bracing themselves for a collision as the *Victory* came on. The French had grappling hooks in their hands, ready to bind the two ships together the moment they touched.

At the last minute, however, the *Victory* suddenly veered to starboard, narrowly avoiding a collision as she passed under the *Bucentaure*'s stern. She sailed so close that her yardarm tangled with the French rigging and her shrouds brushed against the huge tricolour hanging down over the taffrail. A man on the *Victory*'s gangway could have reached out and grabbed the flag if he had had the presence of mind. From a distance of only a few feet, French and English stared open-mouthed at each other for a moment, as if frozen in a tableau. Then they all remembered where they were and sprang into action as the English guns began to fire.

This was the gunners' moment. The *Bucentaure* had already loosed off four broadsides at the *Victory*, but the *Victory* had fired none in return. Advancing at an angle to the enemy, she had had little chance to retaliate before. But she could retaliate now.

The first shot came from the carronade on the *Victory*'s port fo'c'sle. Loaded with one 68-pound shot and a keg of 500 musket balls, the carronade fired straight through the windows of the *Bucentaure*'s upper cabin, spraying death and destruction the length of the ship. It was followed in sequence by the fifty broadside guns on the *Victory*'s port side, each firing in turn as the *Bucentaure*'s stern loomed into view. The effect was devastating. The French were cut down in droves, some torn in half, some blinded and maimed, others mutilated beyond all recognition. Those not killed outright screamed in fear and pain as the destruction hit home. They screamed so loudly that their cries were heard aboard the *Victory* by men whose hearing was already dulled by the noise of the guns. The British had problems of their own, half-suffocated by the smoke of their own weapons, which had come billowing back into the ship. They were so close to the enemy that Nelson and Hardy were covered in dust from the *Bucentaure*'s stern, which had erupted in a shower all over them as the guns did their work.

The moment passed and the *Victory* swept on. Behind her, twenty of the *Bucentaure*'s guns had been destroyed and upwards of 100 of her crew disabled (it seemed like 400 to her officers at the time). The *Victory* was now in clear water on the other side of the enemy line. She came under fire immediately from the French ship *Neptune* (there were three *Neptunes* at Trafalgar, one for each nation). The *Victory*'s foremast and bowsprit were hit and her bows holed in several places. But nothing could be done about it. The *Victory* was under fire from the *Redoutable* as well, some distance away to starboard. Hurriedly sizing up the situation, Captain Hardy decided to board the *Redoutable* and silence her guns before they could do any serious damage. He gave the order for the *Victory* to run alongside.

Captain Lucas was ready for him. He fired one broadside at the *Victory* and then ordered the *Redoutable*'s lower gunports to be closed, to prevent a boarding party from climbing through. The anchors of the two ships clanged into each other as they met, and they would have bounced apart again if their sails hadn't become entangled. As it was, they were hooked together instead, so close that the muzzles of the *Victory*'s lower-deck guns were actually touching the *Redoutable*'s hull.

On the *Redoutable*'s main deck, Lucas's men swarmed over the gangways, ready to repel boarders. To Charles Adair, captain of the *Victory*'s Marines, it was obvious that they were preparing to storm the *Victory*. But Midshipman James Walker, at the other end of the ship, hadn't even seen them in the smoke:

> Captain Adair, at the head of his Marines, rushed from the poop to the forecastle, and, applying his mouth to my ear, bawled into it, 'Are they going to board us?'
>
> I replied, 'Who are going to board us?'
>
> 'Why, this ship in contact with us on the starboard bow' – at the same time elevating his hand, and pointing to the foreyard of the *Redoutable*, dimly seen through clouds of smoke right across our forecastle, and perceiving at the same time an officer in white uniform in the forerigging of that ship, who instantly disappeared, whether shot or not I cannot say.
>
> We of course put our sixty-eight-pounder into immediate requisition, and, I believe, most effectively, but so incessant was the small-arm fire of the enemy, that most of the Marines who came on the forecastle, as also their gallant captain, fell like corn before the sickle; the blue jackets sharing a similar fate.

The sixty-eight-pounder was the *Victory*'s starboard carronade, loaded like the port one with a heavy shot and 500 musket balls. Bosun William Willmet had fired it across the *Redoutable*'s deck with dramatic effect. Scores of Lucas's men had been blown away, cut down as if they had never existed. The planks of the French ship were suddenly slippery with blood and entrails, spilling out bright and glistening as bodies slumped and men fell broken to the deck.

But the fight was far from one-sided. The *Redoutable* fired back at Willmet with grenade-throwing mortars loaded with canister. She had muskets in her rigging and below deck, firing into the *Victory* through the gunports. Both sides were shooting frenziedly at each other, loosing everything they had from a range of only a few feet. Fire and reload, fire and reload. There was no time for anything else.

On the *Victory's* gundecks, the smoke was so intense that the gun crews couldn't see each other any more. Nor could they hear each other either. They were operating by feel and touch, running the guns out and firing blind. They didn't need to aim. They couldn't miss, with their muzzles only inches from the *Redoutable's* side.

But the closeness of the two ships brought dangers of its own. Every gunshot into the *Redoutable* carried the risk of fire. If the *Redoutable* burned, so would the *Victory*. Each gun on the British side had a fireman ready with a bucket of water. As soon as his gun had fired, he stepped forward and leaned out of the port, emptying his bucket at the *Redoutable*. Fire was the enemy of them all aboard ship. It was in everyone's interests to make sure the *Redoutable* didn't go up in flames.

Behind them, coming up fast, the *Téméraire* was hurrying to join in the fight. The *Bucentaure* was there, too, still reeling from the *Victory's* broadside. With dense smoke all around, Villeneuve had little idea of what was happening to the centre and rear of his line. He knew only that Admiral Dumanoir's squadron was continuing to sail ahead, taking no part in the fight. Soon after the *Victory* had raked his stern, Villeneuve had hoisted a signal from the yardarm: 'All ships not engaged because of their positions are to get into action as soon as possible.' The signal was for the whole fleet, but there was no doubt whose squadron it was aimed at. It was to Dumanoir's eternal shame that the signal had to be sent at all.

The duel between the *Victory* and the *Redoutable* had slackened for a moment. The *Redoutable's* main guns had remained silent after their one broadside, leading the *Victory* to assume that she had surrendered. Twice the order was given for the *Victory's* guns to stop firing, in the expectation of a white flag. Twice the order had to be rescinded as the *Redoutable* continued fighting. The French had not surrendered. Far from it. As Captain Lucas understood it, the story was quite different. His men were actually winning the struggle:

There was some delay at the guns. We had to use rope rammers in several cases, and fire with the guns run in. We couldn't run them out because the ports were blocked by the *Victory*'s sides. At the same time, in other places, we were firing muskets into the enemy's ports and preventing them from loading their guns. Before long they stopped firing altogether. What a glorious day for the *Redoutable* if she had only had the *Victory* to deal with! The *Victory*'s guns couldn't fight us any more.

It was then that the enemy tried to board us. I immediately had the bugles sound 'Repel boarders!' Everyone instantly came up from below, in fine style. The officers and midshipmen ran to the head of their men, as if on parade. In less than a minute our decks were swarming with armed men, fanning out across the poop and into the nettings and shrouds. It would be impossible to say who took the lead.

The fighting was fast and furious. Lucas's marksmen raced up the rigging to the tops – platforms halfway up the masts. Armed with muskets and bayonets, they began a murderous fire on the British below. They threw grenades as well, more than 200 by Lucas's account, creating havoc on the *Victory*'s deck.

Second Lieutenant Louis Rotely of the Marines remembered the scene with horror:

The poop became a slaughter-house. The two senior lieutenants of Marines and half the original forty were placed *hors de combat*. Captain Adair then ordered me to bring him up a reinforcement of Marines from the great guns. I need not inform a seaman of the difficulty of separating a man from his gun. In the excitement of action the Marines had thrown off their red jackets and appeared in check shirts and blue trousers. There was no distinguishing Marine from Seaman – they were all working like horses.

I was now upon the middle deck. We were engaging on both sides, every gun was going off. A man should witness a battle in a three-decker from the middle deck, for it beggars all description. It bewilders the senses of sight and hearing. There was the fire from above, the fire from below, besides the fire from the deck I was upon, the guns recoiling with violent reports louder than thunder, the deck heaving and the side straining. I fancied myself in the infernal regions, where every man appeared a devil. Lips might move, but orders and hearing were out of the question; everything was done by signs.

The noise was so bad that some gunners never recovered their hearing. Others suffered hernias as they struggled to keep their weapons firing.

With two sergeants and two corporals to help him, Rotely succeeded in getting twenty-five Marines together, some of whom had to be dragged from their guns by force. It was much safer down below. Perhaps the Marines had guessed why Rotely needed them up above. Whatever the reason, they returned to the main deck to find that the battle had taken a turn for the worse, as Rotely quickly noted:

The *Redoutable* had fallen on board us on the starboard side, and the soldiers from their tops were picking off our officers and men with deadly aim. We were also engaging with the *Santissima Trinidad* and the *Bucentaure* (though at a greater distance) on our larboard. The reinforcement arrived at a most critical moment. Captain Adair's party was reduced to less than ten men, himself wounded in the forehead by splinters, yet still using his musket with effect. One of his last orders to me was, 'Rotely, fire away as fast as you can!' when a ball struck him on the back of the neck and he was a corpse in a moment.

The carnage was appalling. The *Redoutable's* sharpshooters could hardly miss at such short range. The British were no more than forty or fifty feet away. It was like shooting fish in a barrel.

From the *Redoutable's* mizentop, one of the sharpshooters had a view of the *Victory's* quarterdeck, twenty feet below. Two dusty figures were pacing the deck, officers by the look of them. The Frenchman took quick aim, fired at one and ducked down again, swiftly reloading before seeking another target.

Aboard the *Victory*, Lord Nelson slumped to his knees, vainly trying to stop his fall with his hand. The musket ball had torn through the epaulette on his left shoulder, smashing two ribs, severing an artery and shattering his spine. His face hit the deck as Captain Hardy turned round and saw what was happening. Two seamen and Sergeant James Secker of the Marines were already rushing to his aid.

'They have done for me at last,' Nelson told Hardy, as the men gathered him up.

'I hope not,' Hardy replied.

'Yes.' Nelson was in no doubt. 'My backbone is shot through.'

Hardy ordered the men to carry Nelson down to the cockpit, where the surgeon would attend to him. Nelson was badly hurt, but his mind was still on the battle. When he was being handed down the ladder from the middle deck, he saw that the tiller ropes had not yet been replaced. He told a midshipman to go back on deck and ask Hardy to have it done. Then he covered his face with a handkerchief, so the crew wouldn't notice who had been wounded.

Surgeon Beatty was already overwhelmed with casualties as Nelson was brought in. It was a strict rule that they should be seen on a first-come, first-served basis, but the other casualties made an exception for Nelson. 'Mr Beatty,' they cried. 'Lord Nelson is here. Mr Beatty, the admiral is wounded.' Beatty and Purser Walter Burke immediately took hold of Nelson and laid him in a midshipman's berth for examination. They stumbled as they went, causing Nelson to ask who was carrying him. 'Ah, Mr Beatty,' he said. 'You can do nothing for me. I have but a short time to live. My back is shot through.'

Beatty carefully undressed Nelson and investigated the wound. The musket ball had penetrated deep into his chest and was probably lodged underneath his right shoulder blade, since there was no exit hole. Beatty asked Nelson what he could feel:

He replied that he felt a gush of blood every minute within his breast: that he had no feeling in the lower part of his body: and that his breathing was difficult, and attended with very severe pain about that part of the spine where he was confident that the ball had struck; for, said he, 'I felt it break my back.'

Beatty could see that Nelson was doomed, but decided to say nothing for a while. Captain Hardy would have to be told, but no one else outside the cockpit. The rest of the crew wouldn't want to know until the battle was over. Moving Nelson to a more comfortable position against a thick oak timber, Beatty went back to the remainder of the wounded. There was nothing else he could do for Nelson.

On deck, the fight with the *Redoutable* was still raging. The British had suffered so many casualties that the remainder had been ordered below to avoid further slaughter. With no one to stop them, Midshipman Jacques Yon and four French sailors boarded the *Victory* via her anchor and reported back that there wasn't a soul on the quarterdeck. Lucas decided to storm the ship. He gave orders for the *Redoutable*'s mainyard to be dropped on to the *Victory*'s deck to make a bridge for his boarding party. But Lucas was too hasty. With the *Téméraire* closing fast through the smoke, this was not the time to try to take the *Victory*.

For Captain Hardy, it was the most testing moment of his career. A devoted friend of Nelson, he was longing to get down to the cockpit to see how the admiral was doing. But his immediate priority was to beat off the *Redoutable* and win the firefight. It was easier said than done, with bullets flying all around. In addition, Hardy was now in command of the fleet as well, because the *Victory* was still flying the admiral's flag. It was a naval convention that command always vested in the admiral's ship. As soon as he had a chance, Hardy would have to get a message across to Collingwood to tell him what had happened, but for the moment the conduct of the fleet was entirely his responsibility, even though he couldn't see forty yards in the smoke. With the *Redoutable* threatening to storm the *Victory* at any moment, it must have been a nightmare for Hardy, his worst imaginings come true. Everything was going wrong, all at the same time. The loneliness of command could never have weighed more heavily.

At the stern of the ship, nineteen-year-old Midshipman John Pollard had an agenda of his own. Pollard was the only one still alive of the officers and midshipmen originally stationed on the poop. He had taken a splinter in his right arm at the beginning of the fight, but was otherwise unharmed. Pollard knew what had happened to Lord Nelson and realised the shot had come from the *Redoutable*'s mizentop. He could see several Frenchmen up there, hiding behind a canvas tricolour three feet high. They bobbed up to fire, then bobbed down again, reloading out of sight.

Pollard grabbed a dead Marine's musket. One of those Frenchmen had felled Lord Nelson, but Pollard had no idea which. There was only one way to be certain of avenging the admiral. Taking careful aim, Midshipman Pollard set out to kill the lot.

CHAPTER 36

———◦•◦•◦———

THE BATTLE RAGES

In the other British column, Collingwood was still in trouble, fighting alone among the enemy. The *Belleisle* and *Mars* were coming to his rescue, but for the moment the *Royal Sovereign* was surrounded by hostile ships, all firing at her from different directions. Casualties were mounting rapidly. Collingwood himself had felt a great thump in the back – the wind of a passing shot – and had a bad leg wound from a splinter. The ship's master, William Chalmers, had been killed at his side.

A great shot almost divided his body: he laid his head upon my shoulder and told me he was slain. I supported him till two men carried him off. He could say nothing to me, but to bless me; but as they carried him down, he wished he could but live to read the account of the action in a newspaper.

The situation hung in the balance. The *Santa Ana* was one of the Spanish flagships. It had been a bold move to sail straight at her without close support. The *Royal Sovereign* had taken so much punishment that she was effectively crippled – two of her masts were about to fall and she could barely move through the water. But the *Santa Ana* was in an even worse state, her side smashed in by the *Sovereign's* guns. She had only survived for so long because the *Royal Sovereign* was fighting several other ships at the same time, keeping all of them at bay until help arrived from the rest of Collingwood's column.

George Castle was a midshipman aboard the *Royal Sovereign* as she tore into the enemy.

She was fifty-five minutes engaged with them before any other ship came to our assistance, and we were alongside of a great three-decker. I can assure you it was glorious work; I think you would have liked to have seen me thump it into her quarter. I'm stationed at the heaviest guns in the ship, and I stuck close to one gun and poured it into her; she was so close it was impossible to miss her. She behaved very rascally; for when she struck first to us, she went round our bows, and when right ahead of us, up with her Ensign and raked us; but we soon brought our starboard guns to bear upon her.

Crash went her masts, and then she was fairly sicken'd. She was a Spanish Admiral's ship, but the Admiral was kill'd, and after that we made an eighty-four strike to us. I looked once out of our stern ports; but I saw nothing but French and Spaniards round, firing at us in all directions. It was shocking to see the many brave seamen mangled so; some with their heads half shot away, others with their entrails mashed, lying panting on the deck. The greatest slaughter was on the quarter-deck and poop; we had seven ships on us at once.

Several of the enemy ships melted away as the *Belleisle* arrived in support – by most accounts, only five or ten minutes behind the *Royal Sovereign*. The *Belleisle* had been under fire for some time as she approached, but deliberately withheld her own fire until she was within pistol shot of the enemy. Her crew could see what was happening to the *Royal Sovereign*, and knew it would soon be happening to them, too. It was a nerve-racking time for everyone on board as they neared the enemy line. Lieutenant John Owen was on deck with his Marines:

Captain Hargood had taken his station at the forepart of the quarter-deck, on the starboard side, occasionally standing on a carronade slide, whence he issued his orders for the men to lie down at their quarters, and with the utmost coolness directed the steering of the ship. The silence on board was almost awful. It was broken only by the firm voice of the Captain. 'Steady!' or 'Starboard a little!' which was repeated by the Master to the quarter-master at the helm, and occasionally by an officer calling to the now impatient men, 'Lie down there, you sir!'

Sixteen-year-old Lieutenant Paul Nicolas of the Marines was on deck as well:

A shriek soon followed – a cry of agony was produced by the next shot – and the loss of the head of a poor recruit was the effect of the succeeding; and, as we advanced, destruction rapidly increased. A severe contusion in the breast now prostrated our Captain, but he soon resumed his station . . . My eyes were horror-struck at the bloody corpses around me, and my ears rang with the shrieks of the wounded and the moans of the dying. At this moment, seeing that almost every one was lying down, I was half-disposed to follow the example, and several times stooped for the purpose, but – and I remember the impression well – a certain monitor seemed to whisper, 'Stand up and do not shrink from your duty!'

Seeing that our men were falling fast, the First Lieutenant ventured to ask Captain Hargood if he had not better show his broadside to the enemy and fire, if only to cover the ship with smoke? The gallant man's reply was somewhat stern but emphatic: 'No; we are ordered to go through the line, and go she shall!'

This state of things had lasted about twenty minutes, and it required the tact of the more experienced officers to keep up the spirits of those round them, by repeating, '"We shall soon begin our work," when . . . our energies were joyfully called into play by the command "Stand to your guns!"'

The men needed no urging. Within minutes the *Belleisle*'s gun crews were in action, firing at the *Santa Ana* to port and the *Fougueux* to starboard as they crashed through the enemy line. They passed the *Royal Sovereign* and turned starboard to go round the *Indomptable* and attack her on the lee side. But the *Fougueux* came out of the smoke to intercept them, running her foreyard over the *Belleisle*'s quarterdeck. She fired into the *Belleisle* for ten minutes and succeeded in shooting away her mizenmast about six feet above the deck. The *Fougueux* was then chased away by the *Mars*, which had followed the *Belleisle* through the enemy line.

But the *Belleisle* was still in trouble. The sails of her mizenmast had fallen over the stern of the ship, making it impossible for the gun crews at that end to see anything. The *Achille* fired broadside after broadside into her, knowing the British were unable to return fire. The *Aigle*, *San Justo* and *San Leandro* took pot shots as well, from a safe distance. The *Belleisle* was pounded from every side until her other two masts gave way under the strain. Her bowsprit, figurehead, boats and anchors were destroyed too, leaving her a total wreck. Everything collapsed in a heap on the deck, until the *Belleisle* lay little better than a hulk, so swathed in smoke that her crew couldn't even see the colours of the ships that were shooting at her. Lieutenant Paul Nicolas was lucky to escape with his life:

> I was under the break of the poop, aiding in running out a carronade. A cry of 'Stand clear, there! Here it comes!' made me look up, and at that instant the mainmast fell over the bulwarks just above me. This ponderous mass made the ship's whole frame shake; had it taken a central direction it would have gone through the poop, and added many to our list of sufferers.

Without masts, the *Belleisle* was helpless, but certainly not beaten. Her guns continued to fire whenever they could. Captain William Hargood had been bruised from neck to hip by a splinter, which had thrown him into the splinter netting. He untangled himself, cursing horribly, and emerged yelping with rage. 'Let 'em come on!' he bellowed. 'I'm damned if I'll strike. No, never – to nobody whatever!' The story passed rapidly around the ship, to everyone's amusement.

The wind had dropped just as the *Belleisle* and *Mars* reached the enemy, making it difficult for the rest of Collingwood's column to get into the action. The *Belleisle*'s crew had been fighting alone for more than two hours when an unidentified two-decker appeared through the smoke, steering straight towards them. They watched with increasing apprehension until a slight change in the two-decker's course revealed a White Ensign at the stern. The newcomer was the *Swiftsure*. The two crews cheered each other as she swept past. The *Polyphemus* was coming up as well, and the *Defiance*. They tore into the enemy and relieved the pressure on the *Belleisle*.

Not far away, the *Mars* had also been taking a beating. Originally ordered by Nelson to lead Collingwood's column into action, the *Mars* was slow in the water and had suffered the indignity of being overtaken by both the *Royal Sovereign* and the *Belleisle* as they headed for the enemy. She was commanded by George Duff, a gentlemanly Scot much admired by his crew. His twelve-year-old son Norwich was with him, serving as a midshipman. 'Norwich is quite well and happy,' Duff had written to his wife as they turned towards the enemy. 'I have, however, ordered him off the quarterdeck.' Duff knew he would have been answerable to his wife if he hadn't sent their son below as the shooting started.

In the event, it was Duff who was killed, rather than his son. The *Mars* had come under fire from the *San Juan Nepomuceno*, *Pluton*, *Monarca*, *Algesiras* and *Fougueux*. A cannon ball hit him in the chest and ripped off his head, killing two other people as well. The rest of the crew promptly 'held his body up and gave three cheers to show they were not discouraged by it, and then returned to their guns', leaving the body sprawled in the gangway.

Aboard the *Royal Sovereign*, the arrival of other British ships had been a relief to Collingwood as the battle raged. Three enemy ships had immediately sheered off, leaving him free to concentrate on the *Santa Ana*, the flagship of Vice-Admiral Ignatio de Alava. It was a spectacular feat to sail straight for the enemy line and take on their flagship single-handed, surrounded by nothing but hostile ships. Collingwood had been surprised when the *Santa Ana* failed to surrender after his first furious broadside. The Spanish had put up a noble resistance, trading shot for shot with the *Royal Sovereign* until both ships were little more than splintered wrecks, their sides streaked with blood from the drain holes on deck. But it couldn't go on for ever. At length, Vice-Admiral Alava was wounded and Spanish resistance crumbled. The *Santa Ana's* colours eventually came down and she surrendered at last to the *Royal Sovereign*.

By then, though, Collingwood was barely in a position to receive the surrender. His mizenmast had just fallen and the other two were about to follow. If that wasn't enough, a boat had just come alongside from the *Victory*. Lieutenant Alexander Hills had brought a message from Captain Hardy. Lord Nelson had been wounded, Collingwood's dear friend of thirty years' standing.

Collingwood asked Hills if the wound was dangerous. 'He hesitated; then said he hoped it was not; but I saw the fate of my friend in his eye; for his look told what his tongue could not utter.'

There was no time to mourn. The *Royal Sovereign*'s mainmast came crashing down, joining the mizenmast over the side. The ship could no longer move without help. Collingwood hastily signalled to the *Euryalus* to give him a tow. There was still plenty of fighting to be done. The *Royal Sovereign*'s guns could still be brought to bear, with help from Blackwood's frigate to steer her round.

First, though, Collingwood sent Captain Blackwood aboard the *Santa Ana* to receive the Spanish admiral's surrender and bring him back to the *Royal Sovereign*. But Alava was too badly wounded to go anywhere. It was the second-in-command, Captain José Gardoqui, who came instead. He had already been across once, proffering his sword and asking in fractured English the name of the ship he had been fighting. 'I think she should be called the *Royal Devil*,' he is said to have responded when they told him, patting one of the *Sovereign*'s guns admiringly.

While the *Euryalus* took the *Royal Sovereign* in tow, the other ships in Collingwood's column were fighting individual duels of their own – 'every man to take his bird', as an officer on the *Tonnant* put it. They all fought their own actions in the smoke, with little idea of what was happening anywhere else in the fleet.

The *Tonnant* had originally been a French ship, captured at the Nile and recommissioned into the Royal Navy. She was fourth in Collingwood's line, behind the *Belleisle* and *Mars*. Like them, she came under fire as she approached the enemy and took multiple casualties, including a couple of musicians in the band. Frederick Hoffman was the third lieutenant on board:

A French ship of eighty guns, with an Admiral's flag, came up and poured a raking broadside into our stern, which killed or wounded forty petty officers and men, nearly cut the rudder in two, and shattered the whole of the stern, with the quarter galleries. She then, in the most gallant manner, locked her bowsprit in our starboard main shrouds and attempted to board us with the greater part of her officers and ship's company. She had riflemen in her tops who did great execution. Our poop was soon cleared, and our gallant Captain shot through the left thigh, and obliged to be carried below.

The French ship was the *Algesiras*, under Rear-Admiral Magon. Locked at an angle into the *Tonnant's* main shrouds, she was unable to bring her main guns to bear on the British. But the *Tonnant* could bring almost all her quarterdeck guns and carronades to bear on the *Algesiras*, and lost no time doing so. It wasn't long before the *Algesiras's* rigging had been shot to pieces. In desperation, Magon decided to try and board the *Tonnant* to put a stop to the destruction.

Before the battle he had promised a gilded shoulder belt to the first member of his crew to board an English ship. 'The first man to board that ship with me shall have the cross!' he reminded them now. Magon led the charge himself, intending to use the bowsprit as a bridge to the British ship. But a musket ball shot away his hat and wig before he had got more than a few yards. Another hit him in the arm and a third in the shoulder. Bleeding badly, Magon refused to go below and was killed by a cannon ball a little later. The boarding party was taken over by Lieutenant Guillaume Verdreau, but he too was shot down before he could reach the *Tonnant*. Only one Frenchman managed to reach the British ship. He was promptly spiked in the leg with a half-pike and would have been killed if Lieutenant Hoffman hadn't intervened and had him sent down to the cockpit to join the rest of the wounded.

The cockpit was a busy place when the Frenchman arrived. A total of sixteen men had an arm or leg amputated during the course of the action. Surgeon Forbes Chevers was operating by the light of dim tallow candles. 'If you look straight into the wound, and see all that I do, I shall see perfectly,' he told the men holding the lights for him. As soon as Chevers had finished, the amputees were scooped up by Purser George Booth and a petty officer's wife, 'a very powerful and resolute woman', much larger than Booth. Between them, they 'carried the sailors who had been operated upon to their temporary berths, taking them up in their arms as if they had been children, in a manner which Chevers, himself a tall and very strong young man, always spoke of with expressions of wonder'. For all their care, however, only two of the amputees survived their operations.

The fight had continued for half an hour, the two ships locked tightly together, when fire broke out on both of them 'before the cross-trees'. The British immediately brought up their fire engine and sprayed water over the two vessels. It took a long time to put the flames out, and two men were badly injured in the process. Lieutenant Hoffman watched from the *Tonnant*'s deck:

> At length we had the satisfaction of seeing her three lower masts go by the board, ripping the partners up in their fall, as they had been shot through the lower-deck, and carrying with them all their sharpshooters to look sharper in the next world, for, as all our boats were shot through, we could not save one of them in this. The crew were then ordered, with the Second Lieutenant, to board her. They cheered, and in a short time carried her. They found the gallant French Admiral Magon killed at the foot of the poop ladder, and the Captain dangerously wounded . . . We had pummelled her so handsomely that fourteen of her lower-deck guns were dismounted and her larboard bow exhibited a mass of splinters.

The British placed Lieutenant Charles Bennett in command of the captured vessel, with forty-eight men to support him. But that was not the end of the fighting for the *Tonnant*. She was also engaged with Churruca's *San Juan Nepomuceno*. As the French were surrendering, so too were the Spanish, as Lieutenant Benjamin Clement observed:

> I hailed a Spanish officer and asked him if he had struck. When he said 'Yes', I came aft and informed the First-Lieutenant. He ordered me to board her. We had no boat but what was shot, but he told me

I must try, so I went away in the jolly-boat with two men, but had not got above a quarter of the way when the boat swampt.

I cannot swim, but the two men who were with me could, one a black man and the other a quarter-master; he was the last man in her, when a shot struck her and knocked her quarter off, and she was turned bottom up. Macnamara, the black man, staid [sic] by me on one side, and Maclay, the quarter-master, on the other . . . I found myself weak and thought I was not long for this world. Macnamara swam to the ship and got a rope and to me again, and made it fast under my arms, when I swung off, and was hauled into the stern port.

It had been the narrowest of escapes for Clement. He owed his life to Charles Macnamara. For as long as he lived, he never forgot his debt to the black volunteer from Barbados who had saved him from drowning.

Behind the *Tonnant*, the *Bellerophon* was the fifth ship in Collingwood's column as they approached the enemy line. Known to one and all as the *Billy Ruff'n*, she was a hard-fighting ship under a tough captain. John Cooke had never served with Nelson before, but it had long been his ambition to fight a battle under the admiral's command. He was getting his wish at last, standing proudly on the poop as the *Bellerophon* followed the *Tonnant* into action.

They opened their battle earlier than planned, when one of the *Bellerophon*'s midshipmen tripped over a trigger line and fired a gun by mistake. Several enemy ships responded vigorously, assuming the lone gun to be some kind of signal. Like everyone else, Cooke had intended to hold his fire until reaching the enemy, but changed his mind when the *Bellerophon* began to suffer casualties. He opened fire in return, partly to give his men something to do to steady their nerves, but mostly to cover his ship in smoke and reduce her visibility as a target.

They broke the enemy line astern of the Spanish ship *Bahama*. Commanded by Commodore Galiano, the *Bahama* was part of Admiral Gravina's observer squadron, which had now managed to join the action. The *Bellerophon* was turning to port to lay alongside her when another enemy ship emerged from the smoke ahead. The *Bellerophon* backed sails immediately, but too late to avoid a collision. The crew barely had time to see the word *Aigle* on the newcomer's stern before they had run into her, the *Bellerophon*'s foreyard locking into the *Aigle*'s mainyard.

Two other enemy ships joined the fight as well, relentlessly pouring fire into the *Bellerophon* from different angles. But the *Aigle* was her chief opponent. Of the fifty-eight men on the *Bellerophon*'s quarterdeck, fifty-four were eventually cut down by enemy fire. Their numbers included Captain Cooke, as an eyewitness remembered:

He had discharged his pistols very frequently at the enemy, who as often attempted to board, and he had killed a French officer on his own quarter-deck. He was in the act of reloading his pistols . . . when he received two musket balls in his breast. He immediately fell, and upon the Quarter-Master's going up and asking him if he should take him down below, his answer was: 'No, let me lie quietly one minute. Tell Lieutenant Cumby never to strike!'

Cooke died seconds later. Edward Overton, the ship's master, was dying too. Of the three men who had studied Nelson's plan of attack that morning, only William Cumby was still in one piece. Quickly taking command, he saw that the *Bellerophon*'s upper deck had been almost completely cleared by musket fire and grenades from the 150 soldiers aboard the *Aigle*. The French were about to storm the *Bellerophon* and take the ship. But they had reckoned without Cumby.

I ordered all the remaining men down from the Poop and calling the boarders had them mustered under the half-deck and held them in readiness to repel any attempt that might be made by the enemy to board us, their position rendering it quite impracticable for us to board them in the face of such a fire of musquetry so advantageously situated. But whatever advantage they had over us on these upper decks was greatly overbalanced by the superiority of our fire on the lower and main decks . . . Whilst thus closely engaged and rubbing sides with *L'Aigle* she threw many hand grenades on board us, both on our forecastle and gangway and in at the ports. Some of these exploded and dreadfully scorched several of our men. One of them I took up myself from our gangway where the fuse was burning and threw it overboard.

The *Bellerophon*'s decks were covered with loose gunpowder that exploded as well, adding to the list of casualties. One man was so badly burned that he ran aft and jumped overboard rather than take himself to the surgeon. The noise was so awful that Signal-Midshipman John Franklin (later Sir John Franklin, the Arctic explorer) was left slightly deaf for the rest of his life. The *Bellerophon* and *Aigle* were so close together that many Frenchmen tried to jump the gap, as Franklin later remembered. 'In the attempt their hands received some severe blows from whatever the English could lay their hands on. In this way hundreds of Frenchmen fell between the ships and were drowned.'

The fighting was intense, men seizing each other's ramrods and jabbing viciously at each other across the divide. Franklin swore he would never forget the face of a French sharpshooter, falling dead from the *Aigle*'s foretop into the sea. Five other Frenchmen joined him when a British sailor dislodged them from a yardarm. The *Bellerophon*'s colour was shot away three times, giving the impression that she had surrendered. 'That's too bad,' exclaimed Yeoman of Signals Christopher Beatty. 'Those fellows will say we've struck!' Fetching another Union Jack from the flag-locker, Beatty shinned up the mizen rigging to the masthead. The French did their best to kill him until they saw what he was up to. Then they held their fire for a few seconds, apparently allowing him to lash the colour to the mast. Beatty was the only man to climb the English rigging unscathed.

The battle ended in stalemate, neither ship giving way to the other. Both captains were dead, and the *Aigle* had been badly damaged in the struggle. She managed to pull away from the *Bellerophon* after a while, breaking free before she was forced to surrender. With two topmasts down and other bits shot away, the *Bellerophon* was in no state to follow. The *Bellerophon*'s cockpit was so full of wounded that the captain's cabin had to be used for the overflow. Men were queuing outside to have their arms amputated.

They had fought with spectacular courage, but the cost had been high, when they came to count it. Of the 540 men in the *Bellerophon's* crew, almost one in three had been killed or wounded. It was one of the highest casualty ratios in the British fleet.

While the *Bellerophon* assessed the damage, the *Aigle* drifted away, her quarter beaten in. She was raked by the *Revenge* in passing, then attacked by the *Defiance*, the sternmost ship in Collingwood's column. It was the last thing she needed after her long fight with the *Bellerophon*.

The two ships came within pistol range of each other. Already badly mauled, the *Aigle* was in no state to take on the *Defiance*. Her fire soon slackened, suggesting she was ready to surrender. The British decided to board her, but had trouble getting alongside without a wind. They couldn't row across either because the *Defiance's* boats had all been shot to pieces.

Midshipman James Spratt – Jack to his friends – was serving as master's mate on the *Defiance*. He was Irish, one of the handsomest men in the navy. With no other way of getting to the *Aigle*, he decided to swim across. Yelling at his men to follow, he 'plunged overboard from the starboard gangway with my cutlass between my teeth and my tomahawk under my belt' and headed for the *Aigle*.

No one followed. His men had very sensibly failed to hear him in all the noise. Spratt had no choice but to swim on alone, climbing up the *Aigle's* rudder chains and entering the ship through a gun port in the stern. There he made the unwelcome discovery that the French were nowhere near surrender. Undaunted, Spratt fought his way through the ship and emerged on to the *Aigle's* poop, where '[I] showed myself to our ship's crew from the enemy's taffrail and gave them a cheer with my hat on the point of my cutlass.'

Three Frenchmen came at him with bayonets. Swinging from a signal halyard, Spratt disabled two of them and threw the third down on to the quarterdeck. The man took Spratt with him as they fell and they hit the deck together. Spratt survived, but the Frenchman broke his neck.

By this time, others from the *Defiance* had followed Spratt and were climbing aboard the *Aigle*. Fierce hand-to-hand fighting ensued. Spratt spared the life of a surrendering French officer only to be attacked by a soldier who tried to bayonet him in the chest. Parrying the thrust, Spratt was shot in the leg instead. 'I felt something like an electric shock and darted at him but my right leg turned up between my thighs with my shin bone resting on the deck.' Spratt immediately wedged himself between two quarterdeck guns and continued to fight on one foot, holding off the soldier and two others until help arrived.

The *Defiance* meanwhile had managed to get some lines across to the *Aigle* and was busy warping herself alongside. Peering through the smoke, one of the first people Captain Philip Durham spotted on the *Aigle* was Spratt, waving a bloody leg at him over the rail. 'Captain, poor old Jack Spratt is done up at last!' he reported cheerfully. He then swung himself across to the *Defiance* and was taken down to the cockpit, where he refused to have his leg amputated on the grounds that he would never find a match for the other one.

The fight went on without him. The British won control of the poop and quarterdeck and hauled the French flag down from the stern. Lashing it to his body, Lieutenant Thomas Simons delivered the flag to the *Defiance* before returning to the *Aigle*. But the French were still in command of the fo'c'sle and still had sharpshooters in the tops – Simons was shot dead soon after his return. There were plenty of French below deck as well, sheltering behind the big guns and shooting at the British as they came down the ladders. Others were firing into the *Defiance* and lobbing grenades through the gun ports. They were inflicting too many casualties for Captain Durham's liking. He decided to disengage before any more got hurt. Summoning his boarding party back to the *Defiance*, Durham cut his lines to the *Aigle* and allowed the ships to drift a few yards apart, out of musket and grenade range. Then he ordered his big guns to beat the *Aigle* to a pulp.

The cannonade lasted just over twenty minutes. The *Aigle's* rigging was gone by then and most of her guns as well, blown completely off their carriages. Seven officers were dead and another ten wounded. The *Defiance* fired flaming wads, heavily impregnated with sulphur. It wasn't long before fire broke out and the French were forced to give in rather than burn to death. Their colours came down again and they surrendered at last to the British.

'The slaughter on board of her was horrid,' recorded Master's Mate Colin Campbell. 'The decks were covered with dead and wounded. They never heave their dead overboard in time of action as we do.' In all, the *Aigle*'s crew suffered a total of 270 killed and wounded before surrendering. They still had the bodies because it was against Catholic tradition to throw the dead overboard. They were kept in the hold instead, for burial later in consecrated ground.

CHAPTER 37

———◆———

NELSON AVENGED

On board the *Victory*, Midshipman John Pollard was still shooting at the Frenchmen in the *Redoutable*'s mizentop. He was picking them off one by one while an old seaman named King reloaded his muskets for him from the ammunition barrel on the poop.

Pollard continued firing until only one Frenchman remained alive. The man kept changing his position, shooting from the edge of the canvas screen or dodging behind the mast to keep Pollard guessing. Towards the end, he popped up without warning and killed King with a ball between the eyes. Then he abandoned his post, waiting until Pollard had just fired before slipping down the rigging to escape before he had a chance to reload.

But Pollard was too quick for him. Whipping a musket to his shoulder, he loosed off a shot. The Frenchman dropped to the deck with a thump. He was the last of the mizentop sharpshooters to die. Lord Nelson had been avenged.

Was it Pollard who avenged him? Several Frenchmen claimed later that they had killed Nelson and lived to tell the tale, but their claims did not stand up to scrutiny. All the sharpshooters in the mizentop were killed, mostly by Pollard. The only other person Pollard knew of who might have taken the avenging shot was his fellow midshipman Francis Collingwood (no relation of the admiral):

My old friend Collingwood . . . came on the poop after I had for some time discovered the men in the top of the *Redoutable*; they were in a crouching position, and rose breast-high to fire. I pointed them out to Collingwood as I made my aim; he took up a musket, and fired once, and then left the poop, I concluded, to return to the quarter-deck, which was his station during the battle. I remained firing at the top until not a man was to be seen; the last one I discovered coming down the mizen rigging, and from my fire he fell also. King, a quarter-master, was killed while in the act of handing me a parcel of ball-cartridge long after Collingwood had left the poop.

But the Royal Marines had also been firing at the French. After Captain Adair's death, Second Lieutenant Louis Rotely had taken command. He was convinced it was the surviving Marines who had avenged the admiral:

The first order I gave was to clear the mizen top, when every musket was levelled at that top, and in five minutes not a man was left alive in it. Some Frenchman has vaunted that he shot Nelson and survived the battle, and I have heard that a book has been published so stating, but it must be a romance, as I know the man was shot in five minutes after Nelson fell.

There was no time to argue about it. The French were about to board the *Victory*. Lucas's men were massed by the bulwark, poised to clamber across and seize the quarterdeck. The two ships were locked in combat, fighting furiously, heedless of anything else happening around them. They were drifting down towards the *Téméraire*, yet scarcely any of them noticed the other ship in the confusion.

The *Téméraire* did her best to avoid them, but in vain. A collision became inevitable. Captain Eliab Harvey just had time to rake the *Redoutable*'s boarding party with his guns before the two ships crashed together. Still reeling from the broadside, the *Redoutable* now found herself sandwiched between two bigger British ships, both looking down on her from above. Her response was to do to the *Téméraire* what she had already done to the *Victory* – clear her deck with a hail of musketry and grenades from the tops, forcing the British onto the defensive as they took cover below.

In their excitement, the French also threw fireballs – never a good idea with ships locked side by side. The *Redoutable*'s crew managed to set their own ship on fire, and the *Téméraire* as well. The *Victory* was already burning. Her crew put their own flames out, then leaned over the side and emptied buckets of water onto the *Redoutable*'s fo'c'sle to extinguish theirs as well. The situation had become complicated with the arrival of the *Téméraire*. The *Victory*'s gunners were forced to reduce the charges in their guns to avoid shooting straight through the *Redoutable* and hitting the *Téméraire* the other side. The *Téméraire*'s gunners had to do the same. It was only the *Redoutable* that had nothing to lose.

But the *Redoutable* was beaten, and had been since the *Téméraire*'s broadside. The French had been rocked by the blast and found it impossible to recover. They were still fighting magnificently, but they could no longer hope to win. Lucas knew it was over for them now:

All our decks were covered with dead, buried beneath the debris and splinters from different parts of the ship. A great number of wounded were killed on the orlop-deck. Out of the ship's company of 643 men we had 522 disabled, 300 of them killed and 222 wounded.

It was only French pride that kept them going at all.

Yet the *Téméraire* was struggling too. Damaged earlier by the *Santissima Trinidad*, she was also under fire from the French *Neptune*, only 200 yards away. Her colours had been shot away, as had her foreyard, mainmast and much of her rigging. Lashed to the *Redoutable* on one side, with the *Victory* beyond her, the *Téméraire* was drifting helplessly on the swell when a new threat presented itself in the shape of the *Fougueux*, which now loomed up out of the smoke on the *Téméraire*'s starboard side.

The two ships clashed without either wanting to. The *Téméraire*'s crew had their hands full with the *Redoutable*. The *Fougueux* was still bruised from encounters with the *Belleisle* and *Royal Sovereign*. Bracing themselves for this new challenge, they prepared to board each other as their respective vessels came together on the tide.

The *Téméraire*'s starboard guns were loaded and ready. Captain Harvey held his fire until the *Fougueux*'s yardarms were almost touching the

Téméraire's. Then he let French have it, all in one go. At his command, three decks of guns fired simultaneously into the *Fougueux*, from a range of only a few yards.

The effect was catastrophic. The *Fougueux*'s men had been primed to leap aboard the *Téméraire* and sweep all before them before going to the aid of the *Redoutable*. Instead, it was they who were swept away as they came alongside, vanishing as if by magic. Everything else on deck vanished as well, the *Fougueux*'s rigging, her upper works, everything. Her side was smashed in, the gun ports reduced to a long row of splintered matchwood running the length of the ship. If that wasn't enough, her main and mizenmasts collapsed as well, snapped off by the impact as the two warships collided.

Pierre Servaux, the *Fougueux*'s master-at-arms, never forgot the horror of the moment they brushed up against the *Téméraire*.

At once a broadside burst from her upper-deck guns and main battery, with a hot small-arms fusillade, fired right down into us. It swept our decks clear. Even then though, our men rallied. With cries of '*à l'abordage!*' repeated all over the ship, some sixty or eighty of them swarmed up on deck, armed with axes and cutlasses. But the huge English three-decker towered high above the *Fougueux*, and they fired down on us as they pleased with their musketry, until at length they themselves boarded us.

About two or three hundred of them suddenly stormed our ship, boarding via the chains and main-deck ports. Our captain fell dead, shot through the heart with a musket bullet. The few remaining men could do nothing in the face of such numbers. Resistance was out of the question while the enemy's murderous fire continued from the gangways. We had to give way and yield, though we defended the decks port by port. So the *Fougueux* fell into the power of the English.

Servaux exaggerated the odds. The 'two or three hundred' *Téméraire* sailors actually numbered only twenty-nine, under the command of Lieutenant Thomas Kennedy. As soon as the two ships touched, he yelled, 'Boarders away!' and led his men across to the *Fougueux*. They were beaten back at first, but not for long. Captain Harvey ordered his carronades to spray the *Fougueux*'s decks with musket balls. Kennedy's men tried again and quickly carried the ship. With the French captain dead and many other officers dying, Commander François Bazin was now in charge. Badly wounded himself, he could see that further resistance was useless.

I gave orders to cease firing and dragged myself, despite my wounds, to the captain's cabin to get the box containing the signals and ship's orders and throw it into the sea. Back on the quarterdeck, I was captured and taken aboard the English ship. The enemy hauled our colours down and the slaughter ceased entirely after a while.

Bizarrely, there were now four ships lashed together in a row, as if in harbour. The *Victory*, *Redoutable*, *Téméraire* and *Fougueux* were all facing the same way, their fates intertwined. The *Redoutable* had not yet surrendered, but it could only be a matter of time. Some burning canvas on her stern was threatening to engulf them all. Seeing the danger, Captain Hardy of the *Victory* ordered Midshipmen Francis Collingwood and David Ogilvie to take a few men and put it out. The young men couldn't reach the canvas from the *Victory* because of the curvature of the ships' hulls, so they jumped into a boat and rowed round to the *Redoutable*'s stern instead, climbing in through one of the gun ports.

To their surprise, they found themselves 'well received' by the French. The combatants worked side by side to extinguish the flames. Then the British said goodbye to their French hosts and returned to their boat, intending to rejoin the *Victory* and continue the fighting – only to discover that the boat had been cut adrift by a stray shot and they were stranded aboard the *Redoutable*.

But the French ship had had enough. She was so full of holes that she was in danger of sinking. Captain Lucas had only been waiting for this to be confirmed before agreeing to surrender. Reluctantly, seeing no realistic alternative, he gave the order for the colours to be lowered from the mizenmast.

The *Victory* meanwhile was busily disengaging from the *Redoutable*, casting the lines off and pushing clear of the wreck. She was still doing so when the *Redoutable*'s mizenmast collapsed, with her colours still flying. The mainmast fell as well, right across the *Téméraire*'s poop. The *Redoutable* was in such a state now that Lucas was afraid she would sink before he could get the wounded out. He asked the *Téméraire* for help, adding that if he didn't get it he would set fire to his ship, with disastrous consequences for the British ships either side.

The *Téméraire* promptly sent a party aboard, bringing pumping gear to keep the *Redoutable* afloat. But all did not go well, as Lucas later admitted.

One of the English marines, who entered through a lower deck port, was attacked by one of our wounded sailors armed with a musket and bayonet. He fell angrily on the Englishman, shouting, 'I must kill one more of them!' He bayoneted the marine through the thigh, and the man fell between the two ships.

Disgusted, the rest of the *Téméraire*'s party downed tools to return to their own vessel. It was only after some very fast talking by Lucas that they were persuaded to stay.

While all this was going on, Lord Nelson lay in the *Victory*'s cockpit, listening to the men's cheers as the *Redoutable* surrendered and wondering what was happening on deck. He was in great pain, wincing every time the recoil from the guns jolted his back. The chaplain and purser fanned him with a piece of paper and kept him supplied with wine, lemonade and water. With his life ebbing away, Nelson was preoccupied with Emma and Horatia, repeatedly insisting that they must be taken care of after his death. He wanted to know about the battle as well, and kept asking for Captain Hardy. Messages were sent to the quarterdeck, but Hardy never came down to see him. Nelson was convinced something had happened and the truth was being kept from him.

'Will no one bring Hardy to me? He must be killed. He is surely destroyed.'

But Hardy was far too busy to come. He didn't dare leave the deck with so much going on. He had not yet succeeded in getting a boat away to Collingwood, amid all the chaos. Naval regulations required Collingwood as the senior officer after Nelson to come aboard the *Victory* and command the fleet from there. Nelson's flag was to remain flying 'till the Battle is ended, and the Enemy is no longer in sight'. Until Collingwood appeared, however, Hardy was in charge. It was his responsibility, and his alone. Hardy had a silver pencil case with him, for jotting down signals. He chewed on it in moments of stress. The case became a family heirloom after his death – the teeth marks he left in it on the day of Trafalgar are visible still.

Not far away, Villeneuve faced similar problems aboard the *Bucentaure*. He didn't even have control of his own ship, let alone the rest of his fleet. The *Victory's* broadside had been followed by a similar one from the British *Neptune* that had blasted many of the *Bucentaure's* remaining guns off their carriages and killed more than half the men on one of the gun decks. The *Neptune* had then swung to port and fired three more broadsides before moving on to attack the *Santissima Trinidad's* unprotected stern.

The *Neptune* was followed by the *Leviathan*, which fired a broadside into the *Bucentaure's* stern and another into her starboard side. There was very little the *Bucentaure* could do in reply. She had few guns still working and fewer men to work them. Villeneuve's flagship lay at the mercy of her enemies.

Villeneuve himself was wounded, although only lightly. He had his barge ready to transfer his flag to another ship if the masts came down. Before that, though, Villeneuve made one last attempt to get Dumanoir's lead squadron into the fight. Just over an hour after the battle had begun, he hoisted a second signal for Dumanoir, one that was unequivocal in tone. Signal 167 stated simply: 'The van division to wear together.' In laymen's terms, Villeneuve was ordering Dumanoir's squadron to turn round and get into the action.

The signal had barely been hoisted when the *Conqueror* arrived in the wake of the *Leviathan* and fired yet another broadside into the *Bucentaure*. This one brought the mizenmast down and also the mainmast, taking Villeneuve's signal with it.

But the signal had flown long enough for Dumanoir's squadron to see it. They understood the message all too clearly. It could hardly have been plainer.

At least one of the ships was already turning round and sailing back to the fight. Promoted to command the *Intrépide* after the death of the previous captain in Calder's action, Captain Louis Infernet had been appalled by Dumanoir's reluctance to turn about after Villeneuve's first signal. He had waited a long time for Dumanoir to give the order before taking matters into his own hands. Suspecting that Dumanoir had no intention of getting involved, he had begun to wear his own ship round – incidentally colliding with the *Mont Blanc* in the process and smashing her bowsprit – and was now heading back to the fight, aiming straight for the *Bucentaure*. Villeneuve's flagship lay at the heart of the action, surrounded by the enemy. The *Intrépide* was coming to her rescue as fast as conditions would allow.

The rest of Dumanoir's squadron now followed, some glad to be getting into the fight at last, others reluctant to join in at this late stage. Among other things, it wasn't easy to turn about without any wind. Most had to lower boats and tow their ships round manually, as Infernet had done. Even then, sailing into the thick of an action already lost held little appeal for many of them. They advanced only unwillingly towards the fray.

'I observed with regret that I was followed only by the Spanish *Neptuno*,' recalled Infernet, 'four French ships keeping to the wind on the larboard tack standing south and south-south-west, which took them a gunshot to windward of the enemy fleet, under full sail.' The four recalcitrant ships included Dumanoir's *Formidable*, all of them keeping well to the west, clear of the main action. The *Neptuno* eventually joined them, leaving only the *San Augustin* to follow the *Intrépide*.

Three other ships did actually follow the *Intrépide* for a while, but veered to the east as soon as they came under British fire. Among them was the 100-gun *Rayo*, commanded by the Irishman Henry Macdonnell. They were still in the fight, yet keeping the way open for a retreat to Cadiz, if need be. Discretion was definitely the better part of valour for the ships under Dumanoir's command.

CHAPTER 38

VILLENEUVE SURRENDERS

The fight was becoming general now, with most ships engaged one way or another. A few were still delayed by the lack of wind, but the majority had found a target and were shooting at each other with varying degrees of success. A number of French and Spanish ships had been dismasted, but so had several British. The battle was going the British way, yet was far from one-sided. With the exception of Dumanoir's squadron, the French and Spanish made up in courage what they lacked in seamanship. Their tactic of sniping from the tops had proved unexpectedly effective, clearing the British decks and forcing them onto the defensive. The British did not employ similar tactics. Lord Nelson refused to allow sharpshooters in the rigging, in the belief that guns were too much of a fire hazard among the sails. Musket fire only added to the slaughter without influencing the outcome of the battle, in his opinion.

It was the big guns that would decide the outcome, and there the British had the edge. The French and Spanish ships were bigger and better armed, but the British were better sailors. With Nelson and Collingwood coming straight at them, the French and Spanish should have closed their line, forming a solid wall of wood with no gaps for the British to break through. A few ships had managed to close up, but most had not. The British outmanoeuvred them instead to attack from the stern, the least protected part of a ship. It was no accident that both Nelson and Collingwood broke the enemy's line at the stern of a flagship, firing a broadside without hindrance into a rival commander's rear end. No accident either that they had the advantage of the wind at their backs as they manoeuvred. It was seamanship of a high order.

The guns would decide it, but they hadn't done so yet. The cannon were so powerful that they displaced the air around them and were said to have stilled the wind across the sea. They were so loud that they could be heard in Cadiz, far away on the horizon. All afternoon, the people of the city stood listening to them, anxiously crowding the ramparts and shading their eyes to view the distant pall of smoke to the south-west. According to a contemporary account:

> The ships were not visible from the ramparts, but the crowd of citizens assembled there had their ears assailed by the roaring of the distant cannon; the anxiety of the females bordered on insanity; but more of despair than hope was visible in every countenance. At this dreadful moment, a sound louder than any that had preceded it, and attended with a column of dark smoke, announced that a ship had exploded. The madness of the people was turned to rage against England; and exclamations burst forth, denouncing instant death to every man who spoke the language of their enemies. Two Americans, who had mixed with the people, fled, and hid themselves, to avoid this ebullition of popular fury.

The guns were heard south of Cadiz also, across much of Andalusia. The sound carried well inland, passing over the cork woods and orange groves to the hilltop town of Medina Sidonia, a name loathed by the English since the days of the Spanish Armada. People all over the tip of Spain stopped what they were doing and listened to the rumbling out to sea, wondering uneasily what it might signify for them.

The noise was heard in Tangier as well, along the northern coast of Morocco. They could see the smoke from the hills above the town. The guns were heard at sea too, by ships not involved in the fight. The *Canopus* was on her way back from Gibraltar with 300 tons of water for Nelson's fleet. Passing another ship, she learned that firing had been heard off Cape Trafalgar for 'five hours'. To Captain Frank Austen, that could mean only one thing: the French and Spanish had finally put to sea. Just as he had feared, Austen had missed the big battle and all the prize money and promotion that would go with it. Lord Nelson's promise that the *Canopus* would be back in time for the fight had not been fulfilled.

Aboard the *Bucentaure*, Villeneuve wished he was dead and said as much to his senior officers. He had conducted the battle with coolness and courage, making the best of a bad situation, but he bitterly resented the fact that he was still alive, while so many around him had fallen. He wanted to be killed as well, spared the ignominy of survival. Far better to die bravely now than live to rue so black a day.

With his masts shot away by the *Conqueror*, Villeneuve had given orders for his barge to be lowered, to take him and his flag to another ship. But the barge was full of holes and buried under a mass of fallen spars and rigging. All the other ship's boats had been destroyed as well. Villeneuve and his flag were effectively marooned, stuck on a ship with no masts while the rest of his fleet carried on the fight without him.

Villeneuve's men hailed the *Santissima Trinidad* and asked them to send a boat for him. But the *Santissima* was under fire as well and didn't reply. Villeneuve looked round for his repeating frigate to give him a tow, as Blackwood was doing for Collingwood. But the *Hortense* was too far away to reach him in the light breeze. Her captain couldn't see in the smoke and was excessively cautious anyway. None of the other frigates wanted to help either. Villeneuve was on his own.

It was always going to come to this. The whole enterprise had been doomed from the start, right from the day the French fleet left Toulon six months earlier. Villeneuve had hinted as much in countless dispatches to Admiral Decrès, pointing out the deficiencies in his force, begging him to make sure they were put right. Decrès had spoken to Napoleon on numerous occasions, but Napoleon had never listened. And now here they were, despite the best efforts of Villeneuve and many others to prevent the inevitable from happening.

What to do? With so many dead, and no means of defending the *Bucentaure*, the choices were stark. Further resistance would only lead to more slaughter. Villeneuve's duty now was to those still living. He owed it to them to bring the killing to an end, before any more of them died to no purpose.

Being now without any means of repelling the enemy, the upper works and the twenty-four-pounder deck strewn with dead and wounded, the lower-deck guns dismounted or blocked by fallen masts and rigging, the ship isolated in the middle of the enemy and unable to move, I had to yield to fate. It remained only to prevent any further bloodshed. The slaughter was already vast. Any more would have been quite useless.

Villeneuve looked at Lieutenant Fulcran Fournier and gave him the nod. It was time to surrender. He turned away, unable to watch as Fournier lowered the colours and ordered the broken pieces of the Imperial eagle to be thrown overboard. By Villeneuve's account, the *Bucentaure* had lost all of her masts by then. The *Conqueror*'s log, written after the battle, agreed. But William Hicks, a midshipman watching from the *Conqueror*'s quarterdeck, remembered it slightly differently.

We engaged her single-handed for an hour, and she struck to us; after her colours were hauled down two guns from her starboard quarter began to play on us. Sir Israel Pellew, thinking that they were disposed to renew the fight, ordered the guns which could bear on her foremast to knock it away, and her masts were cut away successfully in a few minutes. The officers of the French ship waving their handkerchiefs in sign of surrender, we sent a cutter and took possession of the *Bucentaure*. Then we moved on.

Whatever the truth, Captain Pellew failed to realise that it was the enemy's commander-in-chief who had fallen into his hands. Instead of sending the *Conqueror*'s first lieutenant to take possession of the *Bucentaure*, as was customary, he detached a Marine officer instead. With three other Marines and two seamen, Captain James Atcherley climbed into the cutter and was rowed across to the *Bucentaure*. He was stunned to discover four very senior French officers waiting for him on the quarterdeck. One was Villeneuve, another Captain Jean Magendie. The third was Captain Mathieu Prigny and the fourth Brigadier-General Théodore de Contamine, who had succeeded General Lauriston as commander of the 4,000 troops aboard the French fleet. All four were bowing to Atcherley and offering him their swords.

Villeneuve spoke in halting English. 'To whom have I the honour of surrendering?'

'To Captain Pellew of the *Conqueror.*'

'I am glad to have struck to the fortunate Sir Edward Pellew.' Sir Edward was a distinguished admiral, well known to the French. But Villeneuve had got the wrong man.

'It is his brother, sir,' said Atcherley.

'His brother? What, are there two of them? *Hélas!*'

'*Fortune de la guerre,*' shrugged Magendie, who had been captured by the Royal Navy twice before.

Atcherley told them to keep their swords until they could surrender to the more senior Captain Pellew. Leaving the French on deck, he took his men below to secure the magazines. They were staggered by what they saw:

> The dead, thrown back as they fell, lay along the middle of the decks in heaps, and the shot, passing through these, had frightfully mangled the bodies . . . More than 400 had been killed and wounded, of whom an extraordinary proportion had lost their heads. A raking shot, which entered in the lower deck, had glanced along the beams and through the thickest of the people, and a French officer declared that this shot alone had killed or disabled nearly forty men.

But not everyone was dead. Atcherley's arrival, in his bright red coat, had been noticed by the British deserters on the lower deck. A British officer was the last person they wanted to see. Capture by the Royal Navy meant only one thing for them – execution by hanging. They would be court-martialled and strung up from the yardarm without any hope of clemency. There was no mercy for deserters in time of war, particularly not ones who had fought against their own side.

With nothing to lose, one of these desperate men attempted to fight his way out. Grabbing a sword, he lunged out of the gloom at Atcherley's party. But they were too quick for him. One of his seamen hit back with a cutlass, virtually decapitating the man with a single blow.

Atcherley locked up the magazines and pocketed the keys. Posting the Marines as sentries on the admiral and flag-captain's cabins, he went back on deck to take Villeneuve and the others across to the *Conqueror*. Prigny was too badly hurt to go, but Villeneuve, Magendie and de Contamine climbed into the cutter, along with two aides. The *Conqueror* had moved on by then to attack the *Santissima Trinidad*, so Atcherley needed another British ship for his prisoners. Looking around, he spotted the *Mars* not far away and ordered his men to pull towards her.

A few minutes later, Admiral Villeneuve was climbing aboard. The first thing he saw on deck was Captain Duff's headless body, as Midshipman Thomas Robinson recalled:

> The French commander-in-chief came aboard about the middle of the battle and seeing Captain Duff lying dead upon Deck began to smile to some of his attendants which one of our sailors observing came running up to him and laid hold of him and said when my captain lived he was able to avenge an insult now he is dead it is my duty to revenge it for him at the same time throwing Villeneuve from him covered the dead body with a flag that was laying near him.

With Duff gone, Lieutenant William Hennah was now in command of the *Mars*. He received Villeneuve politely and accepted his sword in token of the French commander's surrender.

The *Conqueror* meanwhile had joined the British ships surrounding the *Santissima Trinidad*. She arrived just in time to see the Spanish four-decker dismasted, as one of her officers later recounted:

> The *Bucentaure* had just surrendered and the *Conqueror* passed on to take a station on the quarter of the *Trinidada*, while the *Neptune* continued the action with her on the bow. In a short time this

tremendous fabric gave a deep roll with the swell to leeward, then back to windward; and on her return every mast went by the board, leaving her an unmanageable hulk on the water. Her immense topsails had every reef out, her royals were sheeted home but lowered, and the falling of this mass of spars, sails and rigging, plunging into the water at the muzzles of our guns, was one of the most magnificent sights I ever beheld. Immediately after this a Spaniard showed an English Union on the lee gangway, in token of submission.

That was not quite the end of it. The little *Africa*, at sixty-four guns less than half the *Santissima's* size, lay to windward and didn't see the Union Jack. The Spanish were showing no colours of their own, though, and had ceased firing, so the *Africa* assumed they wanted to surrender. Captain Henry Digby impudently sent Lieutenant John Smith over in a boat to take possession.

Smith arrived to find that the Spanish had changed their minds about surrendering. They had just noticed Dumanoir's squadron in the distance, heading back towards the battle. Smith was received with courtesy, but was assured that the *Santissima* had no intention of giving up. The ship had only stopped firing, they told him, because they were busy getting more ammunition up from the magazines. It was just an oversight that their colours were no longer showing. Politely escorting Smith back to his boat, the Spanish retained command of their floating hulk and remained in the fight for a while longer, hoping to hang on until the new arrivals came to their aid.

But Dumanoir's squadron had also been spotted by Captain Hardy. He immediately hoisted a signal from the *Victory* ordering his column to keep their wind and engage the enemy's van. Seven British ships acknowledged and brought their bows round, turning slowly northwards to meet this new threat. The remainder either didn't see the signal or were in no state to go anywhere.

Dumanoir's ten ships were already dividing into three groups, each going their own way. He had intended the whole squadron to sail southwards to the west of the battle, from where they would be well placed to turn to port at length and advance towards the action on the swell, with the wind at their backs, as the British had done. If Dumanoir had given that order hours earlier, the battle would have been looking very different by now. But only four of Dumanoir's ships had obeyed the order to follow him. Two more were heading straight for the British and the other three were hanging back towards the east, looking nervously over their shoulders towards Cadiz. Dumanoir's force was fatally divided just when it needed to be together.

Dumanoir pressed on anyway. Immediately in front of him lay the *Minotaur* and *Spartiate*. They were the last two ships of Nelson's column and were still proceeding towards the battle. Dumanoir headed towards them, intending to cut them off with his five ships before they could reach what remained of Villeneuve's line.

CHAPTER 39

───◆◆◆───

GRAVINA ORDERS A RETREAT

While Dumanoir headed south, Captain Hardy found time at last to go below to visit Nelson. It was more than an hour now since the admiral had been hit. Hardy was glad to find him still alive when he reached the cockpit.

'How goes the battle?' demanded Nelson.

'Very well, my Lord. We have twelve or fourteen of the enemy's ships in our possession, but five of their van have tacked and show an intention of bearing down upon the *Victory*. I have therefore called two or three of our fresh ships round us, and have no doubt of giving them a drubbing.'

'I hope none of *our* ships have struck, Hardy?'

'No, my Lord. There is no fear of that.'

Nelson was fading rapidly. 'I am a dead man, Hardy. I am going fast. It will be all over with me soon. Come nearer to me. Pray let my dear Lady Hamilton have my hair, and all other things belonging to me.'

Embarrassed by this, Burke the purser moved away, not wanting to intrude. But Nelson told him to stay.

'I hope Mr Beatty can yet hold out some prospect of life,' Hardy ventured.

'Oh no.' Nelson knew he was dying. 'It is impossible. My back is shot through. Beatty will tell you so.'

Hardy didn't reply. He couldn't stay any longer with Dumanoir closing fast. Gripping Nelson warmly by the hand, he left him and went back to the battle. Nelson insisted that Beatty should leave as well to attend the rest of the wounded. But he sent for him again a few minutes later to say that he had lost all power of movement or feeling below his chest.

It was a bad sign. There had been a similar case aboard the *Victory* a few months earlier – a seaman paralysed with a broken back who had taken thirteen days to die. Nelson understood the implications all too well.

Beatty felt Nelson's legs without getting any response. 'My Lord,' he admitted, 'unhappily for our country nothing can be done for you.' He turned away to hide his tears.

'I know it,' Nelson agreed. 'I feel something rising in my breast which tells me I am gone.'

He was fanned and given something to drink. 'God be praised,' he kept repeating. 'I have done my duty.'

Beatty asked if the pain was still bad. Nelson replied that it was so severe he wished he was dead. 'Yet one would like to live a little longer, too.' He lay sunk in thought for a while before speaking again. 'What would become of poor Lady Hamilton if she knew my situation?'

Beatty had no answer to that. He returned instead to the rest of the wounded, who still needed his attention.

A mile to the west, Dumanoir's five ships had reached the tail end of Nelson's line and were bearing down on the *Minotaur* and *Spartiate*. The two British ships were unimpressed. Keeping steadily to their course, they hove to in front of Dumanoir's bows and began firing at him from a range of only fifty yards. 'At the distance of pistol-shot, they did me considerable damage,' he later commented. His column also came under fire from the seven British ships ordered north by Hardy. The Spanish *Neptuno* was badly damaged, her captain knocked out by a falling mast. Seeing her predicament, the *Minotaur* and *Spartiate* closed in for the kill, forcing the *Neptuno* to surrender while the rest of Dumanoir's ships abandoned her to her fate and continued hurriedly southwards.

Through his telescope, Dumanoir could see that the *Bucentaure* and *Santissima Trinidad* had been dismasted as well. Many other ships had lowered their colours and were surrendering to the British. Those still fighting were looking to Dumanoir for help. As soon as he was in range, he loosed off a few shots at the *Victory* and *Téméraire* to show that he was doing something. Some of the shots hit the *Redoutable* instead, killing a number of Frenchmen who had surrendered to the *Téméraire*. Whether he noticed or not, Dumanoir decided there was little to be gained from getting any more closely involved. He maintained his course instead.

> I continued towards our rearguard, which I found in part surrendered. I engaged twelve vessels in succession, four of which were three-deckers and gave us a hard time. Only thirteen French and Spanish vessels still remained on the field of battle, all of them surrendered. There were also fifteen English ships, of which only one had been dismasted. I was thus cut off from the rest of the combined fleet, which was sailing before the wind.
>
> The *Neptuno*, a Spanish ship, had tacked about with us but had been left a long way behind. She was surrounded by the enemy, dismasted and forced to surrender. My division, consisting now of only four disabled ships, was cut off to windward, the rest of the combined fleet being two leagues away and bearing off under full sail. To rejoin them, I would have had to tackle the English squadron, which remained intact between us. I would have been heading for certain destruction, with no prospect of doing any real damage to the enemy.

Dumanoir's division was not as badly hit as he made out. His own ship had suffered sixty-five casualties and was holed below the waterline, but two others had sustained no casualties at all, and the fourth only a few. Dumanoir decided nevertheless to distance his division from the battle and effect what repairs he could before reviewing the situation next day.

His decision did not impress those still fighting under far worse conditions, as one captain bitterly recorded:

> We were all mixed together in total confusion. It was painfully apparent that the British flag predominated amongst the combatants, when at length Admiral Dumanoir's division appeared under sail on the larboard tack. The French and Spanish were heartened by the sight. They invested all their hopes in Dumanoir's division. But their

hopes were dashed when the ships – the *Formidable*, *Scipion*, *Duguay Trouin* and *Mont Blanc* – edged off to windward and fired a few useless broadsides before departing the scene entirely.

Unlike Dumanoir's ships, dancing around the edges of the action, Captain Infernet of the *Intrépide* had sailed right into the middle of it, heading straight for the *Bucentaure*. It was a stupid thing to do, with Villeneuve's ship already overwhelmed, but Infernet didn't care. Like Captain Lucas of the *Redoutable*, he was of humble origin, risen on his merits. His instinct was always to head for the sound of the guns. Marquis Gicquel des Touches, one of the *Intrépide*'s lieutenants, admired his courage:

> It was into the thick of this fray that our Captain Infernet led us. He wanted, he said, to rescue Admiral Villeneuve and take him on board, and then to rally around us the ships still capable of fighting. It was a reckless, forlorn hope, a mad enterprise – and he himself did not doubt it. It was the pretext Infernet gave for continuing the fight. He would not have it said that the *Intrépide* had quit the battle while she could still fire a gun or hoist a sail. It was noble madness, but though we knew it, we all cheerfully supported him – and wish others had done the same!

The *Intrépide* never got near the *Bucentaure*. She was set upon by the *Leviathan*, *Africa*, *Agamemnon* and *Orion* and attacked without mercy. Her port lids were shot away and she was quickly riddled below the waterline. Before long, her masts were tottering as well. It was as much as Infernet could do to keep the ship afloat, let alone rescue Villeneuve.

From his post on the fo'c'sle, des Touches watched a British ship bearing down on them:

> While the fighting was very hot, the British *Orion* crossed our bows to rake us. I got my boarding party ready and sent a midshipman to the captain with a request to lay our ship aboard the *Orion*. Seeing the spirit of my men, I already imagined myself master of the British seventy-four, taking her into Cadiz with her colours under ours! I

waited tensely, but the *Intrépide* did not change course, so I hurried to the quarterdeck myself.

On the way, I found my midshipman lying flat on the deck, terrified at the sight of the *Téméraire* [des Touches probably meant the *Britannia*] which had come abreast of us within pistol shot and was thundering into us with her batteries. I treated my messenger as he deserved – gave him a hearty kick – and then continued aft to speak to the captain personally. By then though it was too late. The *Orion* swept across our bows, loosing off a murderous broadside, and we never got another chance.

The French fought with great courage, but the outcome was never in doubt. The *Intrépide*'s masts were shot away and most of her guns disabled. She had eight feet of water in her hold and 306 men killed or wounded – almost half her crew. Even then, though, Captain Infernet refused to surrender. He had to be forcibly held down as the colours were lowered at length to prevent any further slaughter.

Humphrey Senhouse, a lieutenant watching from the *Conqueror*, was full of admiration. 'Her captain surrendered after one of the most gallant defences I ever witnessed. The Frenchman's name was Infernet, a member of the Legion of Honour, and it deserves to be recorded in the memory of those who admire true heroism.'

But that was little consolation to Infernet. He had sworn to Napoleon that he would defend his ship to the death. In despair, he was taken aboard the *Orion* with his eleven-year-old son – by French accounts, swimming across with the boy on his shoulders, by English, being fetched in the ship's boat. Once on board, he was well received by Captain Codrington, who shared the general admiration for his gallant opponent. Infernet, he later told his wife:

is much like us in his open manner, is a good sailor, and I have no doubt a good officer, has more delicacy in his conduct, although perhaps more boisterous in his manner, than any Frenchman I have before met with: and endeavours to make himself agreeable to all in the ship. He fought most stoutly, and had I not had the advantage over him of position and a ready fire whilst he was engaged with others, we should not have escaped as well as we did.

Wretched and bedraggled, Infernet had been taken aboard the *Orion* with nothing to his name except the clothes on his back. A Canadian captain later gave him £100 to buy some more.

Among the Spanish commanders, the situation was every bit as grim. They too had fought outstandingly, only to see their courage and sacrifice go for nothing as ship after ship was battered into submission, forced to surrender by the superior gunnery and seamanship of the British.

Aboard the *San Juan Nepomuceno*, at the southern end of the battle, Commodore Cosma de Churruca had been full of gloom from the start, convinced that Villeneuve was leading them all to disaster. 'Write to your friends that you are going into a battle that will be desperate and bloody,' he had advised his nephew, who was on board with him. 'Tell them also that they may be certain of this – I, for my part, will meet my death there. Tell them that I shall sink my ship rather than surrender. It is the last duty an officer owes his king and country.' Churruca's words were melodramatic, but he meant what he said. He would never allow his ship to be taken while he was still alive to prevent it.

The *San Juan* was part of Gravina's observer squadron, unable to get into the action until Collingwood's column had smashed through the enemy line. Thereafter, Churruca had steered for the *Bellerophon*, only to be intercepted by the *Tonnant*, *Defiance* and *Dreadnought*. The *San Juan* had been hopelessly outgunned. Churruca himself was hit almost immediately in the thigh by a cannon ball, but insisted that the fight should go on. His last order before being taken below was for the colours to be nailed to the mast.

He died a few minutes later, after leaving a farewell message for the bride he had married five months earlier. Without him, the crew swiftly lost heart. They conceded defeat when Lieutenant Clement hailed them from the *Tonnant* to ask if they had struck. Clement's boat was swamped before he could take possession, so the *San Juan* ended up surrendering to the *Dreadnought* instead.

*

Aboard the *Bahama*, also part of the observer squadron, it was a similar story. Commodore Alcala Galiano exchanged a few shots with the *Bellerophon* at close range, then moved on to tackle the *Colossus* in an extended fight. Galiano was hit in the foot early on and gashed in the head by a splinter, but refused to go below. Like Churruca, he too had nailed his colours to the mast. He was standing on the quarterdeck at about 3 p.m. when the wind of a passing shot sent him staggering back and knocked the telescope out of his hand. His coxswain picked it up and was about to return it when a cannon ball cut him in two. Galiano himself was killed a moment later when another ball took off part of his head.

A flag was hurriedly thrown over Galiano's body, but too late to hide the truth from his men. News of the captain's death spread rapidly around the ship. The *Bahama* had been holding her own in the fight with the *Colossus*, but with Galiano gone and other officers wounded, the crew began to waver. Galiano had been a brave man and a strict disciplinarian. Without his steadying hand, the men were less determined. After a hasty consultation, the surviving officers appear to have panicked, tearing down their flag instead of fighting on, and raising the Union Jack in its place. The *Colossus* then moved in smartly to take their surrender before they had a chance to change their minds.

All of this was bad news for Admiral Gravina, the Spanish commander. His best officers were going down like ninepins, taking their flags with them. The British seemed to be everywhere, scattering all before them. Gravina himself had been badly wounded in the arm after a lengthy fight with several of Collingwood's ships. He had been taken below to have the wound dressed, but had insisted on being carried back on deck, only to faint from loss of blood. He had recovered quickly and remained in command, with the help of his chief of staff Rear-Admiral Antonio de Escano.

If that wasn't enough, they were now in command of the whole fleet as well, supposed to rally the remaining ships and turn the battle in their favour. It was a hopeless task with the *Santissima Trinidad* dismasted, Villeneuve's flag down and many other ships surrendering. Fighting had already ceased along much of the line. The only squadron still in contention was Gravina's, and most of his ships were surrendering as well. It would only be reinforcing failure to carry on now.

The alternative was to run for Cadiz, taking the remains of the fleet with him. It was not a happy prospect, but Gravina could see no other choice. Better that than surrendering meekly to the British. Better by far to escape while he still could, rather than lose every single ship to the enemy.

Reluctantly, Gravina gave the order. The signal was hoisted to the masthead: all ships to rally on his. At the same time, with two of her masts wobbling alarmingly, the *Principe de Asturias* began to extricate herself from the battle, edging slowly away from the fight and pointing her bows towards the north-east, the direction of Cadiz.

CHAPTER 40

———◆———

KISS ME, HARDY

It was not only Gravina's masts that had been hit. His sails were in tatters as well. The *Principe de Asturias* was so badly damaged that she would never make it back to Cadiz without a tow.

The nearest frigate was the *Themis*. Downwind of the bigger ships, Captain Jugan had been lost in smoke for much of the battle, unable to see what was happening. He knew only that firing had ceased along much of the line, although he could hear at least one ship still in action.

> In a little time, about a quarter to five, the smoke had entirely drifted away and I made out the *Principe de Asturias*, Admiral Gravina's flagship, dragging herself very slowly off to leeward with what remained of her ragged sails. In response to her signals, I immediately headed for the *Principe* and passed close astern of her.

Jugan was ordered to take the *Principe* in tow, because her masts were threatening to come down at any moment.

> I obeyed as soon as possible, and at the same time all firing ceased as well. Several of our ships were now following the *Neptune's* example and keeping close to the wind. They seemed to be waiting for Admiral Gravina to join them, so I towed the Spanish flagship in their direction.

All the ships that could still move rallied to Gravina, steering away from the battle in the direction of Cadiz. They were followed immediately by the British. At the northern end of the line, the *Conqueror* changed course to intercept a French ship that was trying to escape with only a foremast still standing.

Her Captain stood upon the poop, holding the lower corner of a small French jack, while he pinned the upper with his sword to the stump of the mizenmast. She fired two or three guns, probably to provoke a return, which might spare the discredit of a tame surrender. The *Conqueror's* broadside was ready; but Captain Pellew exclaimed: 'Don't hurt the brave fellow; fire a single shot across his bow!' Her Captain immediately lowered his sword, thus dropping the colours, and, taking off his hat, bowed his surrender.

But the pursuit did not last long. With night coming on and many of their own ships damaged, the British were in no state for a lengthy chase. A signal from Collingwood to come to the wind soon brought them back. In all, eleven enemy ships were allowed to escape, limping towards Cadiz as fast as they could go. The smoke cleared after they had gone and the guns fell silent at last. Five hours after it had started, the great sea battle off Cape Trafalgar had finally come to an end.

While this last act was being played out, Hardy had been to see Nelson again. Grasping the admiral by the hand, he congratulated him on a brilliant victory. He didn't know how many enemy ships had surrendered, but he was sure it was fourteen or fifteen at least.

'That is well,' agreed Nelson, 'but I bargained for twenty.' His mind was dwelling on the heavy swell. With so many ships dismasted or rudderless, the fleet might easily be driven aground after the battle and dashed to pieces on the rocks. Nelson had earlier signalled his captains to anchor at the close of day. He wanted to be sure the message had sunk in. 'Anchor, Hardy,' he reminded his captain. '*Anchor!*'

'I suppose, my Lord, Admiral Collingwood will now take upon himself the direction of affairs.'

'Not while I live, I hope, Hardy.' Nelson struggled to raise himself from his makeshift bed. 'No. Do *you* anchor, Hardy.'

'Shall we make the signal, sir?'

'Yes, for if I live, I'll anchor.'

But Nelson was not going to live. He told Hardy he would be dead in a few minutes. He was keen to avoid the usual fate of sailors killed in action. 'Don't throw me overboard, Hardy.'

'Oh no! Certainly not!'

'Then you know what to do. Take care of my dear Lady Hamilton, Hardy. Take care of poor Lady Hamilton. Kiss me, Hardy.'

Kneeling down, Hardy kissed him on the cheek. 'Now I am satisfied,' said Nelson. 'Thank God I have done my duty.'

After a minute or two, Hardy knelt again and kissed Nelson's forehead. 'Who is that?' demanded Nelson.

'It is Hardy.'

'God bless you, Hardy.'

Hardy returned sombrely to the quarterdeck, leaving Nelson with his steward, Burke the purser and Alexander Scott, the chaplain. Nelson's voice was growing fainter by the minute. 'Doctor,' he insisted to Scott, 'I have not been a *great* sinner. Remember, I leave Lady Hamilton and my daughter Horatia as a legacy to my country.'

Scott rubbed his chest continually while the others fanned his face and moistened his lips. But Nelson was fading fast. He could hardly breathe now, let alone talk. 'Thank God, I have done my duty,' he kept repeating, until at length the words tailed off altogether. His attendants waited quietly, not wanting to disturb him, for another five minutes. Then his steward fetched the surgeon.

Beatty felt Nelson's hand. It was very cold, with no pulse in the wrist. His forehead was cold, too, but Nelson was still clinging to life. He opened his eyes briefly when Beatty touched his brow.

It couldn't be much longer now. Beatty returned to the other casualties, but hadn't been gone long when he was called back by the steward. With Scott rubbing his chest and Walter Burke supporting his shoulders, Horatio Nelson had died at 4.30 p.m., just as the last shots were being fired in the greatest naval victory his country had ever known.

*

There was no time to grieve. The battle wasn't over yet. Shooting was still sporadic. The *Victory*'s mizenmast was about to collapse and a fire aboard the French *Achille* was hopelessly out of control. With wreckage everywhere, ships drifting into each other and the wounded crying out for help, there was still plenty to do before the storm developing in the west came on.

Hardy's first priority was to report to Admiral Collingwood. Taking the only one of the *Victory*'s boats that hadn't been shattered, he had himself rowed across to the *Royal Sovereign*. Collingwood's eyes misted over at the news of Nelson's death. Hardy told him that Nelson's last order had been for the fleet to anchor after the battle.

'Anchor the fleet!' exclaimed Collingwood. 'Why, it is the last thing I should have thought of.' With so much else on his mind, Collingwood had not considered the dangers of running aground on the gathering swell. He wasn't even sure that Nelson was right.

While Hardy rowed over to the *Royal Sovereign*, Henry Blackwood of the *Euryalus* had come the other way, hurrying across to the *Victory* to see Nelson before he died. Nelson's earlier forecast that he would never see him again was ringing in his ears. Scrambling up the *Victory*'s side, Blackwood asked for the admiral and was told he was still alive. He went straight down to the cockpit to discover it wasn't true. Nelson had died a few minutes earlier and Blackwood had just missed him. Nelson's gloomy prophecy had proved only too accurate.

All eyes turned now towards the *Achille*, burning furiously from end to end. The fire had begun in the foretop, where an arms chest had exploded. The foretop had collapsed before the French could get the flames under control, apparently destroying the ship's fire engine as it fell. The flames had then spread unchecked and were threatening to burn the entire ship down to the waterline. The British were doing all they could to take off survivors, but they were worried that the *Achille*'s powder magazine would blow as well, taking everyone with it. To add to the danger, her guns were still loaded and going off at random, ignited by the heat. The *Achille* was a hazard to all the ships around her as she drifted out of control on the swell.

The French were even more worried than the British. With the *Achille*'s captain dead, Sub-Lieutenant Alphonse Cauchard had opened the bilge cocks to flood the ship before ordering all hands on deck. He set them to work throwing debris overboard for the men to cling to when they abandoned ship. They were desperate to escape. Those who could swim were already stripping off and jumping into the sea, determined to put a safe distance between themselves and the ship before she blew. The rest were still on board, terrified of the flames, terrified also of the water. There was nothing they could do, nowhere they could run to. They knew they were all doomed unless a miracle came to save them.

Among those trapped on board were at least two women, one of them the young wife of a maintopman. Jeanne Caunant, known as Jeanette, had been ordered ashore when the fleet left Cadiz, but had remained aboard, apparently disguised as a sailor. She had worked in the forward magazine during the battle, handing up powder for the guns. As soon as the firing stopped she had gone to look for her husband, only to discover that the ladders to the main deck had been removed or shot away. Jeanette was trapped below as fire engulfed the ship. With dead and dying all around, everyone else on deck and the bilge flooding rapidly, she ran to and fro in shock, not knowing what to do. She was still undecided when the deck above her burned away and the guns began to fall through. Hurrying to the ship's stern, she climbed out through a gun port, preferring to brave the water rather than be crushed by a gun or scorched to death.

Grabbing hold of the rudder chain, Jeanette worked her way round to the back of the rudder and huddled there for some time, praying for the ship to blow up and put her out of her misery. Instead, the lead lining of the rudder-trunk began to melt as the flames caught hold. It dripped down in a molten cascade, burning her neck, shoulders and legs dreadfully. She would be scalded to death if she stayed there any longer. The only refuge now was the sea.

Stripping naked, Jeanette plunged in. She floundered towards a group of crew members clinging to a flimsy piece of wreckage. They weren't pleased to see her. One of them bit and kicked her to make her go away. Fortunately for Jeanette, another man saw her distress and swam over with a length of plank. He placed it under her arms to keep her afloat. By her own account, she was still clinging to it two hours later when a boat from the *Naiad* found her at last and picked her up.

The *Achille* had long gone by then. The ship blew up about 5.30 p.m., taking most of her crew with her. In one mighty explosion, so loud that they heard it in Cadiz, the powder magazine went up, flinging bodies and debris high into the air in a great ball of smoke and fire. Most of those still aboard were killed instantly. The onlookers could do nothing except wince in horror as the bodies twisted helplessly through the air before plummeting back into the sea. The British could scarcely bear to watch, as one officer aboard the *Defence* remembered:

> It was a sight the most awful and grand that can be conceived. In a moment the hull burst into a cloud of smoke and fire. A column of vivid flame shot up to an enormous height in the atmosphere and terminated by expanding into an immense globe, representing, for a few seconds, a prodigious tree in flames, speckled with many dark spots, which the pieces of timber and bodies of men occasioned while they were suspended in the clouds.

Jeanette's husband was probably among them. She herself was more dead than alive, badly blistered by the molten lead. A British sailor gave her his trousers when she was hauled into the *Naiad*'s boat. Another gave her his coat and a third a handkerchief for her head. She was taken to the *Pickle*, already overflowing with French survivors. The tiny schooner had somehow managed to cram 160 Frenchmen on board, many of them stark naked. Jeanette was sent to join them, miserable and wretched without her husband. The headroom below was only four foot three, which could only have added to her distress.

In all, perhaps 200 of the *Achille*'s crew survived the disaster. Some were taken aboard the *Euryalus*, where they recovered their spirits with astonishing rapidity. Midshipman Hercules Robinson remembered 'getting hold of a dozen of her men who were hoisted into the air out of the exploding ship, cursing their fate, *sacre*-ing, tearing their hair, and wiping the gunpowder and the salt water from their faces; and how, in the evening these same fellows, having got their supper and grog and dry clothes, danced for the amusement of our men under the half-deck'.

Robinson also helped save a black pig, which scrambled gratefully aboard the *Euryalus* in the belief that it had been rescued, only to discover that its faith in the Royal Navy was wholly misplaced. There were pork chops all round for supper that night.

Aboard the *Belleisle*, a mile away, there were too many casualties for anyone to think of dancing, or even enjoying the victory. With no masts and men lying wounded everywhere, the *Belleisle* had problems enough just keeping afloat. The first concern for most people in the immediate aftermath of the battle was to find out who among their friends had been killed, and who were still alive.

'Eager inquiries were expressed and earnest congratulations exchanged, at this joyful moment,' recalled Lieutenant Paul Nicolas. 'The officers came to make their report to the Captain, and the fatal results cast a gloom over the scene of our triumph.' Among the officers, the first lieutenant had predicted his own death at breakfast that morning and had indeed been killed, as had the junior lieutenant and many others. Paul Nicolas went to see their bodies:

These gallant fellows were lying beside each other in the gun-room preparatory to their being committed to the deep; and here many met to take a last look at their departed friends, whose remains soon followed the promiscuous multitude, without distinction of either rank or nation, to their wide ocean grave. In the act of launching a poor sailor over the poop, he was discovered to breathe. He was, of course, saved, and after being a week in hospital the ball, which had entered at his temple, came out of his mouth.

The upper deck presented a confused and dreadful appearance: masts, yards, sails, ropes and fragments of wreck were scattered in every direction; nothing could be more horrible than the scene of blood and mangled remains with which every part was covered, and which, from the quantity of splinters, resembled a shipwright's yard strewed with gore.

From our extensive loss – thirty-four killed and ninety-six wounded – our cockpit exhibited a scene of suffering which rarely occurs. I visited this abode of suffering with the natural impulse which led many others thither – namely, to ascertain the fate of a friend or companion. So many bodies in such a confined space and under such distressing circumstances would affect the most obdurate heart. My nerves were but little accustomed to such trials but even the dangers of battle did not seem more terrific than the spectacle before me.

On a long table lay several men anxiously looking for their turn to receive the surgeon's care, yet dreading the fate he might pronounce. One subject was undergoing amputation, and every part was heaped with sufferers: their piercing shrieks and expiring groans were echoed through this vault of misery: and even at this distant period the heart-sickening picture is alive in my memory. What a contrast to the hilarity and enthusiastic mirth which reigned in this spot the preceding evening.

At 5 p.m., Captain Hargood summoned the *Belleisle*'s surviving officers to tea in his cabin. They were glad to be asked. The smoke had left them all parched, and they were exhausted, physically and mentally. Hargood also invited a Spanish officer, the second captain of the *Argonauta*, who had come aboard to surrender. The man was a little bemused to find himself attending this most English of ceremonies with the battle still sputtering outside.

Tea was barely over when a lieutenant from the *Entreprenante* arrived with the news of Nelson's death. He could hardly have dispensed more gloom.

The melancholy tidings spread through the ship in an instant, and its paralysing effect was wonderful. Our Captain had served under the illustrious chief for years, and had partaken in the anxious pursuit of the enemy across the Atlantic, with the same officers and crew. 'Lord Nelson is no more!' was repeated with such despondency and heartfelt sorrow that every one seemed to mourn a parent. All exertion was suspended: the veteran sailor indulged in silent grief; and some eyes evinced that tenderness of heart is often concealed under the roughest exterior. [Even the Spanish captain] joined in our regret.

It was the same across the rest of the fleet, although not everyone heard the news at once. Aboard the *Royal Sovereign*, a sailor named Sam gave an account of it to his father in a letter home.

Our dear Admiral Nelson is killed! So we have paid pretty sharply for licking 'em. I never sat [sic] eyes on him myself, for which I am both sorry and glad; for, to be sure, I should like to have seen him – but then, all the men in our ship who have seen him are such soft toads they have done nothing but blast their eyes, and cry, ever since he was killed. God bless you! Chaps that fought like the devil sit down and cry like a wench.

Sam himself had lost three fingers in the battle, but didn't even notice until it was over. Fortunately for him, they were on his left hand.

Aboard the *Bellerophon*, they did not know what had happened, but guessed something was amiss when darkness fell and no lights shone from the *Victory*. With the *Royal Sovereign* crippled, Collingwood transferred his flag to the frigate *Euryalus* at the end of the battle. After dark, he carried the lights of the commander-in-chief as well, which confirmed to the rest of the fleet that Nelson must have been killed. Even then, though, they didn't want to believe it. An officer going aboard the *Euryalus* next morning had breakfast with Collingwood and received his orders without either of them even mentioning the subject.

On the *Victory* herself, they felt the loss worst of all, but still had no time to mourn. The mizenmast had come crashing down after Nelson's death and the other two were threatening to follow. The crew were struggling to secure them with runners and tackles. Midshipman Pollard was with them, helping to oversee the rigging of a temporary jury mast. Once it had been done, he was summoned to the wardroom and congratulated by Captain Hardy and the other officers for avenging Lord Nelson's death.

While all that was going on, Admiral Villeneuve came aboard, expecting to dine with Lord Nelson. The Royal Marines hastily produced a guard of honour under Second Lieutenant Rotely. In full dress uniform, 'as if on parade on shore', the men stood smartly to attention and presented arms as the enemy commander stepped onto the deck. 'What cannot the English do?' Villeneuve demanded in astonishment, as he acknowledged their salute.

Elsewhere, men were still in shock from the battle, reeling from the horror of everything they had seen and heard during the past few hours.

Aboard the *Leviathan*, they spoke of Thomas Main, whose arm had been shot off while he manned a gun on the fo'c'sle. Refusing all help, Main made his own way down to the surgeon and insisted on waiting his turn, although more badly hurt than most. He sang 'Rule, Britannia' in a firm, steady voice as the surgeon sawed off the rest of his arm near the shoulder, conducting himself with great composure throughout.

On the *Victory*, seventeen-year-old Midshipman William Rivers had similarly waited his turn, cutting pieces of flesh and bone from his own leg until the surgeon had time to amputate it. The midshipman also submitted without a murmur. 'It is nothing at all. I thought it had become much worse.'

On another ship, they remembered a man cut off at the knees by a passing shot. His body was blown overboard, but his legs remained upright on deck 'with all the firmness and animation of life'.

On the *Britannia*, a shot had struck the muzzle of a gun, killing or wounding almost the entire crew. Among them 'was a man named Pilgrim, an Italian, who was stooping to take up a shot for the gun, when it was split, and both his arms were blown off'.

Aboard the *Achilles*, Marine Stephen Humphries remembered the bad behaviour of a seaman at breakfast, pushing and shoving to get an extra helping of rice from the copper.

The first round shot from the enemy, that told amongst the crew, caught this fellow just on the side of his head, and smashed it to pieces; and his tongue was dashed against the still-hot copper, where it stuck and remained a long time. This was talked of as a judgement upon him for many a day after.

Aboard the *Revenge*, the ship's cobbler had been knocked out when his head collided with another man's under gunfire.

No one doubted but that he was dead. As it is customary to throw overboard those who, in an engagement, are killed outright, the poor cobbler, amongst the rest, was taken to the porthole to be committed to the deep, without any other ceremony than shoving him through the port: but, just as they were about to let him slip from their hands into the water, the blood began to circulate, and he commenced kicking. Upon this sign of returning to life, his shipmates soon hauled the poor snob in again and, though wonderful to relate, he recovered so speedily that he actually fought the battle out.

On the *Conqueror*, they had cleared for action in a hurry that morning, throwing equipment overboard rather than carrying it down to the hold. They had thrown the ship's dog as well, a Sardinian pointer belonging to an officer. The dog hadn't fallen into the sea, however. It had managed to survive somehow and was discovered after the battle 'lodged on the ridge of the swinging-boom on the side engaged'. With guns going off all round it and the French firing into the ship's side, the dog had been in the thick of the action all day. It emerged without a scratch, but was noticeably subdued as the crew hauled it inboard again.

On every ship, men lay listless and weary, riven by their exertions. They had fought magnificently and won a brilliant victory, but there was little euphoria among the exhausted survivors. Even their own survival left them unmoved. Four hundred and forty-nine of their comrades had been killed and another 1,214 wounded, many of whom would die in the days to come. Among the dead was Lord Nelson, the greatest naval commander the English had ever produced. There seemed little to celebrate as the men struggled to come to terms with what had happened. For most of them, it was enough that they were still in one piece as night closed in and the long, dreadful day came to an end at last.

CHAPTER 41

---∴◆∴---

THE STORM AFTER
THE BATTLE

Morning brought little respite. The fleet was still in shock from the battle. The men wanted only to sit and rest for a while, gradually recovering from their ordeal. But there was no rest for any of them with squalls coming on and the barometer rapidly falling. The fight had to go on, against the elements now, rather than the French and Spanish.

Captain Prigny, Villeneuve's chief of staff, was amazed at the Royal Navy's composure.

> The act that astonished me the most was when the action was over. It came on to blow a gale of wind, and the English immediately set to work to shorten sail and reef the topsails, with as much regularity and order as if their ships had not been fighting a dreadful battle. We were all in amazement, wondering what the English seamen could be made of.

Nursing his wounded leg aboard the *Euryalus*, Admiral Collingwood had all sorts of problems to deal with before the weather got any worse. He had spent most of the night on deck, 'now and then tugging at the waistband of his unmentionables . . . his only food a few biscuits, an apple and a glass of wine every four hours'. Collingwood's immediate priority was to regroup his scattered forces and get the damaged vessels and prize ships back to Gibraltar as soon as possible. With so many casualties in men and materiel, it was the obvious course to take. But the wind was against Gibraltar for most of the day and he also needed to maintain the blockade of Cadiz. His overriding duty was to keep up the pressure on Cadiz, to prevent the enemy from emerging again. With only twelve ships of the line still fully operational, Collingwood didn't have nearly enough vessels for everything he had to do.

To make matters worse, Collingwood had not anchored his ships after the battle, as Nelson had wanted. He had ordered them westwards instead, away from the treacherous coastline. He had changed his mind later, only to discover that many ships couldn't anchor anyway because their cables had been shot away. His fleet was all over the place as a result, widely scattered by the time dawn broke on the day after the battle.

Most ships were heading west as ordered, towing their prizes towards a rendezvous with the *Royal Sovereign* out to sea. But some had anchored and a few were already in trouble, as Nelson had forecast. The *Fougueux* had lost her tow to the frigate *Phoebe* and was drifting inexorably towards the shore. She ran aground later and was smashed to pieces on the rocks. With heavy seas and the wind whipping up from the south, Collingwood was worried that other ships would suffer a similar fate before the day was out.

Aboard the *Victory*, they spent the early part of the morning repairing the rigging and reinforcing the remaining masts while they still had the chance. They understood the dangers as well as Collingwood. The men worked hard, but their minds were not on their work as they laboured. The *Victory* was an unhappy ship that morning, with fifty-seven men dead, 102 wounded and their beloved admiral lying stiff and cold below.

Many went down to see him before his body was removed for the journey back to England. Among them was Louis Rotely of the Royal Marines, who was one of the first to pay his respects. Rotely wanted a lock of Nelson's hair as a memento, but found that Captain Hardy had got there before him. In accordance with Nelson's wishes, Hardy had cut off the admiral's queue for Lady Hamilton. All that remained was a small tuft at the back of his neck which Rotely promptly removed for himself. He also got hold of Nelson's breeches and stockings and kept them for the rest of his life.

Clad only in a shirt, Nelson's body was later removed from the cockpit and carried up to the middle deck by two seamen. A wooden cask had been lashed to the mainmast to receive it. Rotely tipped Nelson in head first and replaced the lid. The cask was then filled with brandy to preserve the corpse for burial. Rotely placed a twenty-four-hour guard on it to keep it safe. There was a rumour going round that some other ship would have to take Nelson home, but the men of the *Victory* were determined that would never happen. The Royal Navy would have a mutiny on its hands if anyone tried to take Nelson away from them.

On every ship, as soon as they could find the time, they were writing up the ship's log for the previous day, giving a terse account of the battle for the record. In several cases, the log-keeper had been killed and the log was written in an alien hand, by someone who hadn't been expecting to do it. All across the fleet, there was earnest debate as officers struggled to remember the precise details of what had happened during the battle, and at roughly what time. Their watches all told a different time, which didn't help. Their recollections were all different as well, hazy impressions of gunfire coming from somewhere and ships drifting in and out of the smoke, a kaleidoscope of different experiences from a variety of sources that was impossible to reconcile. Armchair sailors have been grappling with it ever since.

Among the French, too, the surviving ships' captains would soon be preparing their own version of events for posterity. For those who were prisoners of the British, their versions would be taken to England and then forwarded to Paris. For those who had escaped, they would go directly to Napoleon. All would tell of immense derring-do, in which the captain had fought heroically against overwhelming odds before being forced to surrender. All were quite clear that wherever the blame for the disaster lay, it certainly wasn't with them. Everyone had fought superbly by their own accounts – and indeed many of them had.

Aboard the *Algesiras*, they had no time yet for the penning of reports. Formerly the flagship of Rear-Admiral Magon, the *Algesiras* had been dismasted during the battle and taken over by a skeleton crew from the

Tonnant. Without a serviceable anchor, she had drifted away from the British fleet during the night and like the *Fougueux* was heading straight for the reefs north of Cape Trafalgar. The only thing that could save her was a jury mast, but with hundreds of prisoners below deck, Lieutenant Charles Bennett didn't have enough men to guard the French and erect a mast as well.

Against his own inclinations, Bennett was forced to return the ship to the French – but only after receiving an assurance that the British would be set free as soon as they reached port. The French came up on deck at once and began to erect topgallants as jury masts. Seven hours later, after narrowly avoiding the reefs, the *Algesiras* sailed safely into Cadiz while Bennett and his prize crew looked on with distinctly mixed feelings.

By evening, the storm had worked itself up into a fury. The rain came lashing down and the wind screamed through the rigging at sixty knots. Collingwood's ships pitched and rolled, their crews powerless to do anything except batten down the hatches and say their prayers as the waves broke over the deck. For the exhausted seamen, struggling at the pumps while the wounded continued to die, it was the last thing they needed after everything they had been through already.

The *Redoutable*, which had fought so bravely against the *Victory*, was being towed by the *Swiftsure*. Her only surviving mast collapsed under the strain. With water flooding in as well, the prizemaster was forced to send out distress signals at 5 p.m. The *Swiftsure* immediately hove to and lowered her boats. The British prize crew was rescued and as many of the French as could be managed before darkness fell. But the sea was too rough for the rest to be saved. The *Redoutable* went down just after 10 p.m. that night, taking perhaps 300 people with her. The *Swiftsure* was able to pick up a few survivors next morning, when the weather abated for a while, but the death toll was still severe. Added to the men already killed in action, the *Redoutable* had lost a total of 474 dead and another seventy wounded. It was a bitter price to pay for all the courage and resolution they had displayed over the past two days.

The improvement in the weather lasted a few hours into the morning of 23 October before deteriorating again. The lull brought an unexpected development from Cadiz, where Admiral Gravina's ships had arrived the previous day after fleeing the battle. Most were in no state to put to sea again, but a few were still fit for duty. After the drubbing they had received from the British, they were determined to retrieve something from the debacle and regain their professional pride.

Captain Julien Cosmao-Kerjulien was the senior surviving French officer. From the walls of Cadiz, he could see the captured *Santa Ana* only two miles away, being towed by the *Thunderer*. Both were struggling against the swell. Other ships were struggling as well. It was clear to Cosmao-Kerjulien that the few British ships in sight had their hands full with their prizes and were in no position to think about anything else. Taking advantage of the lull in the storm, he decided to lead a sortie from Cadiz to recapture the prizes and bring them back into harbour.

The sortie consisted of five ships of the line, five frigates and two brigs. It was successful at first. The *Thunderer* was forced to abandon the *Santa Ana* to defend herself. The *Conqueror* similarly had to cut the *Bucentaure* loose and the Spanish *Neptuno* was recaptured too. But the British formed a battle line of ten ships to protect the rest of their prizes and the wind suddenly changed direction again, bringing the storm back with it. Cosmao-Kerjulien was compelled to order a retreat to Cadiz while it was still feasible.

Unfortunately, the storm overtook his force before they could get back. Three ships of the line were lost. One anchored safely outside the harbour, but was driven ashore after the cable broke. Another couldn't make the harbour and had to surrender to the British after losing her masts. The third ran aground just north of Cadiz with enormous loss of life. If that wasn't enough, the newly liberated *Bucentaure* broke up as well, sinking at the entrance to Cadiz harbour, within a mile of the ramparts. Cosmao-Kerjulien had made a brave attempt, but his sortie had ended in a very costly failure for the French.

At sea, the British were not much happier. If anything, the storm was worse for them because they had nowhere to run to until it was over. Their only option was to keep the hatches battened and ride it out as best they could.

Unhappiest of all were the prize crews aboard the captured vessels. They had to fight the storm and keep control of their prisoners as well. Aboard the Spanish *Monarca*, the British were outnumbered ten to one by their captives. The ship had become so unmanageable by 24 October that they all thought they were going to die – a prospect the British sailors greeted by getting drunk, as Midshipman Henry Walker of the *Bellerophon* recalled:

> You will imagine what have been our sufferings, in a crippled ship, with 500 prisoners on board and only fifty-five Englishmen, most of whom were in a constant state of intoxication. We rolled away all our masts except the foremast; were afterwards forced to cut away two anchors, heave overboard several guns, shot etc to lighten her; and were, after all, in such imminent danger of sinking that, seeing no ship near to assist us, we at length determined to run the ship on shore on the Spanish coast, which we should have done had not the *Leviathan* fortunately fallen in with us and saved us, all but about 150 Spaniards . . . who were afraid of getting into the boats.
>
> I can assure you I felt not the least fear of death during the action, which I attribute to the general confidence of victory which I saw all around me; but in the prize, when I was in danger of, and had time to reflect upon the approach of death, either from the rising of the Spaniards upon so small a number as we were composed of, or what latterly appeared inevitable, from the violence of the storm, I was most certainly afraid, and at one time, when the ship made three feet of water in ten minutes, when our people were almost all lying drunk upon deck, when the Spaniards, completely worn out with fatigue, would no longer work at the only chain pump left serviceable, when I saw the fear of death so strongly depicted on the countenances of all around me, I wrapped myself up in a Union Jack and lay down upon deck for a short time, quietly awaiting the approach of death.

Happily, Walker rallied and later returned safely to the *Bellerophon*. The *Monarca*, however, ran aground and was wrecked.

*

Other ships were in trouble, too. Aboard the *Intrépide*, Lieutenant Gicquel des Touches was struggling to keep the situation under control.

> In the midst of the gloom, while the storm was still gathering strength, we had to pass through a leeward gunport more than eighty wounded who were incapable of moving into the small English boats. We succeeded in this with infinite trouble, by means of a bed-frame and capstan bars. Afterwards, we were towed by an English frigate, which we followed while rolling from side to side and leaking everywhere. I became aware that the pumping was slowing down, and I was warned that the doors of the storeroom had been broken down, and that everyone, English and French, had rushed there to get drunk. When I arrived amongst these men, reduced to the state of brutes, a cask of brandy had just been broken, and the liquid was running over the floor and lapping against the foot of a candle which had been set up there. I only just had time to stamp out the flame, and in the darkness threatening voices rose against me . . . With kicks and punches I had the storeroom cleared, I barricaded the door, and I agreed with the English officer how to avert the danger that was threatening.

The storm had reached hurricane force by now, so bad that it was threatening to hurl the entire fleet against the Spanish shore. Collingwood despaired of saving all the prize ships captured in the battle. Rather than see them fall back into enemy hands, he decided at length to destroy the crippled ones instead. He gave the order for the crews to be transferred to British ships and the prizes sent to the bottom, those that weren't sinking already.

He did so with great reluctance. The prizes were worth a fortune to the British – just under £4 million, by Collingwood's reckoning. For an admiral, that was enough to buy a country estate and build a gracious stately home. For a junior officer, it was an essential supplement to his pay, which was inadequate to support a family. For an ordinary seaman, if he was very lucky, it might be enough to take a lease on a pub and call it the *Lord Nelson*. The money was crucial to everyone aboard the British fleet. It was their nest egg, security for their old age. It wasn't to be sent to the bottom lightly.

But the storm had left them no choice. The crippled prizes simply couldn't be saved. Lieutenant John Edwards was aboard the *Santissima Trinidad*, the biggest prize of all:

'Tis impossible to describe the horrors the morning presented, nothing but signals of distress flying in every direction, guns firing, and so many large ships driving on shore without being able to render them the least assistance. After driving about four days without any prospect of saving the ship or the gale abating, the signal was made to destroy the prizes. We had no time before to remove the prisoners, and it now became a most dangerous task; no boats could lie alongside, we got under her stern, and the men dropped in by ropes; but what a sight when we came to remove the wounded, which were between three and four hundred.

We had to tie the poor mangled wretches round their waists, or where we could, and lower them down into a tumbling boat, some without arms, others no legs, and lacerated all over in the most dreadful manner. About ten o'clock we had got all out, to about thirty-three or four, which I believe it was impossible to remove without instant death. The water was now at the pilot deck, the weather dark and boisterous, and taking in tons at every roll.

Midshipman Badcock too was aboard the *Santissima*. 'Her beams were covered with blood, brains and pieces of flesh and the after part of her decks with wounded, some without legs and some without an arm.' The Spanish crowded the gangway as the last British boats pulled away. A father and son became separated, the son jumping into the sea and clinging to the gunwales of an overloaded boat as his father tried to haul him aboard. Terrified of being swamped, the British cut the son's fingers off with a cutlass to get rid of him. The father then made to leap overboard and drown with his son, whereupon the British relented and pulled his son into the boat. They all survived somehow and were taken safely to the *Revenge*.

The *Santissima*'s cat survived as well. The *Ajax*'s boat had shoved off from the starboard quarter when the cat ran out along a gun muzzle and gave a plaintive mew. The boat returned and took the animal on board. But some people still had to be abandoned, according to a sailor from the *Revenge*:

> On the last boat's load leaving the ship, the Spaniards who were left on board appeared on the gangway and ship's side, displaying their bags of dollars and doubloons and eagerly offering them as a reward for saving them from the expected and unavoidable wreck; but however well inclined we were, it was not in our power to rescue them, or it would have been effected without the proffered bribe.

Soon afterwards, the *Santissima* went down in the darkness, the Spaniards' money no use to them as the waters closed over their heads. The ship's fate was shared by many others. Of the twenty French and Spanish vessels originally captured at Trafalgar, one blew up and two were recaptured by Cosmao-Kerjulien. Four remained in British hands and were taken to Gibraltar after the storm was over to be valued at the prize office. The rest were either scuttled, burned or wrecked on shore.

CHAPTER 42

---·◆·---

THE BODIES COME ASHORE

The storm blew itself out after four terrible days and the ships still afloat won a breathing space at last. They needed it badly after the traumas of the previous week.

As soon as the weather had calmed down, Collingwood was able to send an account of the battle to the Admiralty. He had written a long dispatch immediately after the action, beginning with the death of Nelson and ending with details of the victory. Two days later, he added a second dispatch about the storm and the loss of some of the prizes. On the morning of 26 October, he gave both dispatches to Lieutenant John Lapenotiere, captain of the *Pickle*, and told him to sail to England at once and deliver them personally to the Admiralty in London.

It was the chance of a lifetime for Lapenotiere. Despite his name, he was from Devon, descended from French Huguenots who had come to England with William of Orange. As captain of the *Pickle* – the second-smallest ship on either side – he had played no active part in the battle beyond dancing attendance on the bigger ships. Instead, he had endured the polite but condescending stares of Midshipman Hercules Robinson and others as they looked down on his tiny little schooner from the poops of their two- and three-deckers. The *Pickle* had been called the *Sting* before the Admiralty renamed her. It was difficult for the rest of the fleet to take her seriously under her new name. But she was one of the fastest ships Collingwood had available to get the news back to England, and he was said to have owed Lapenotiere a favour. This was a crucial moment in Lapenotiere's career.

He rowed straight back to the *Pickle* after seeing Collingwood. It was a huge honour to be entrusted with the dispatches. There would be money in it when he arrived at the Admiralty – Lapenotiere could expect to receive £500 in cash and promotion to commander. For a man of thirty-five with a new young wife to support, it was a very welcome boost to his career.

First, though, the remaining French prisoners had to be released from the *Pickle*'s bilge and transferred to the *Revenge*. Lapenotiere waited impatiently while the men were ferried across in the jolly boat. The work was finished by noon. A few minutes later, the *Pickle* hoisted her sails and turned north-west, bearing her precious dispatches for the 1000-mile journey back to England.

Aboard the *Revenge*, the young Frenchwoman Jeanette Caunant had been transferred from the *Pickle* the day after the battle. She hadn't eaten for twenty-four hours when she arrived and looked 'the picture of misery and despair', according to one of the *Revenge*'s lieutenants. He lent her his cabin for a dressing room and had a berth erected for her outside the wardroom, protected by a canvas screen. The purser supplied her with two shirts and a blanket, and the chaplain gave her a pair of shoes. Another lieutenant gave her a piece of sprigged muslin looted from a Spanish ship. Before long, Jeanette had made a dress for herself and was feeling strong enough to start asking after her husband, lost somewhere in the *Achille*'s sinking. According to one account, he had been killed in the fighting, but nobody knew for sure. With the storm threatening to engulf them all, the *Revenge*'s lieutenant had had too many other things to think about, without worrying about Jeanette's problems:

> For several days I was so much busied in securing the ship's masts, and in looking after the ship in the gales which we had to encounter, that I had no time to attend to my *protégée*. It was on about the fourth day of her sojourn that she came to me in the greatest possible ecstasy and told me that she had found her husband, who was on board among the prisoners and unhurt. She soon afterwards brought him to me, and in the most grateful terms and manner returned her thanks for the attentions she had received. After this, Jeanette declined

coming to the wardroom, from the very proper feeling that her husband could not be admitted to the same privileges.

On the *Euryalus*, Collingwood was playing host to Admiral Villeneuve, who had been aboard for several days. He was an object of keen interest to the *Euryalus's* officers and men. Midshipman Hercules Robinson was one of many who examined him curiously:

> Villeneuve was a thinnish, tall man, a very tranquil, placid, English-looking Frenchman. He wore a long-tailed uniform coat, high and flat collar, corduroy pantaloons of a greenish colour, with stripes two inches wide, half-boots with sharp toes, and a watch-chain with long gold links.

Collingwood was impressed by his guest, much more so than he had been expecting. In Villeneuve he recognised a professional sailor much like himself. 'Admiral Villeneuve is a well-bred man, and I believe a very good officer: he has nothing in his manner of the offensive vapouring and boasting which we, perhaps too often, attribute to Frenchmen.'

But Villeneuve's calm exterior must have belied his inner feelings. Good officer or not, he had failed miserably in what he had set out to do. He was on the *Euryalus's* deck one day, leaning against a capstan, when he fell into conversation with Philip Durham, captain of the *Defiance*.

'Sir,' Villeneuve asked him, 'were you in Sir Robert Calder's action?'

Durham confirmed that he was.

Villeneuve sighed. 'I wish Sir Robert and I had fought it out that day. He would not be in his present position, or I in mine.'

True enough. If Villeneuve had fought Calder and won, he could have pressed on to Boulogne as ordered. If he had appeared off Boulogne on the day Napoleon marched his army down to the waterfront, the army would have crossed safely to England. If Villeneuve had had ships under his command of the calibre of Nelson's, there never would have been a Battle of Trafalgar and Great Britain would be a French dominion by now. If, if, if. But none of it had happened, and now it never would.

*

The *Victory* was heading for Gibraltar, under tow from the *Neptune*. She arrived on the evening of 28 October and dropped anchor in Rosia Bay. Next day, her wounded were carried ashore, some to be buried later in the Trafalgar cemetery. Nelson's body remained on board in its cask. A discharge of air from his corpse had lifted the lid off three days after his death, frightening the daylights out of the sentry. It was later rumoured that the brandy had been drawn off and drunk by the crew before the cask was refilled.

As the men had feared, there had been a move to transfer Nelson to another ship for the journey back to England, but it had come to nothing in the end. The authorities had conceded that the *Victory* should have the honour. Marine James Bagley applauded the decision in a letter to his sister:

> They have behaved very well to us. They wanted to take Lord Nelson from us, but we told Captain as we brought him out we would bring him home; so it was so, and he was put in a cask of spirits.

But they could not start for a while yet. They needed several days to erect proper jury masts and fit new rigging. By 2 November, the *Victory* was ready for sea again and was ordered to leave her anchorage to make room for other crippled ships. She sailed for Morocco to take on fresh water, but was forced back by a change in the wind. She finally left Gibraltar on 3 November, towed now by the *Polyphemus*, with orders to make all possible speed back to Portsmouth.

The *Revenge* too had headed for Gibraltar after the battle, carrying a shipload of prisoners. The Spanish were to be returned to Spain in an exchange of captives, but the French prisoners were mistakenly put ashore at Gibraltar as well. Among them were Jeanette and her husband, happy to be together again. The *Revenge*'s lieutenant was sorry to see Jeanette go:

> We all considered her a fine woman. On leaving the ship, most, if not all of us, gave her a dollar, and she expressed her thanks as well as she was able, and assured us that the name of our ship would always be remembered by her with the warmest gratitude.

Jeanette had been a hit on the lower deck as well. 'On leaving our ship, her heart seemed overwhelmed with gratitude,' remembered William Robinson. 'She shed abundance of tears and could only now and then, with a deep sigh, exclaim "Les bons Anglois".' The crew all missed her after she had gone. It had been a long time since any of them had seen a woman.

Along the Spanish coast, the bodies were beginning to pile up, washed ashore by the swell. From Cape Trafalgar all the way up to Cadiz, more arrived with every tide, drifting aimlessly in the shallows amid wreckage from the battle. Among them was William Ram, an Irish lieutenant from the *Victory* who had ripped the bandages from his own body in order to bleed to death more quickly.

In Cadiz, wounded were coming ashore as well, so many of them that every carriage in the city had been commandeered and all the hospitals were filled to bursting point. Churches and convents had to be used for the overflow. Masses were being sung for the dead, offices besieged with enquiries about the missing. The city was full of distraught people – women in tears, Spanish sailors still in shock, French soldiers wandering the streets listlessly with nowhere to go. The calamity had hit them all.

Arriving in Cadiz soon after the battle, an English merchant found the place in turmoil:

Ten days after the battle, they were still employed bringing ashore the wounded; and spectacles were hourly displayed at the wharfs, and through the streets, sufficient to shock every heart not yet hardened to scenes of blood and human suffering. When, by the carelessness of the boatmen, and the surging of the sea, the boats struck against the stone piers, a horrid cry, which pierced the soul, arose from the mangled wretches on board.

Many of the Spanish gentry assisted in bringing them ashore, with symptoms of much compassion, yet as they were finely dressed, it had something of the appearance of ostentation; if there could be ostentation at such a moment. It need not be doubted that an Englishman lent a willing hand to bear them up the steps to their litters, yet the slightest false step made them shriek out, and I even yet shudder at the remembrance of the sound.

On the top of the pier the scene was affecting. The wounded were carried away to the hospitals in every shape of human misery, whilst crowds of Spaniards either assisted or looked on with signs of horror. Meanwhile their companions, who had escaped unhurt, walked up and down with folded arms and downcast eyes, whilst women sat upon heaps of arms, broken furniture and baggage, with their heads bent between their knees.

I had no inclination to follow the litters of the wounded, yet I learned that every hospital in Cadiz was already full, and that convents and churches were forced to be appropriated to the reception of the remainder.

If, leaving the harbour, I passed through the town to the Point, I still beheld the terrible effects of the battle. As far as the eye could reach, the sandy side of the isthmus bordering on the Atlantic was covered with masts and yards, the wrecks of ships, and here and there the bodies of the dead.

There was little animosity towards the British for all this suffering. Those forced ashore by the storm received nothing but kindness from the Spanish. The prize crew of the *Rayo* were given food and drink as soon as they landed. Their officer found a carriage waiting for him, full of cordials and confectionery. Women and priests presented him with 'delicacies of all sorts' as the carriage drove him through the streets towards lodgings with a bed and clean linen. He found himself wondering if Spanish sailors wrecked off the English coast in similar circumstances would have had such a reception. Two Americans in his crew promptly deserted and were not seen again.

On another prize ship, the British sent their former prisoners ashore first and followed later. They found the prisoners waiting for them with bread, figs and wine. A seaman from the *Spartiate* was so badly injured that he couldn't stand up.

One of the Spaniards, seeing the state I was in, was kind enough to get two or three more of his companions, and lifted me up in one of the bullock-carts in which they had brought down the provisions for us, and covered me up with one of their great ponchos, and he tapped me on the shoulder, and said 'Bono English!' And, being upon the cart, I was out of the wind and rain – for it blew a heavy gale of wind – and I felt myself quite comfortable, only my leg pained me a good deal; but, thanks be to God, I soon fell into a sound sleep, and, as I heard afterwards, the French soldiers came down and marched the rest of my shipmates up to Cadiz, and they put them into the Spanish prison. As for my part, I was taken up to Cadiz in the bullock-cart and my kind friend took me to his own house, and had me put to bed, where I found myself when I woke.

The good relations were brokered by Captains Prowse and Blackwood, who had been sent to Cadiz under flags of truce with an offer to repatriate the Spanish wounded. Marquis Solana, the town's governor, was delighted. Inviting Blackwood to dinner, he sent Collingwood some wine and a supply of grapes, figs, melons and pomegranates in appreciation. Collingwood was delighted in his turn:

Nothing can exceed the gratitude expressed by him for this act of humanity. All this part of Spain is in an uproar of praise and thankfulness to the English. Solana sent me a present of a cask of wine, and we have a free intercourse with the shore. Judge of the footing we are on, when I tell you he offered me his hospitals, and pledged the Spanish honour for the care and cure of our wounded men. Our officers and men who were wrecked in some prize ships were most kindly treated: all the country was on the beach to receive them, the priests and women distributing wine, and bread, and fruit amongst them. The soldiers turned out of their barracks to make lodging for them.

It was a curious response to the defeat they had just suffered, but the Spanish had never wanted a war with the British. They had fought bravely at Trafalgar and had nothing to be ashamed of. Their relations with the British were often cordial – at Gibraltar, for instance, the officers frequently dined together, although they were supposed to be at war. The Spanish regretted Nelson's death and contrasted Collingwood's humane treatment of their wounded with the awfulness of the French, whom they accused of abandoning them in the heat of battle. It wasn't long in fact before the Spanish were persuaded to change sides altogether and join the fight against Napoleon, something many of them had been waiting to do all along.

CHAPTER 43

TAKING THE NEWS TO
ENGLAND

West of Cadiz, the *Pickle* was making slow progress towards England. She was aiming to clear Cape St Vincent and then turn north up the Portuguese coast, but it was a hard slog against the weather. The *Pickle* had not been designed for such waters. Her crew of forty-two were often wet through for days at a time, so disaffected that they had twice threatened to desert to the French in the past two years.

A quarter of the crew were Irish. Some had sworn on a book entitled *The Rights of Ireland* to 'aid and assist Bonaparte with all his power and might on every occasion'. In January, Lieutenant Lapenotiere had asked the Admiralty for an extra corporal and six Marines to help him keep order, but no help had been forthcoming. The situation had improved of its own accord once Villeneuve put to sea, but the *Pickle* was still not a happy ship.

She was approaching Cape St Vincent on 29 October when she met the sloop *Nautilus* coming the other way. The *Nautilus's* captain came aboard and heard the news of Trafalgar. He immediately turned his ship about and set off for Lisbon to tell the British ambassador, leaving the *Pickle* to continue towards England.

By 31 October, she was heading past Cape Finisterre into the Bay of Biscay when she sprang a leak forward. The pumps couldn't work fast enough, so the crew had to form a human chain and bail the water out with buckets. They laboured all night but were still forced to throw four carronades overboard next morning, to lighten the ship and improve her stability. Even then the situation remained precarious. It was not until the evening of 1 November that Lapenotiere managed to get it under control again.

Next day, the *Pickle* passed Ushant and entered the English Channel. She was within a day's sailing of the Lizard when the weather played another cruel trick and the wind dropped away to nothing, leaving the *Pickle* becalmed. It was the last straw for Lapenotiere, with all of England waiting for the news that he had in his dispatches.

Worse was to follow. The *Nautilus* was now heading for England as well. Captain John Sykes had decided that the news of Trafalgar was too important to be left to the *Pickle* alone, in case she was captured or sank on the way. After leaving a message for the British ambassador in Lisbon, the *Nautilus* had turned north and quickly caught up with the *Pickle*. They had spotted each other several times as they hurried towards home, each determined to be the one with the news. The race was on to see who would get there first.

Further up the French coast, the rest of the Royal Navy still knew nothing of Trafalgar. The blockade of Boulogne remained as tight as ever, even though the bulk of the Grand Army had long since marched away. The *Immortalité* under Captain Owen lay at anchor outside the harbour, keeping a sharp eye on the inshore traffic. She was rewarded at the end of October with the unusual sight of a French pinnace approaching from the shore, with a small punt in tow.

After setting the punt adrift within reach of the British, the pinnace retreated to shore. Intrigued, Owen sent a crew to investigate. They returned with the punt, which contained a short note from Commodore Robin, probably at the behest of Admiral La Crosse. Robin was pleased to inform the British that a brilliant victory had been won. 'The Austrian army of 100,000 men is no more. General Mack is a prisoner at Ulm, and Prince Ferdinand is put to flight.'

The British were thunderstruck. It couldn't possibly be true. It was inconceivable that Mack could have surrendered. Surely the French were exaggerating, as they so often did?

Midshipman Abraham Crawford echoed the general disbelief:

An account that seemed so wholly improbable, and which, if true, would have been so ruinous to the allies, was scarcely credible. That an army, which had only quitted the vicinity of Boulogne in the early part of September, should have traversed such an extent of country – crossed rivers – forced defences – fought battles – and, after annihilating an army of 100,000 men, and capturing its commander-in-chief, have established itself in Ulm, the key of all the Austrian movements and positions, upon the strengthening and storing of which so much pains had been bestowed, and all in the brief space of six or seven weeks, seemed so far to exceed all that one had ever heard or read of in ancient or modern warfare, that the account was considered a fabrication, and wholly disbelieved.

Captain Owen sent the French boat back with a politely sceptical note, expressing his opinion that the victory at Ulm was probably as illusory as other French triumphs that had later turned out to be nothing of the kind. The French read his letter and were outraged that he did not believe them.

In Canterbury, the Reverend William Nelson was waiting for news of his brother and the British fleet. Rumours were flying in all directions, but nobody knew anything for certain. If there had been a victory, the church bells would surely have rung by now, sounding out across the town. Yet they remained stubbornly silent, with no message to impart. If there was anything to celebrate, no word of it had reached the authorities yet.

The best place to find out what was happening was Bristow's reading room on the Parade. Nelson went there at eight every morning to scan the newspapers and see what he could learn. The papers always had the news before anyone else. But there was nothing in them about a battle, no word of Lord Nelson's fleet, or Villeneuve's, either. Perhaps it was good news that there was no news. Or perhaps it wasn't. Either way, they must surely hear something soon. It couldn't be much longer now.

Back at Merton after her visit to Canterbury, Emma Hamilton kept busy by supervising the remodelling of the kitchen, as agreed with Nelson during his last home leave. She also went up to London to oversee the redecoration of her house in Clarges Street. She had persuaded herself that Nelson would be home soon, retired for ever from the sea. She wanted Merton looking wonderful for him when he came.

Emma couldn't bear to be alone at such an anxious time. She prevailed on Nelson's younger sister Susannah Bolton to keep her company at Merton. Susannah was ill, but came anyway. Emma was ill, too, so sick with worry that she had broken out in a rash. She spent some time in bed, suffering from nerves. Like William Nelson in Canterbury, she was longing for an end to the suspense – but the church bells at Merton were just as quiet as those at Canterbury. They hadn't pealed out joyfully across the fields, as they would have done if there had been a great victory to report. Instead, they remained silent as the grave.

In Downing Street, William Pitt was also feeling the strain. As Prime Minister, the waiting was probably worse for him than for anyone else. He was worn out from long years of worry, growing sicker and more haggard by the day.

The rear windows of No. 10 looked across to the Admiralty, giving Pitt a clear view of the shutter telegraph on the Admiralty roof. One line went to Deal in Kent; the other via the Royal Hospital, Chelsea and Putney Heath to the naval base at Portsmouth. Both lines were busy during daylight hours, constantly sending and receiving signals. The shutters never stopped chattering. But none of it ever culminated in the cheerful figure of Lord Barham skipping across the parade ground with glad tidings in his hand.

What came instead, on the morning of 3 November, was a bundle of newspapers from the Continent. The papers were in Dutch, full of news about Napoleon. It was a Sunday, so there was no one around to translate for Pitt. Fortunately, Lord Malmesbury lived nearby, round the side of the Admiralty. Malmesbury was a former ambassador to The Hague and had spent a year learning the language in his youth.

> Pitt and Lord Mulgrave came to me in Spring Gardens about one o'clock, with a Dutch newspaper in which the capitulation of Ulm was inserted at full length. As they neither of them understood

Dutch, and as all the offices were empty, they came to me to translate it, which I did as well as I could.

The news could hardly have been worse. The fall of Ulm was a disaster of epic proportions. It meant that the alliance against Napoleon was defeated before it had even got off the ground. All the Prime Minister's good work over the past year and a half had come to nothing. He slumped visibly as the implications began to sink in.

I observed but too clearly the effect it had on Pitt, though he did his utmost to conceal it . . . His manner and look were not his own, and gave me, in spite of myself, a foreboding of the loss with which we were threatened.

What it meant was another decade of war. Pitt was certain of it. Another ten years of Europe in turmoil, while Napoleon rampaged unrestricted from one end of the Continent to the other. Ten more years of strife, chaos and disorder, a prospect no responsible statesman could relish. It was particularly devastating for Pitt, after everything he had done to try to prevent it. His life's work lay in ruins.

At sea, the *Pickle* had spent four hours becalmed, her sails quite useless without a breath of wind. In desperation, Lieutenant Lapenotiere set his men to work on the sweeps – huge three- or four-man oars – to propel the ship forward. They were urged on by acting Second Master George Almy, one of two Americans in the crew from Newport, Rhode Island. Most of their efforts went into keeping the ship pointing in the right direction, ready for the wind when it came. The work was back-breaking. The *Pickle* desperately needed to reach England, but however hard she tried, she seemed only to be treading water, going nowhere at all.

The wind picked up eventually and continued sporadically throughout the following night. The *Pickle* made progress again, coming in slowly past the Scilly Isles towards Cornwall. At 2 a.m. on 4 November, she spotted the lighthouse on Lizard Head, nine miles away on the port bow. A few hours later, she was approaching Falmouth Bay in the early-morning light.

By 10 a.m. she had heaved to and was dropping anchor in the shadow of Pendennis Castle.

Lapenotiere was rowed ashore at once. He was dressed in his best uniform, carrying Collingwood's dispatches in a pouch. London lay 266 miles away, a journey of twenty-two stages by post chaise. The trip usually took a week, but Lapenotiere needed to do it much quicker than that if he was to get there before Captain Sykes of the *Nautilus*. He could probably arrive by the following night if he drove non-stop all the way.

Hiring a coach, Lapenotiere set off immediately. Within a few minutes, he had left Falmouth behind and was on his way to Truro with the Trafalgar dispatches safely in his possession.

CHAPTER 44

A NATION IN MOURNING

From Truro, Lapenotiere continued to Bodmin, and from there to Launceston, Okehampton and Crockernwell. His coach rattled onwards for the rest of that day and all of the following night. By lunchtime next day, he was only an hour ahead of Sykes, as a bystander later reported from Dorchester:

> Yesterday about Noon, two officers of the navy came through this Town, following each other, at about an hour's Space of Time, in two Post-Chaises and four Horses to each, from the Westward; the first reported that he brought good News of great Importance, and the second, that his Dispatches contained the best and most capital News that the Nation ever experienced.

The way ahead lay through Salisbury and Andover towards Basingstoke and Hertford Bridge. By late afternoon, Lapenotiere had passed through Bagshot and was on his way to Staines. Night had fallen again by the time he reached Hounslow – Guy Fawkes Night, a time of bonfires for the children and fireworks in the dark. London lay in front of him now, the capital wreathed in a coal fog as his coach sped forward along the turnpike.

The fog was so thick by the time Lapenotiere reached the outskirts that the traffic had slowed to a crawl and drivers were struggling to find a way through the gloom. Some of them had dismounted and were walking at their horses' heads to feel for the road. Others were knocking on doors to ask where they were. For Lapenotiere, sitting in frustration on his dispatches, the delay was intolerable. Even on this last lap, so close to the finishing line, the weather still seemed to be conspiring against him.

It was already midnight when he passed Kensington and pushed on towards Knightsbridge and Hyde Park Corner. By 1 a.m. he had reached Whitehall at last and was turning into the Admiralty forecourt, still ahead of Captain Sykes. Weary and travel-stained after a thirty-seven-hour journey, Lapenotiere presented himself to the night porter with his dispatches. He was taken upstairs immediately and shown to the board room, where the secretary William Marsden was just finishing work for the night.

Lapenotiere did not stand on ceremony. 'Sir, we have gained a great victory, but we have lost Lord Nelson.'

Shocked, Marsden listened briefly to Lapenotiere's story. Then he went to tell Lord Barham. The First Lord had a bedroom somewhere in the building, but Marsden wasn't sure exactly where. He found it after a while and went in. Barham was awake in an instant, listening intently to the news. He got out of bed and began issuing a stream of instructions as to what should be done now.

The first task was to make several copies of Collingwood's dispatches. One was rushed across the parade ground to Downing Street, where the Prime Minister had just gone to bed after writing a letter to Nelson. William Pitt was perfectly accustomed to being woken in the middle of the night with momentous news. He usually managed to go back to sleep again afterwards, but not this time. Pitt was so shaken by Nelson's death that he couldn't sleep any more. He decided to get up instead, even though it was still only 3 a.m.

Another copy of the dispatches went to the king at Windsor. It was getting on for 7 a.m. by the time the Admiralty messenger reached the castle. King George was so dumbstruck that he couldn't speak for five minutes. His wife and daughters burst into tears. It was some considerable time before they had recovered sufficiently to go to St George's Chapel and give thanks for the victory. Later, the Staffordshire Militia paraded in Little Park and fired three volleys in celebration, although what kind of victory they were celebrating with Nelson dead, no one was quite sure.

Guns were fired in London also, at Hyde Park and the Tower. Emma Hamilton heard them far away at Merton, where she lay sick in bed. 'I think I hear the Tower guns,' she told Susannah Bolton. 'Some victory perhaps in Germany, to retrieve the credit lost by Mack.'

'Perhaps it may be news from my brother,' said Susannah.

'Impossible, surely. There is not time.'

Five minutes later, a coach drew up at the door. The servants announced Captain John Whitby from the Admiralty.

'Show him in directly,' said Emma.

Whitby was ashen-faced, not looking forward to this at all. 'We have gained a great victory,' he told Emma faintly.

'Never mind your victory.' Emma wanted to hear from Nelson. 'My letters, give me my letters.'

Whitby didn't answer. His eyes were full of tears.

Emma understood at once. 'I believe I gave one scream and fell back, and for ten hours after I could neither speak nor shed a tear – days have passed on, and I know not how they end or begin – nor how I am to bear my future existence.'

In Canterbury, William Nelson was equally distraught. He heard the news from Mr Bristow, owner of the reading room on the Parade. To spare him the indignity of learning about it in a public place, Bristow came to tell Nelson in person. He found him just inside the cathedral gate and broke the news as gently as he could. Nelson still took it badly, crying freely and wiping his eyes with a handkerchief. It was a while before he managed to pull himself together again and turn back towards his house to tell his family.

In London, the news cast a gloom over the whole city. The Admiralty was besieged from early morning, as were the newspaper offices. A *London Gazette Extraordinary* was rushed into print, giving full details of Collingwood's dispatches. The victory was glorious, a magnificent triumph for the Royal Navy, but it wasn't the victory that the public wanted to know about as they crowded round for more news. It was Lord Nelson. Nothing else seemed to matter, with the nation's favourite son snatched from them at the moment of triumph.

'Mingled pride and consternation' was the universal reaction, according to Lady Elizabeth Hervey. She was at the Admiralty that morning, watching the crowds pressing for more information.

As we came away, there was a vast rush of people, but all silent, or a murmur of respect and sorrow; some of the common people saying, 'It is bad news if Nelson is killed,' yet they knew that twenty ships had been taken. A man at the turnpike gate said to Sir Ellis, who was going through, 'Sir, have you heard the bad news? We have taken twenty ships from the enemy, but Lord Nelson is killed!'

According to *The Times*:

There was not a man who did not think that the life of the Hero of the Nile was too great a price for the capture and destruction of twenty sail of French and Spanish men of war. No ebullitions of popular transport, no demonstrations of public joy, marked this great and important event. The honest and manly feeling of the people appeared as it should have done: they felt an inward satisfaction at the triumph of their favourite arms; they mourned with all the sincerity and poignancy of domestic grief their Hero slain.

The victory was duly celebrated, but with little overt enthusiasm. People's hearts were not in it as they went through the motions. Church bells rang to announce the news, but their peals alternated with the solemn, muffled toll of mourning to indicate that all was not well. Candles were placed in windows, and houses were half-heartedly illuminated, but the lights were often removed again after a while because nobody felt like cheering, as Lord Malmesbury observed:

I never saw so little public joy. The illumination seemed dim and as it were half-clouded by the desire of expressing the mixture of contending feelings; every common person in the streets speaking first of their sorrow for him, and then of the victory.

Within hours, thousands of people were wearing cockades with Nelson's name on, or else black crepe scarves of mourning. Shop windows were draped in black and shrines erected in Nelson's honour – medallions bearing his image, coloured lamps spelling out his name, clusters of laurels and oak branches 'sacred to the memory of the immortal Nelson'. All the main public buildings were lit up in his honour – the Admiralty, Treasury, Royal Exchange, Mansion House, Bank of England – and many commercial buildings as well. At Covent Garden, the theatre was adorned with a huge 'N' picked out with violet lamps and topped by an anchor lit up with red. In a hasty addition to the published programme, the cast finished their performance with a spirited rendering of 'Rule, Britannia', sung against a naval backdrop while a portrait of Nelson descended from the clouds. Not to be outdone, the German theatre erected a giant transparency of Britannia with a lion at her side, holding up an image of Nelson and the legend 'Victorious Nelson, I will avenge thy death'.

All over the country, it was the same as the news spread. In every marketplace, the victory was formally announced by the local mayor, to be greeted by a stunned silence as the price became clear. There were guns and fireworks across the land, but mourning and sadness too. Even the little children understood that something dreadful had happened and remembered the day for the rest of their lives.

Abroad, too, the news was met with widespread dismay. In Jamaica, a funeral pyre forty-seven feet high was erected at Kingston, one foot for every year of Nelson's life. Forty-seven guns were fired and forty-seven rockets soared into the sky as Jamaica's governor saluted the man who had delivered the island from Villeneuve's fleet. Off Denmark, within sight of Hamlet's castle, 'all the ships in the road of Elsineur fired three discharges in celebration of the victory off Cadiz. Immediately afterwards their flags were lowered and three minute-guns fired, on account of the death of Lord Nelson'. And at Boulogne, where the French had recently been so complacent about Ulm, it was the turn of the British to present their compliments and announce a great victory. Sir Sidney Smith delivered a copy of the *Gazette* to the French coast containing full details of Trafalgar. He apologised for sending it in an unmanned boat, but observed acidly 'that the last flag of truce he sent in, the officer was very *honourably* detained'.

The news reached Napoleon on 18 November. He was at Znaim in Moravia, just sitting down to a meal, when Marshal Berthier put the dispatch in his hand. By some accounts, Napoleon immediately flew into a rage. By others, he reacted with uncharacteristic calm, saying nothing about it and displaying no visible emotion. Whatever the truth, he penned a note to Admiral Decrès demanding more information about the battle. 'All this makes no difference to my plans,' he announced defiantly. 'I am annoyed that all is not ready yet. They must start without delay.'

To Berthier, however, he privately expressed a wish that the American Paul Jones was still alive, in whom France might have had an admiral to match Nelson. And he was in a much fouler mood next morning, noticeably sullen and angry as he spurred his horse to an unnecessary gallop. The news was kept from the Grand Army at first, but they found out soon enough from Russian and Austrian prisoners only too eager to let them know. The Austrians in particular were delighted to see the French humiliated after the debacle at Ulm.

Yet it didn't really matter any more. The invasion of England was no longer Napoleon's prime concern. His aim now was to complete the rout of the alliance that had begun at Ulm. He did so two weeks later, when he caught up with the Austrians and Russians in a muddy field near 'a poor little thatched village, with an old castle'. The village's name was Austerlitz.

While Napoleon pursued the Austrians, Villeneuve was being taken to England as a prisoner. He and Captain Magendie arrived off Spithead on 29 November and were put ashore at Gosport. They walked up through the town and were escorted to the Crown Inn for the night. Villeneuve seemed 'melancholy, but not despondent', according to a local journalist. By next morning, however, he was feeling thoroughly depressed, so ill with spasms that a doctor had to be called. The two Frenchmen were taken to Bishop's Waltham at first, but transferred later to more suitable accommodation at Sonning, near Reading. Villeneuve stayed there as the guest of Henry Addington and was later visited by William Pitt.

At the Reading depot, the two Frenchmen were joined by Captain Lucas of the *Redoutable* and Captain Infernet of the *Intrépide*. All four gave their parole not to escape and were allowed a substantial measure of freedom in return. They were treated with sympathy by the locals as they strolled unhappily through the town. The gentry in particular went out of their way to be hospitable. Captain Lucas was in great demand after his exploits at Trafalgar and soon found himself swamped with invitations to London, where he was a big success at parties. Infernet went to London as well and was looked after by Jane Codrington, wife of the *Orion*'s captain. She did her best for him but found her guest rather uncouth, more at home on the poop of a warship than in a London drawing room.

Other French prisoners arrived throughout December, aboard ships coming home for repair. Collingwood had wanted to leave them all at Gibraltar, to be exchanged for British prisoners in France, but Napoleon disliked exchanges and his officials had no authority to agree a deal. As a result, the French were brought to England instead. The officers gave their parole and were interned in small country towns across the south and midlands. The ordinary sailors were separated from their shipmates to prevent trouble and then dispersed to Portchester Castle and other prisons, or else incarcerated aboard the prison hulks in the harbours. Thousands of them remained there for years.

Among the later arrivals was Rear-Admiral Dumanoir. He had escaped capture at Trafalgar by leading his squadron away from the battle and continuing south towards Gibraltar, but had subsequently doubled back in the darkness and headed for Rochefort instead. A few days after the battle, his crippled ships ran into another British squadron and were unable to escape. They took 750 casualties before surrendering. Dumanoir was brought to Britain, but did not join Villeneuve and the other senior officers at Reading. As well as fleeing Trafalgar and firing on Lucas's ship by mistake, he was suspected of firing on several Spanish ships after they had surrendered and would not have been welcome at Reading. He was interned at Tiverton instead.

Nelson was coming home as well, making slow progress in his damaged flagship. It wasn't until 4 December that the *Victory* arrived off the Isle of Wight. She waited there six days before being ordered up to the Thames, where Nelson's body was to be delivered to the Royal Naval Hospital at Greenwich.

The orders came as a relief to Surgeon Beatty, faced with the task of keeping Nelson in a good state of preservation for the funeral. He had been hoping for some professional help when he reached Portsmouth, but none had been forthcoming. Beatty had twice renewed the brandy in Nelson's cask on the journey home, but was unsure of what he was doing. En route to the Thames, therefore, he opened the cask again and was relieved to find that Nelson's body was still in good condition, although his bowels were beginning to putrefy. Beatty removed them before they could corrupt the rest of the body. He extracted the fatal musket ball as well and found it embedded with gold lace from Nelson's epaulette. Then he wrapped Nelson's remains in cotton bandages and replaced them in a leaden coffin filled with brandy and a solution of camphor and myrrh.

The *Victory* proceeded slowly along the coast and was forced to anchor at Dover for five days until the weather improved. Every ship she encountered gave her a cheer. To the irritation of the *Victory*'s crew, she was inundated with sightseers at Sheerness, wanting to inspect the damage. 'We scarce have room to move the ship is so full of Nobility coming down from London to see the ship looking at shot holes,' complained one of her crew.

An old shipmate of Nelson's came aboard as well, bringing Nelson's preferred coffin with him, the one made out of wood salvaged from the *Orient*. Nelson's face had swollen up by now, but a hard rub with a napkin restored him to a semblance of his normal self. He was dressed in a shirt, stockings, small clothes, waistcoat, neck cloth and nightcap before being placed in the new coffin, which was then enclosed in a leaden outer coffin and soldered up immediately. The ensemble was transferred to the yacht *Chatham* for the remainder of the journey to Greenwich. All the forts and ships along the way fired their minute-guns and flew their flags at half-mast as Nelson's body sailed past.

The yacht reached Greenwich on the afternoon of Christmas Eve. The Royal Naval Hospital's governor wanted the body to remain aboard the *Chatham* until after Christmas, but was advised that everyone in London would insist on coming to inspect it. A crowd of sightseers was already forming. They dispersed after being told that Nelson's body would not be landed until the following Thursday. As soon as they had gone, the coffin was carried ashore under cover of darkness and taken to the Hospital, where it was to lie in the Painted Hall for a few days before the funeral at St Paul's Cathedral.

CHAPTER 45

NELSON'S FUNERAL

The original plan had been for the coffin to lie open in the Painted Hall, so that people could see Nelson's face as they filed past. But Beatty's attempts to restore his features had not been successful enough for that, so the coffin remained closed for the viewing. It was encased in a magnificent casket, custom built for the occasion, adorned with seahorses, Nile crocodiles and gilded heraldic devices. In keeping with ancient tradition, a helmet, surcoat, shield and gauntlets were also on display. The catafalque was surrounded by flags and the walls of the Hall were hung with black cloth, all lit by hundreds of candles in sconces.

The first mourner was the Princess of Wales, who made a private visit on the afternoon of 4 January 1806. Next morning, the doors were opened to the public and ordinary people were admitted as well.

A written notice was posted up, that the public would be admitted at 11 a.m. by which time many thousands were assembled. Punctually at that hour, the doors were thrown open, and though express orders had been given that only a limited number should be admitted at once, yet the mob was so great as to bear down everything in its way. Nothing could be heard but shrieks and groans, as several persons were trodden under foot and greatly hurt. Vast numbers of ladies and gentlemen lost their shoes, hats, shawls etc, and the ladies fainted in every direction. One man had his eye literally torn out, coming into contact with one of the gate-posts.

Things were no better next day. The Royal Naval Hospital governor became so alarmed that he wrote to the Home Secretary, warning that the funeral procession might be disrupted if firm action wasn't taken:

> The Mob assembled here is so very numerous and tumultuous that it is absolutely necessary that your Lordship should apply for a very strong party of Cavalry to line the street on each side from Deptford Bridge to the entrance of the Hospital and to attend the other Gates early on Wednesday morning or it will not be possible for the procession to move from here – the mob consisted yesterday of upwards of 30,000 and equally so today and more outrageous – Townsend and the other peace officers from Bow Street say they never saw anything like it before.

In the event, the procession passed off without incident. Nelson's coffin was taken from the Painted Hall on 8 January and transferred to a royal barge, originally built for Charles II, for the journey to Westminster. Rowed by sixteen men from the *Victory*, it was escorted by dozens of other barges and innumerable smaller craft as it set off for Whitehall Stairs. Minute-guns boomed from the Tower and thousands watched from the bank as the barge proceeded upriver. At Whitehall, Nelson's coffin was unloaded and carried to the Admiralty, where it was to remain overnight before the funeral. His body was placed in the small waiting room immediately to the left of the front door – a room well known to him in life. Nelson had waited there often as a young man, impatient to see someone about his next command.

William Marsden, the Admiralty secretary, watched him arrive:

> I have had a good view of the water procession from the top of the building, and of its entry into the court and house from my own window. The Mackenzies and the Wilkins are to be here at ten o'clock tonight (through the garden door) to be introduced to the tomb of the Capulets.

Nelson's chaplain Alexander Scott was there as well, unable to tear himself away from the body. He had been with Nelson when he died and had hardly left his side ever since.

The weather next morning was unusually fine for January. The funeral cortège formed up on Horse Guards Parade for the procession to St Paul's. The Royal Scots Greys led the way, heading a column so long that they had reached the cathedral before Nelson's funeral car had even left the Admiralty. The column consisted mostly of soldiers, carriages and military bands, with relatively few sailors among its ranks. Apart from forty-eight Greenwich Pensioners, the only other naval contingent came from the *Victory*. One of them had proudly written home:

> There is three hundred of us Pickt out to go to Lord Nelson Funral. We are to wear blue Jackets and white Trowsers and a black scarf round our arms and hats besides gold medal for the battle of Trafalgar Valued £7 round our necks.

In fact, only forty-eight sailors marched in the column, followed by a further seven carrying the three shot-riddled flags that the *Victory* had flown during the battle. They held the flags up as they marched, so the crowd could see the holes. Amidst all the pomp and ceremony, the sailors were the star attraction, according to Lady Elizabeth Hervey. 'The show altogether was magnificent, but the common people, when the crew of the *Victory* passed, said, "We had rather see *them* than all the show!"'

Nelson's funeral car came towards the end of the procession. It was an elaborate affair, decked out to look like the *Victory*, with a figurehead in front and cabin windows in the rear. The crowds fell silent as it approached, the only sound a noise like the murmur of waves along the seashore as thousands removed their hats in respect.

At St Paul's, the coffin was lifted from the funeral car by twelve of the *Victory*'s crew. They carried it up the steps and into the cathedral. Six admirals in full dress uniform held a canopy over the coffin as it proceeded to the choir past the enemy flags captured at Trafalgar. A giant wooden amphitheatre seventeen tiers high had been built to provide seating for 7,000 mourners. The Duke of York was among them, and the Prince of

Wales – a total of seven royal dukes in all. There were also sixteen earls, thirty-six admirals and 100 Royal Navy captains. No women had been invited, so Lady Nelson had remained at home, as had Emma Hamilton. A few fashionable ladies had found seats in the organ loft, but they were there unofficially, without any tickets.

Prominent among the mourners was William Nelson, the admiral's brother. He was now Earl Nelson of Trafalgar, having been raised to the peerage three days after the news of his brother's great victory. Parliament was also going to give him money, enough to buy a country estate and live according to his new station. His tears at Canterbury had rapidly given way to demands for water paints as he sketched designs for the livery to be worn by his staff after the mourning was over.

William Nelson had made a dreadful nuisance of himself over the funeral arrangements, fussing about precedence and his own importance in the proceedings. He had demanded six mourning coaches in the procession and insisted that tickets should not be issued to relations until they had shown 'undoubted evidences of their pedigree'. He was universally considered an ass, quite unworthy of his brother.

Yet he was not the only one to have made a fuss about the arrangements. The Prince of Wales had announced himself to be the chief mourner, only to be overruled by the government. The Lord Mayor had claimed precedence over everyone, including the Prince of Wales, because St Paul's lay within the boundaries of the City. The Speaker of the House of Commons had refused to sit with the Privy Councillors, citing a 1689 Act of Parliament that entitled him to sit with peers of the realm. There had been a great deal of jockeying for position before anyone got seated at all.

Some people boycotted the service. Every admiral in England was invited, but nineteen chose not to attend. Some couldn't make it, but quite a few stayed away because they hadn't cared for Nelson, considering him a publicity-seeker and a charlatan with a sordid private life. His old friend Lord St Vincent was one of those who didn't come. The two had been involved in a lawsuit over prize money, but it was the codicil to Nelson's will leaving Emma Hamilton to the nation that had upset St Vincent. Emma was a 'bitch', in his opinion. The Admiralty asked him twice to attend the funeral, but twice he declined, claiming his eyes were too sore. He stayed at home instead.

Two men who did attend were Admiral Villeneuve and Captain Magendie. They came up from Hampshire to do honour to their adversary. Nelson's peers may have been equivocal about him, but the Frenchmen were in no doubt as to his greatness. They came to salute their conqueror, the man who had reduced them to nothing. According to some accounts, Captain Lucas came as well.

The service was very moving. Fifes and muffled drums had played the 'Dead March' from *Saul* as the cortège wound through the streets. In the cathedral, the choir sang Purcell and Greene during the proceedings. At the committal, they all rose for Handel's funeral anthem 'The Ways of Zion Do Mourn', muting the words 'His body is buried in peace', then bursting into full cry for the line 'But his name liveth evermore'. After the words had died away, Nelson's coffin slowly disappeared, vanishing dramatically through a trapdoor into the crypt below. There wasn't a dry eye in the house as he went.

Following ancient tradition, three white staves signifying Nelson's ranks of knight, baron and viscount were ceremonially broken in two and thrown into the grave as the coffin descended. The flags from the *Victory* were supposed to be folded up and dropped into the grave as well, but the sailors had other ideas. They began to tear up one of the flags for souvenirs. They were joined by a few members of the congregation, despite the disapproval of the rest. A midshipman named Dent 'was so moved that he bit off a piece of the flag covering the coffin'. It was an unseemly display, but the sailors were determined to have their way. They held on tight to the tattered bits of flag and kept them as mementoes of an extraordinary day. Many of them still exist.

Nelson was buried in the crypt of St Paul's, directly below the cross on the dome. His sarcophagus of Italian marble was designed for Cardinal Wolsey, but had later passed into Henry VIII's hands. With him were buried any French hopes of invading Great Britain. They never tried again. By tacit agreement, the Royal Navy reigned supreme and remained unchallenged for the next 100 years. Nelson's death may have been a disaster for the nation, but he and the other British sailors who lost their lives at Trafalgar had certainly not died in vain.

CHAPTER 46

───◆●◆───

THE CAPTAINS AND THE KINGS DEPART

Three months after the funeral, a small boat left the Sussex coast under a flag of truce and crossed the Channel to Brittany. It carried Admiral Villeneuve. He had been exchanged for four British post-captains and was on his way home.

Villeneuve was glad to be leaving England, yet apprehensive about what lay ahead. He knew his life would not be easy after the disaster at Trafalgar. Napoleon had threatened to have him hanged in the past. Villeneuve must have wondered if that was the fate that awaited him when he returned home.

At Morlaix, as soon as he was off the boat, he wrote to Admiral Decrès announcing his arrival and asking for instructions. He was hoping to go to Paris for an audience with the Emperor. Meantime, he would await Decrès' reply at the Hôtel de la Patrie in Rennes.

During his stay there, he read in the newspaper that Captains Lucas and Infernet had been promoted to rear-admirals. They had been exchanged a few weeks earlier and were to be received by the Emperor at St-Cloud. They were also to receive the Légion d'honneur in recognition of their heroism at Trafalgar. It was important to the French to salvage some pride from the disaster.

Villeneuve wrote to congratulate Lucas. 'If all the captains had acted as you did at Trafalgar, victory wouldn't have been in doubt for a moment. No one understands that better than I do.' He asked Lucas for help in preparing his report for the court of inquiry. Villeneuve intended to name and shame the officers who had disgraced themselves in the battle. He wanted Lucas as a witness.

But no orders came from the Minister of Marine. Villeneuve arrived at Rennes on 17 April and waited four days without hearing anything. Apparently, Decrès was deliberately delaying his answer to avoid compromising his own position with the Emperor. Whatever the reason, Villeneuve became increasingly agitated when no reply was forthcoming. His mood changed to deep depression. He saw only too clearly that he was to take all the blame for Trafalgar, even though much of it hadn't been his fault. He was going to be the scapegoat for everything that had gone wrong.

He was thoroughly unhappy when he went to bed on the evening of 21 April. Next morning, he could not be roused. His bedroom door was locked and the key was on the inside. When they finally got into the room, it was to find Villeneuve lying dead on the bed with six stab wounds and a table knife buried in his chest. Nearby was a letter to his wife and several small gifts of money. He had left his telescope to Infernet and his speaking trumpet to Lucas. By some accounts, he had also left a rude letter to Napoleon, which promptly disappeared.

Did Villeneuve really stab himself? Six times in the chest? Or was he quietly murdered before the court of inquiry, when he would have had plenty to say that others didn't want to hear? The inquest was in no doubt that Villeneuve had died of self-inflicted wounds, but the rest of France was not so sure. Rumours arose at once that Villeneuve had been secretly liquidated, just as General Pichegru had been, and others opposed to Napoleon. The Emperor's enemies had a habit of suddenly killing themselves when they became a danger to him. Perhaps Villeneuve had been ordered to take his own life, warned that if he didn't, a prison cell awaited him in Paris and strangulation by Mamelukes. Napoleon was always ruthless in pursuit of his own ends.

Whatever the truth, it was the last of Villeneuve. He was buried at night, without military honours. His personal effects were forwarded not to his wife but to Fouché, the Minister of Police in Paris. The contrast between Villeneuve's dismal end and Nelson's could not have been more marked.

*

Admiral Gravina was dead too. Badly wounded at Trafalgar, he lingered in hospital for four and a half months while doctors argued over whether to amputate his arm. Gravina declined amputation, only to see mortification set in. 'I am a dying man,' he is said to have announced ruefully, 'but I die happy. I am going, I hope and trust, to join Nelson, perhaps the greatest hero the world has produced.' He went on 9 March 1806.

Rear-Admiral Dumanoir remained in England for a while, vigorously defending himself against accusations of cowardice at Trafalgar. A week before Nelson's funeral, he had had a long letter in *The Times*, denying that he had been a 'mere spectator of the combat . . . precipitately taking to flight'. He denied too that his ships had fired on the *Santissima Trinidad* and other Spanish vessels that had surrendered to the British.

Dumanoir was court-martialled on his eventual return to France and condemned for his conduct during the battle. But he appealed against the verdict and was ultimately exonerated. Julien Cosmao-Kerjulien, by then an admiral, was so outraged at this that he broke his own sword in disgust when Dumanoir's was returned to him after the verdict. Dumanoir resumed his career and was created a count in 1814, at the restoration of the monarchy.

On the British side, Vice-Admiral Collingwood was also raised to the peerage, the same day as Nelson's brother. He was still at sea when he received the news. He shared it with his dog, Bounce:

> I am out of all patience with Bounce. The consequential airs he gives himself since he became a right honourable dog are insufferable. He considers it beneath his dignity to play with commoners' dogs, and truly thinks that he does them grace when he condescends to lift up his leg against them.

In truth, though, a peerage was a mixed blessing for Collingwood. With the Trafalgar prize money gone to the bottom, he could not afford to live like a lord. Even if he had been able to, he was still needed at sea and had no immediate prospect of going home. In the event, Collingwood remained with the fleet for the rest of his life. He died at sea in 1810 without ever seeing England again.

Sir Robert Calder was preparing for his court martial when he heard the news of Trafalgar. To the disgust of his fellow officers, he immediately claimed a share of the little prize money from the battle. He reckoned he had done his bit in forcing Villeneuve's fleet to back down and turn away from England.

The court martial took a different view. It was held aboard the *Prince of Wales*, in Portsmouth harbour, on 23 December 1805. Calder was acquitted of cowardice, but found guilty of not doing his utmost to renew the action against Villeneuve when he had the chance. Severely reprimanded, he remained in the navy but never had another seagoing command.

Captain Hardy was made a baronet in 1806 and later became First Sea Lord. There was speculation that Hardy had misheard Nelson on his death bed, mistaking 'Kismet' – fate – for 'Kiss me'. Hardy remained tight-lipped on the subject, but Surgeon William Beatty and Chaplain Alexander Scott were both adamant that Nelson had asked to be kissed.

Scott himself was deeply traumatised by the battle and Nelson's death. He could never bring himself to speak of it, but remained haunted for years afterwards. In modern terms, he was a victim of severe post-traumatic stress disorder.

John Roome, the press-ganged sailor who had hoisted Nelson's famous signal, deserted after the battle. In common with many others at Trafalgar, he had never wanted to be in the Royal Navy and escaped at the first opportunity. He was discovered penniless in 1846, selling watercress and red herrings through the streets of London. As a deserter, he was ineligible for a Royal Navy pension, but an exception was made and Roome was admitted to Greenwich Hospital. His arrival caused consternation among the other pensioners, several of whom had been making a good living out of claiming to be the man who had hoisted the signal.

John Yule was a lieutenant aboard the *Victory*, but he too received a Greenwich pension from 1835. He died six years later and was buried in the shirt he had worn at Trafalgar.

Benjamin Clement, the *Tonnant* lieutenant who had nearly drowned during the battle, never forgot his debt to the black seaman who had saved him. Clement kept in touch with Charles Macnamara all his life and left him money when he died in 1836.

Midshipman Jack Spratt, the *Defiance's* handsome swordsman, fought like a Hollywood star during the battle but never walked properly again. He remained a strong swimmer, though, and at the age of nearly sixty won a fourteen-mile race against a Frenchman for a bet.

Lieutenant John Lapenotiere enjoyed his fifteen minutes of fame as the man who had brought the Trafalgar dispatches to the Admiralty. He was presented with a valuable sword by Lloyd's Patriotic Fund and invited to meet George III to give him an eyewitness account of the battle. Promotion and his gratuity of £500 proved more elusive. Lapenotiere had to write several times to William Marsden to remind him of the Admiralty's obligations. He got his reward in the end, but not without a struggle.

Henry Blackwood had been hoping for promotion to a ship of the line on the morning of Trafalgar. Two captains had left vacancies when they went home for Calder's court martial. In the event, Blackwood remained with his frigate and later delivered Villeneuve to England, which at least enabled him to attend Nelson's funeral. He became a baronet in 1814 and retired as a vice-admiral.

Several Trafalgar veterans subsequently fought at Waterloo as well. Two British midshipmen took commissions in the army and one sailor fought as a colour-sergeant. They were joined by General Miguel de Alava, nephew of Rear-Admiral Alava, who had been aboard the *Principe de Asturias* at Trafalgar, but later served as aide-de-camp to the Duke of Wellington after Spain had switched sides. As Spanish ambassador to

Holland, Alava witnessed the battle from Wellington's headquarters and dined alone with him afterwards.

Perhaps the oddest story of all was that of Major Antoine Drouot of the French artillery. He escaped from Trafalgar with Admiral Gravina and then joined the Grand Army. After surviving the retreat from Moscow, Drouot was promoted to command the Imperial Guard at Waterloo. He survived Waterloo as well, but gave up fighting after that, retiring to a quieter life as president of the Agricultural Society in Nancy.

William Nelson became very grand after his elevation to the peerage. 'Never mind the battle of Trafalgar,' he told his wife, in front of a scandalised audience. 'It has made me an earl and thee a countess.' Parliament gave him the money for a 3,400-acre estate near Salisbury and a pension 'in perpetuity'. The pension continued to be paid to the Nelson family until 1947.

Emma Hamilton went into a spiral of despair after Trafalgar. The codicil to Nelson's will was never honoured. She lived in reduced circumstances for the rest of her life, fleeing to Calais in 1814 to escape her creditors. She died there on 15 January 1815 and was buried in the local cemetery. It is said that all the British ships at Calais flew their flags at half-mast on the day of the funeral, and all the ships' captains attended the service.

William Pitt died on 23 January 1806, only two weeks after Nelson's funeral. His spirit had been broken by the disasters at Ulm and Austerlitz. 'Roll up that map,' he told his staff bitterly. 'It will not be wanted these ten years.' Pitt died a failure in his own eyes, but had succeeded in his primary aim of diverting Napoleon's army away from England.

Lord Melville deserved some of the credit for Trafalgar after initiating a massive ship-building programme as First Lord of the Admiralty. His trial for high crimes and misdemeanours was held in May 1806. Melville was acquitted on all ten charges, but never held public office again.

*

Sir John Moore continued to fight the French and was killed at Corunna in 1809, as was Major Stanhope, Lady Hester's favourite brother.

Upset by these two deaths, as well as Pitt's, Hester Stanhope left England for good in 1810 and settled eventually in the Lebanon. Dressed as a Turkish man, she liked nothing better than to smoke a pipe and surround herself with slaves and stray cats. She died in 1839.

Robert Fulton continued to experiment with torpedoes, but lost the British government's support after Trafalgar. He demanded a large sum to keep his designs secret, but was rebuffed. Undaunted, he returned to the United States in the autumn of 1806 and turned his attention to building steamboats instead.

Field Marshal Mack was stripped of his rank after Ulm and sentenced to two years in prison.

HMS *Victory* returned eventually to Portsmouth and is still there, still commissioned in the Royal Navy. Equipped with a new set of masts, she flies the flag of the commander-in-chief, Naval Home Command. She last saw action in the Second World War, when she was hit by a German bomb. The portrait of Emma Hamilton that hung in Nelson's cabin on the morning of Trafalgar hangs now in the National Maritime Museum in Greenwich.

England and France remain as close as ever, and as far apart. Since Napoleon's youth, the French system of government has embraced one Terror, two empires, three monarchies, five republics, a directorate and a Vichy. The British continue with their monarchy.

And Napoleon? As Pitt had forecast, it took another ten years to bring him down. After his defeat at Waterloo he fled south, pursued by troops from several nations calling for his immediate execution. If the Prussians caught up with him, they were planning to shoot him in the same moat at Vincennes as he had shot the Duc d'Enghien. His only hope of escape was to reach the coast before them and take passage to America.

On 2 July 1815, two weeks after Waterloo, Napoleon arrived at Rochefort on the Bay of Biscay. The provisional government formed after his abdication wanted him off French soil without delay. Napoleon was ready to sail to America, but the way was blocked by the Royal Navy, which refused to guarantee him safe passage. The navy's orders were to bring him to England instead.

Bowing to the inevitable, Napoleon surrendered to the British. They had a long tradition of harbouring political refugees – Napoleon's brother Lucien had been in England since 1810. He decided to put his faith in British justice and throw himself on their mercy.

On the morning of 15 July, Napoleon and his retinue were received aboard HMS *Bellerophon* – the same *Bellerophon* that had fought so bravely at Trafalgar. The deck where Captain Cooke had died and Lieutenant Cumby had grappled with French boarders now played host to Napoleon and his staff, with their wives and children, to the number of thirty-three people in all. There was no room for a further seventeen, who were taken aboard the *Myrmidon* instead.

It was an exciting moment for the *Bellerophon*'s crew. Napoleon was the most famous man in the world, the tyrant they had been fighting all their adult lives. Now here he was, being rowed towards their ship.

Bosun Manning, an Irishman from Limerick, stood ready to pipe him aboard. 'Manning,' a midshipman told him, 'this is the proudest day of your life.'

Manning nodded happily.

'Along with the great Napoleon, the name of Manning, the bosun of the *Bellerophon*, will go down to posterity. And as a relic of that great man, permit me, my dear Manning, to preserve a lock of your hair.' The midshipman pulled out some of Manning's whiskers and fled before the bosun could catch him.

Napoleon appeared soon afterwards, preceded up the ship's side by General Bertrand. The ex-Emperor wore his trademark black hat and a greatcoat buttoned to his chin. The British recognised him at once, even though he looked nothing like the evil dwarf of the cartoons. He carried himself with the easy assurance of someone long accustomed to command.

'Napoleon Bonaparte is about five feet seven inches high,' reported Lieutenant Bowerbank, 'rather corpulent, remarkably well made. His hair is very black, cut close, whiskers shaved off; large eyebrows, grey eyes, the most piercing I ever saw.'

Others thought him only five foot two, so short that he walked on tiptoe to look taller. All agreed though that Napoleon had a pot belly and all were mesmerised by his eyes. They were like a hawk's, according to another officer. It was a characteristic he shared with Hitler.

Climbing to the quarterdeck, Napoleon removed his hat and addressed Captain Frederick Maitland in French. 'I have come to throw myself on the protection of your prince and your laws,' he announced.

Maitland bowed and led Napoleon to his cabin. He was lending it to him for the journey to England. They chatted for a while and Napoleon asked to meet the other officers. 'Well, gentlemen,' he told them, 'you have the honour of belonging to the bravest and most fortunate nation in the world.' He then went on a tour of the ship.

Napoleon had never been aboard a British warship before. Many years earlier, back in the days when his elder brother was still called Giuseppe and his younger brother Luigi was only a baby, little Nabulione Buonaparte had dreamed of being a British sailor. As a child, he had seen Royal Navy ships in Corsica and had been impressed by their smartness and efficiency. He had fantasised about joining the Royal Navy and fighting to liberate Corsica from France. But fate had dictated otherwise. Napoleon had learned French instead and gone to military school on the mainland.

He still admired the Royal Navy, though. He stood on deck as the *Bellerophon* got under way, watching everything that was going on. 'What I admire most in your ship,' he told Maitland, 'is the extreme silence and orderly conduct of your men. On board a French ship everyone calls and gives orders, and they gabble like so many geese.'

At dinner that night, he discussed Trafalgar with the British and spoke approvingly of Nelson. Napoleon owned a bust of the admiral and had had the words '*La France compte que chacun fera son devoir*' (the French equivalent of 'England expects . . .') prominently displayed on every French man-of-war after the battle. He saw the fight between the two nations as a struggle between a whale and an elephant.

The *Bellerophon* headed for England and reached Torbay on 24 July. The country looked very beautiful to Napoleon. As soon as the ship had anchored, a number of rowing boats set out from Brixham to sell fruit and vegetables to the crew. But the *Bellerophon* had orders to keep Napoleon's presence a secret, in case anyone tried to rescue him. The rowing boats were seen off by sentries with muskets. Those that returned were threatened with violence if they didn't stay away.

One or two persisted, however. Some schoolboys with bread to sell circled the ship, but were driven back towards her by the tide. They spotted a sailor at one of the lower gun ports trying to attract their attention without alerting the sentry. He furtively dropped a black bottle into the water. The boys waited until it had drifted well clear of the *Bellerophon* before retrieving it and reading the message inside.

'We have got Bonaparte on board.' As messages go, it could hardly have been more electrifying. The boys didn't waste a moment. They turned their boat round at once and raced back to shore with the news. The *Bellerophon's* secret was out.

Before long, she was surrounded by sightseers, paddling furiously from shore in every boat they could find. The *Bellerophon* was overwhelmed. None of the boats was allowed alongside, but there were far too many to chase away. And it was no good pretending Napoleon was not on board. People had seen him through the stern windows.

Around 3 p.m., he came on deck to meet his public. He wore a green Chasseur uniform with red facings, white waistcoat and tall boots. This was the man who had set Europe aflame for a generation, the man who by one calculation had caused someone else's death for every minute of his self-appointed reign. The mere mention of his name was enough to make children sit up and behave, because he would come down the chimney and get them if they didn't. The British hated him particularly because they held him responsible for that newest and most outrageous of government impositions – a tax on income to pay for the war. Napoleon was the devil incarnate to the good people of Brixham. They gave him a cheer as he appeared at the ship's side.

Napoleon took off his hat and bowed. He was delighted with his reception. He had convinced himself that the British would take him to their hearts. Caesar would have paraded him in chains through the streets, but Napóleon was expecting to receive the Order of the Garter from the king before buying a country house somewhere, under discreet guard, to begin work on his memoirs. English girls were nice, too. He had noticed lots of pretty ones in the boats around the *Bellerophon*. 'What charming girls!' he kept saying, as he bowed to them. 'What beautiful women!'

But it was not to be. The British wouldn't even allow him ashore. He would have legal rights, once he was ashore. Their European allies wanted to put him up against a wall and shoot him without further ado. In England, though, seven centuries of common law stipulated that Napoleon must have a fair trial first. He had committed no crimes on English soil and there was no guarantee that he would be found guilty even if he had. Napoleon had his share of admirers in Britain, people who could see in meritocracy rather than aristocracy the kernel of a good idea.

The *Bellerophon* was ordered to Plymouth while the authorities discussed what to do with him. The harbour was safer at Plymouth, full of warships to prevent a rescue attempt. The *Bellerophon* arrived there on 26 July.

Once again she was surrounded by sightseers. Every inn for miles was swamped as people came from far and wide to view the ogre. At the height of the excitement, it was calculated that 10,000 people lay in a thousand different boats around the ship, waiting for him to show his face. Several drowned in the crush. The *Bellerophon*'s crew hung notices over the ship's side detailing his progress: 'At Breakfast', 'In Cabin With Captain Maitland', 'Writing With His Officers'. The one they were all waiting for was 'Coming On Deck'.

He was not impressed when they mentioned St Helena to him. He felt betrayed. Napoleon was a guest of the British, not a prisoner. He had voluntarily subjected himself to British law. How could they send him to St Helena when he didn't want to go?

St Helena it was, though. The *Bellerophon* was ordered to transfer Napoleon to the *Northumberland* for the journey. It had to be done quickly, because there was a lawyer in a boat waving a writ for Napoleon.

The entire ship's company formed up on the *Bellerophon*'s deck to see him off. It was a poignant moment. Those Frenchmen not going with

Napoleon were in tears. The British were subdued as well. The crew of the *Bellerophon* had fallen under Napoleon's spell during his twenty-four days on board. They recognised a leader of men when they saw one.

The *Northumberland* sailed for St Helena on 11 August 1815. Napoleon got a glimpse of France next day. 'Adieu, land of the brave!' He removed his hat. 'Adieu, France! Adieu!' He never saw his country again.

After his death in 1821, he was buried on St Helena and remained there until 1840, when his body was repatriated to France for reinterment at Les Invalides in Paris. Nicolas Soult and Emmanuel Grouchy were among the marshals from the old days who joined almost a million Frenchmen watching the procession. Napoleon's coffin had been opened after his exhumation and his body was reported to be in good condition, although his nails had continued to grow after his death.

There was no mention of his penis, which was said to have been removed after his autopsy in 1821. It was very small, according to the report. Something described variously as a mummified tendon, a maltreated strip of buckskin shoelace or shrivelled eel, or a short length of dried leather in a blue morocco box has since been sold several times at auction. When last heard of, it was the property of an American urologist who bought it to spare Napoleon further indignity. If it really is his penis, and if it really is only an inch long and shaped like a grape, then it might explain why Napoleon felt such a pressing need to fight the whole world.

EPILOGUE

In the autumn of 1804, when they were still poised to invade England, the men of the Grand Army clubbed together to build a monument to Napoleon at Boulogne. It was to be a column 160 feet high, topped by a statue of the Emperor in imperial dress, looking down across the vale of Terlincthun towards the British Isles in the distance. Marshal Soult laid the foundation stone on 6 November 1804.

For various reasons, the column was not completed until 1841, shortly after Napoleon's reinterment at Les Invalides. On 15 August that year – his birthday – a crowd of dignitaries gathered for the formal inauguration of the statue. The ceremony was solemn and dignified, marred only by the discovery that somebody had been there in the night and scratched the word 'Waterloo' across Napoleon's left eyeball. The ceremony went ahead anyway and the statue was hoisted into position. Napoleon was placed magisterially on his column, looking down across the natural amphitheatre of Terlincthun, where he had sat on Dagobert's throne all those years ago, handing out Légions d'honneur to his troops before the invasion of England.

The place has changed remarkably little since Napoleon's time. A modest obelisk marks the site of his throne, surrounded now by crisp packets and old Coca-Cola bottles. The Calais train clatters across the valley floor and there are council flats and a trailer park further up the hill. A Commonwealth War Graves cemetery stands to one side. Otherwise, though, Terlincthun remains the same as ever, a natural amphitheatre of green, bordered at the edge by the sea and a view of England beyond.

It was here that Julius Caesar stood on the cliffs in 55 BC, looking at the island of Britannia on the horizon. Here, too, that Napoleon laid his plans. And it was here also, on a lovely day in May 1940, that a line of sinister grey figures appeared on the crest of the hill around Napoleon's column and swept down rapidly across Terlincthun towards the sea.

The figures were German. They were descended from the rough forest tribes that had given Caesar so much trouble (they called him 'Kaiser' in their own ungainly tongue). They had since emerged from the forest, swarmed and multiplied, moving ever outwards in their quest for more living space. Now they had reached the sea.

As the Germans hurried across Terlincthun, others were sweeping towards Boulogne from the south, encircling the town in a classic pincer movement. Their leader was General Heinz Guderian, a man well versed in the art of war. There were not enough French troops to stem their advance. A battalion each of the Irish and Welsh Guards had arrived by sea the day before, to reinforce the garrison, but it was all too little, too late. Boulogne could not be held. The order was given for the British troops to withdraw again twenty-four hours after they had arrived. On the evening of 23 May, British destroyers moved into Boulogne under gunfire to take them off from the pier.

It was a terrifying experience. As well as being dive-bombed by Stukas, the destroyers came under attack from tanks and snipers in the town. The Germans were firing at them across open sights. Aboard HMS *Keith*, Captain David Simpson did what so many captains at Trafalgar had done and ordered his men below to reduce casualties. He himself was the last man on the bridge. He was about to join the rest when he fell dead, shot through the chest by a German sharpshooter. He was the same age as Nelson when he died.

On the quays, a last stand was made after the destroyers had left. The fiercest fighting was around the Bassin Napoleon, the semicircular inner harbour that Napoleon had constructed for his invasion barges. British stragglers held one side of it, Germans the other. The battle was bravely fought, but there was never any doubt as to the outcome. With no hope of escape, and no chance of reinforcement, the British were forced to surrender when their ammunition ran out.

These were the same quays that the Grand Army had occupied while waiting to embark for England on the morning of 21 August 1805. Believing the invasion was really going to happen this time, they had sold their rings and watches on the dockside so as to have spending money in London. As the Germans searched their British prisoners, another exchange of rings and watches took place, but without any money changing hands. The Germans simply helped themselves to whatever they wanted.

Afterwards, they went up to the cliffs to look at England through their scissor telescopes. Another few weeks and they would be marching up the Mall, something Napoleon had never achieved. The Germans already knew what to do when they had conquered England. They would arrest everybody on Dr Goebbels' list to begin with, all the prominent Britons likely to cause trouble for the new regime. They would ban cars and radios, seize control of the newspapers and dismantle the heavy industry, transporting the machinery back to Germany for reassembly in the Ruhr. They would also dismantle Nelson's column in Trafalgar Square and re-erect it in Berlin as a trophy.

After that, they would turn their attention to other matters. There would be a host of new regulations as to exactly which British citizens were allowed to own a business or sit in the park or go to the cinema. There would be a visitation of the universities, German troops clumping up the staircases of Oxford and Cambridge to drag out the Jews and homosexuals and make a bonfire of their books. There would be executions of left-wingers and slave labour for all men between seventeen and forty-five. And there would be photographs – partisans decapitated in the Welsh mountains with cigarettes dangling from their lips, East End rabbis with their ringlets cut off, passers-by strung up like poultry in the market place, lone English girls cowering naked among grinning, strutting men in jackboots. All of that there would be, and a lot more besides, when the Germans were safely across the Channel.

They folded their telescopes after a while and went down to the harbour again to begin clearing up. The Bassin Napoleon was their first priority. They wanted it back in working order as soon as possible. They needed it for their landing craft.

Behind them, just across the water, the fishermen and ploughboys of the Walmer Home Guard patrolled the beach where Caesar had landed, wondering if rifles would be delivered to them any time soon. Royal Navy warships patrolled further out, defending the approaches to the shore. And the Channel rolled ever onwards, with its tides and cross-currents, its shifting sands and treacherous undertows, its unpredictable swells and atrocious, never-to-be-relied-on weather. To the British, it is the most beautiful stretch of water in the world.

BIBLIOGRAPHY

Adkins, Roy, *Trafalgar*, Little, Brown and Co., London, 2004.

Ammon, Harry, *James Monroe*, New York, 1971.

Aspinall, A., *The Later Correspondence of George III*, Cambridge University Press, Cambridge, 1968.

Asprey, Robert, *The Rise and Fall of Napoleon Bonaparte*, Little, Brown and Co., London, 2000.

Atteridge, A. Hilliard, *The Bravest of the Brave*, Methuen, London, 1912.

Baring-Gould, Sabine, *The Life of Napoleon Bonaparte*, London, 1897.

Beatty, William, *The Death of Lord Nelson*, The War Library, 1894.

Bennett, Geoffrey, *The Battle of Trafalgar*, Batsford, 1977.

Blond, Georges, *La Grande Armée*. Robert Laffont, Paris, 1979.

Blythe, Legette, *Marshal Ney*, Jarrolds, 1937.

Bonaparte, Napoleon, *Correspondence de Napoleon*, Paris, 1858–70.

Brooks, Richard, *The Royal Marines*, Constable, 2002.

Bryant, Arthur, *The Years of Victory*, Collins, 1944.

Burne, Alfred, *The Noble Duke of York*, Staples, London, 1949.

Castelot, André, *Napoleon*, Harper and Row, 1968.

Chandler, David, *The Campaigns of Napoleon*, Weidenfeld & Nicolson, London, 1967.

Clayton, Tim and Craig, Phil, *Trafalgar*, Hodder & Stoughton, London, 2004.

Coignet, Jean-Roch, *The Notebooks of Captain Coignet*, Peter Davies, 1928.

Coleman, Terry, *Nelson*, Bloomsbury, London, 2001.

Constant, Louis, *Mémoires de Constant*, Jean de Bonnot, Paris 1969.

Cooksey, Jon, *Boulogne*, Pen and Sword, 2003.

Corbett, Julian, *The Campaign of Trafalgar*, Longmans, 1910.

Cordingley, David, *Billy Ruff'n*, Bloomsbury, London, 2003.

Crawford, Abraham, *Reminiscences of a Naval Officer*, Chatham, 1999.

Cresson, W. P., *James Monroe*, Hamden, Connecticut, 1971.

Cronin, Vincent, *Napoleon*, Collins, London, 1971.

Cruikshank, Dan, *Invasion*, Boxtree, London, 2001.

Desbrière, Edouard, *Projets et tentatives de débarquement aux Îles Britanniques*, 1900.

Dickinson, H. W., *Robert Fulton*, Bodley Head, 1913.

Dodge, Theodore, *Great Captains*, A. P. Watt, 1904.

Epton, Nina, *Josephine*, Weidenfeld & Nicolson, London, 1975.

Esdaile, Charles, *The Wars of Napoleon*, Longmans, 1995.

Forshufvud, Sten, *Who Killed Napoleon?* Hutchinson, 1962.

Fournier, August, *Napoleon I*, Longmans, 1911.

Fraser, Edward, *The Enemy at Trafalgar*, Hodder and Stoughton, London, 1906.

Fraser, Edward, *The Sailors Whom Nelson Led*, Methuen, London, 1913.

Fraser, Flora. *Beloved Emma*, Weidenfeld & Nicolson, London, 1986.

Furber, Holden, *Henry Dundas, 1st Viscount Melville*, Oxford University Press, Oxford 1931.

Furse, George, *A Hundred Years Ago*, William Clowes, London, 1905.

Gardiner, Robert (ed.), *The Campaign of Trafalgar*, Chatham, 1997.

Gengembre, Gérard, *Napoleon*, Hachette, Paris, 2003.

Glover, Richard, *Britain at Bay*, George Allen and Unwin, London, 1973.

Green, Ivan, *The Book of Deal and Walmer*, Buckingham: Barracuda, 1983.

Hardwick, Mollie, *Emma, Lady Hamilton*, Cassell, London, 1969.

Hibbert, Christopher, *Napoleon: His Wives and Women*, HarperCollins, London, 2002.

Hibbert, Christopher, *Nelson*, Penguin, London, 1995.

Holland Rose, J., *William Pitt and the Great War*, G. Bell, 1911.

Holmes, Thomas, *The Semaphore*, Stockwell, 1983.

Honan, Park, *Jane Austen: Her Life*, Weidenfeld & Nicolson, London, 1987.

Howarth, David, *Trafalgar*, Collins, London, 1969.

James, William, *Naval History of Great Britain*, London, 1822.

Junot, Laure, *Memoirs of Laure Junot, Duchess D'Abrantes*, London, 1833.

Kemble, James, *Napoleon Immortal*, John Murray, 1959.

Kielland, Alexander, *Napoleon's Men and Methods*, Owen, 1907.

King, Dean, *Every Man Will Do His Duty*, Conway, 1997.

Knapton, Ernest, *Empress Josephine*, Harvard University Press, 1964.

Landreth, Helen, *The Pursuit of Robert Emmet*, Browne and Nolan, Dublin, 1949.

Legg, Stuart, *Trafalgar: An Eyewitness Account*, Hart-Davis, 1966.

Longmate, Norman, *Island Fortress*, Hutchinson, 1991.

Mackenzie, R. H., *The Trafalgar Roll*, George Allen, 1913.

Maine, Rene, *Trafalgar*, Thames and Hudson, 1957.

Marbot, Baron, *The Memoirs of the Baron de Marbot*, Longmans, 1892.

Marchand, Louis-Joseph, *In Napoleon's Shadow*, Proctor Jones, 1998.

Markham, Felix, *Napoleon and the Awakening of Europe*, Harmondsworth, 1975.

Marriott, Leo, *What's Left of Nelson*, Dial House, 1995.

Matcham, Mary Eyre, *The Nelsons of Burnham Thorpe*, Bodley Head, 1911.

Maurice, Sir John, *The Diary of Sir John Moore*, Edward Arnold, 1904.

McLynn, Frank, *Invasion*, Routledge & Kegan Paul, 1987.

Mossiker, Frances, *Napoleon and Josephine*, Victor Gollancz, London, 1965.

Mundy, H. G., *Journal of Mary Frampton*, London, 1885.

Napoleon, Prince (ed.), *The Memoirs of Queen Hortense*, Butterworth, 1928.

Nelson Dispatch, Journal of the Nelson Society, B. B. and Co., Norwich, 1982.

Newnham Collingwood, G. L., *Correspondence of Vice-Admiral Lord Collingwood*, London, 1838.

Nicolas, N. H., *The Dispatches and Letters of Vice-Admiral Lord Viscount Nelson*, London, 1846.

Nicolay, Fernand, *Napoleon at the Boulogne Camp*, Cassell, London, 1907.

Oman, Carola, *Britain Against Napoleon*, Faber & Faber, London, 1942.

Oman, Carola, *Sir John Moore*, Hodder and Stoughton, 1953.

Pocock, Tom, *The Terror Before Trafalgar*, John Murray, 2002.

Pope, Dudley, *England Expects*, Chatham, 1998.

Rawson, Geoffrey, *Letters From Lord Nelson*, Staples Press, 1949.

Richardson, Frank, *Napoleon's Death: An Inquest*, William Kimber, 1974.

Roberts, Andrew, *Napoleon and Wellington*, Weidenfeld & Nicolson, London, 2001.

Saunders, Andrew, *Fortress Britain*, Beaufort, 1989.

Saunders, Andrew and Smith, Victor, *Kent's Defence Heritage*, Kent County Council, 2001.

Sherrard, O. A., *A Life of Emma Hamilton*, Sidgwick and Jackson, 1927.

Shirley, F. J. (ed.), *Reminiscences of the Reverend George Gilbert*, Privately printed, 1938.

Sichel, Walter, *Emma, Lady Hamilton*, Constable, 1905.

Sloane, W. M., *The Life of Napoleon Bonaparte*, Appleton-Century, 1939.

Sparrow, Elizabeth, *Secret Service*, Boydell Press, 1999.

Stanhope, Earl, *Life of William Pitt*, 1867.

Stanhope, Lady Hester, *Memoirs*, London, 1845.

Thompson, J. M., *Napoleon Bonaparte*, Blackwell, 1990.

Tomalin, Claire, *Jane Austen: A Life*, Viking, 1997.

Tours, Hugh, *The Life and Letters of Emma Hamilton*, Victor Gollancz, London, 1963.

Trafalgar Chronicle, Hoylake, periodical.

Vincent, Edgar, *Nelson*, Yale University Press, 2003.

Warner, Oliver, *Emma Hamilton and Sir William*, Chatto and Windus, London, 1960.

Werner, Jack, *We Laughed at Boney*, London, 1943.

Wheeler, H. F. B. and Broadley, A. M., *Napoleon and the Invasion of England*. Bodley Head, 1908.

INDEX